BIOGRAPHICAL ESSAYS

BIOGRAPHICAL ESSAYS

F. MAX MULLER, K.M.

GYAN

Published by

GYAN

Gyan Publishing House
5, Ansari Road
Daryaganj, New Delhi-110002
Phone: 011-47034999, 9811692060
E-mail: books@gyanbooks.com

Distribution Network
gyanbooks.com
India, USA, Canada, UK, Australia, France

ISBN: 978-81-212-8899-6 (PB)
First Published, 1884

2nd Impression 2023

Printed at: Gyan Press, Delhi.

BIOGRAPHICAL ESSAYS

AUTHOR: F. MAX MULLER

BIOGRAPHICAL ESSAYS.

BIOGRAPHICAL ESSAYS

BY

F MAX MÜLLER, K. M.

MEMBER OF THE FRENCH INSTITUTE

RÂMMOHUN ROY, KESHUB CHUNDER SEN
DAYÂNANDA SARASVATÎ
BUNYIU NANJIO AND KENJIU KASAWARA
MOHL AND KINGSLEY

NEW YORK
CHARLES SCRIBNER'S SONS
1884

The Riverside Press, Cambridge:
Electrotyped and Printed by H. O. Houghton & Co.

TABLE OF CONTENTS.

RÂJAH RÂMMOHUN ROY.

(1774–1833.)

ADDRESS DELIVERED IN THE BRISTOL MUSEUM, SEPTEMBER 27, 1883, THE FIFTIETH ANNIVERSARY OF THE RÂJAH'S DEATH.

It is only fifty years ago that Râjah Râmmohun Roy, who had come to Bristol to pay a visit to Dr. Carpenter and other friends, died here on the 27th of September, 1833. He drew his last breath at twenty-five minutes past two o'clock in the morning.

On the 18th of October his body was committed to the earth, under the shadow of some fine old elm-trees in the garden of Stapleton Grove, where the Râjah had been staying, since the beginning of September, as the guest of Miss Castle, a ward of Dr. Carpenter's.

Lastly, in 1843, on the 29th of May, the remains of the Râjah were transferred from Stapleton Grove to the beautiful cemetery of Arno's Vale. There, as you enter, on the right hand side, many of those whom I have the honor to address here to-night, have no doubt gazed and wondered at a strange Oriental monument, which was erected over the tomb of the Râjah by my old friend, Dvârkânâth[1] Tagore, who was himself a follower of the great religious reformer, and soon after shared his sad fate of dying an exile

[1] Dvârakânâtha, like Dvârakesa, is a name of Krishna.

in a foreign country. Let me read you the lines inscribed on the monument: —

BENEATH THIS STONE
REST THE REMAINS OF RÂJAH RÂMMOHUN ROY BAHADOOR,
A CONSCIENTIOUS AND STEADFAST BELIEVER IN THE
UNITY OF THE GODHEAD;
HE CONSECRATED HIS LIFE WITH ENTIRE DEVOTION
TO THE WORSHIP OF THE DIVINE SPIRIT ALONE.

TO GREAT NATURAL TALENTS HE UNITED A THOROUGH MASTERY OF MANY LANGUAGES, AND EARLY DISTINGUISHED HIMSELF AS ONE OF THE GREATEST SCHOLARS OF THE DAY.

HIS UNWEARIED LABORS TO PROMOTE THE SOCIAL, MORAL, AND PHYSICAL CONDITION OF THE PEOPLE OF INDIA, HIS EARNEST ENDEAVORS TO SUPPRESS IDOLATRY AND THE RITE OF SUTTEE, AND HIS CONSTANT ZEALOUS ADVOCACY OF WHATEVER TENDED TO ADVANCE THE GLORY OF GOD AND THE WELFARE OF MAN, LIVE IN THE GRATEFUL REMEMBRANCE OF HIS COUNTRYMEN.

THIS TABLET RECORDS THE SORROW AND PRIDE WITH WHICH HIS MEMORY IS CHERISHED BY HIS DESCENDANTS.

HE WAS BORN IN RÂDHÂNÂGORE, IN BENGAL, IN 1774, AND DIED AT BRISTOL, SEPTEMBER 27TH, 1833.

These are the bare facts which connect this ancient city of Bristol with the memory of Râjah Râmmohun Roy, the great religious reformer of India. You wished for an interpretation of these facts, and I only wish you could have found a more competent and more eloquent interpreter. But as an old admirer, and I feel proud to say, as a sincere follower of Râmmohun Roy, so far as he went in his religious reforms, I felt it almost impossible to decline the kind invitation which was addressed to me by my friend, our Chairman, in the name of your Society, to be present here on the fiftieth anniversary of the death of Râjah Râmmohun Roy, and to say a few words on his life, and, what is more important, on the work of his life, — on that which has outlived his life, and has secured to him that best of all immortalities, — the gratitude of mankind.

If I tell you that Râmmohun's life-work was the restoration of the old religion of India, as contained in the Veda, and that a great part of my own life has been spent in making the Veda accessible to the students of Europe, by collecting the ancient MSS. of the Sacred Writings of the Brâhmans, and publishing for the first time the text and commentary of the Rig-Veda, the oldest book of the whole Aryan race, you will easily understand the strong sympathy I feel for the Indian Reformer, whose ashes rest among the ashes of your own forefathers; but I am afraid I shall hardly convey to you by these few words a very clear idea either of what the Râjah tried to achieve as a reformer, or what I myself hoped to accomplish as a scholar. It will be necessary therefore, before proceeding further, to turn our eyes together to the past, in order to gain a kind of historical background from which the religious reformer of India, to whose memory we wish to do honor to-night, may step forward as you see his stately figure advancing towards you in that excellent picture which has to-night been placed in this hall, and which, I hope, may always retain a place of honor in your Museum.[1]

Great men, depend upon it, do not come down from the sky like shooting stars. They come in the fulness of time; and if we want to understand their true character, we must try to understand that fulness of time, that is, the time that lay behind and the time that lay before them. We must know the

[1] The life-size portrait by Biggs was bought by Miss Castle, and presented to the Bristol Museum. The Râjah himself did not like it, possibly because he thought the complexion too dark. There is also a miniature by Newton, and a bust by Clarke.

work that others had done before them, in order to understand the work that they themselves were meant to do.

Râmmohun Roy, the originator of the Indian Reformation, a reformation that is still going on slowly, silently, but, for all that, irresistibly, died fifty years ago. Now fifty years may not seem to some of us a very long time. It is quite possible that a few who are present here to-night may remember the Râjah's visit to Bristol. Yet fifty years are half a century, and remember that, according to the received chronology, not more than sixty such centuries are supposed to form the canvass for the whole history of the world, or, at least, for as much of it as we shall ever know. Remember that we have accustomed ourselves to believe that only one hundred and twenty such short periods as have passed since the death of Râmmohun Roy, that is to say, no more than six thousand years — a stretch of time that might almost be spanned by the memory of sixty men — separate us from what will always remain the most miraculous of all miracles, and, at the same time, the most certain of all facts — the appearance on this earth of a being, capable of language, that is, of reason; a being which, when it came to be conscious of its dignity, called itself *Man*, or, in Sanskrit, *Manu*, which means the measurer, the thinker, the discoverer, and the giver of laws.

I do not mean to imply that I myself believe that the age of man is six thousand years and no more. I only wish to measure the time that has elapsed since the death of Râmmohun Roy with the time that is commonly believed to have elapsed since the birth of man.

I doubt whether Astronomy will ever be able to measure the age of the solar system in which our planet moves as a very small star among larger stars, all held together by the same central force.

I doubt whether Geology will ever be able to fix the time when, after the long interval that must have followed on the glacial period, the highest plateaus of the earth became fit for human occupation.

But I feel perfectly certain that no one who has carefully studied the origin, growth, and decay of all that we call human, our thoughts, our words, our religions, our arts, our sciences, our laws and literature, can really believe, or can make it even intelligible to himself, that no more than sixty centuries, no more than one hundred and eighty generations, should have passed since the first fire was lighted, the first flint chipped, the first word uttered.

Let us think of our language only. It is said that the New English Dictionary, which has been prepared during the last twenty-five years by the members of the Philological Society, and the first part of which, edited by Dr. Murray, will soon issue from the University Press at Oxford, is to contain one quarter of a million of words. Every one of these words is a work of art; it is the workmanship of human genius. And every one of these words had not only to be fashioned, but it had to be accepted; it had to be recognized as the current coin of the realm by millions and millions of speakers. The history of that primeval coinage, its dispersion over the whole inhabited world, the losses which it suffered by wear and tear, the alloys which it had to admit, the ever-increasing rapidity with which the ever-increasing wants of the intellectual Exchange of the whole world were supplied, — all this forms a study with which, to my mind, no other study can vie, call it astronomy, geology, or even philosophy. That study certainly leaves the impression on every unprejudiced scholar that, to account for it all, we want rather the fabulous periods of Hindu chronology than the narrow limits of the dates which have been deduced by mediæval scholars from the Sacred Books of the Jews.

Well, let us consider now what a lesson of history is conveyed by the fact that Râmmohun Roy, when he came to England from the far East, spoke a language, the Bengâli, which in one sense, and in a truly scientific sense, may be called the same language as English. Not only the material elements, but the original formal elements too, are the same in English and Bengâli; and turn it as you like, you cannot escape from the conclusion that Râmmohun Roy, however strange his language may have sounded to his friends at Bristol, was not a mere stranger when he arrived in Europe, but was returning, in reality, to his own intellectual kith and kin. I say *intellectual* kith and kin, because that kinship is far more important than the mere kinship of blood. Blood may be thicker than water, but language is thicker than blood, at least to beings who, though for a time identifying themselves with flesh and blood, are themselves something very different from mere flesh and blood.

We have now reached a point from which the journey of Râmmohun Roy from India to Europe, and his stay in England, will appear to us in an entirely new light. The Science of Language, and, in fact, every true science, is like a hardy Alpine guide that leads us from the narrow, though it may be the more peaceful and charming valleys of our preconceived opinions, to higher points, apparently less attractive, nay often disappointing for a time, till, after hours of patient and silent climbing, we look round, and see a new world around us. A new horizon has opened, our eyes see far and wide, and as the world beneath us grows wider and larger, our own hearts seem to grow wider and larger, and we learn to embrace the far and distant, and all that before seemed strange and indifferent, with a warmer recognition and a deeper human sympathy. We form wider concepts, we perceive higher truths.

The Indian and the European grow into one, the Indo-European, speaking the same speech, thinking the same thoughts; and Râmmohun Roy, the dark-skinned stranger, when landing on the shores of these distant isles, is recognized at once, and greeted as one of ourselves, estranged from us by no greater changes than what some thousand years may have wrought in that language which his ancestors and ours once spoke together under the same sky, it may be, under the same roof, and which still lives on, however disguised, in his speech and in our own, in Bengâli and in English.

And now let us ask another question, in order to understand and properly to appreciate the hidden springs and the real purport of Râmmohun Roy's visit to England. Why did he come to England?

We shall see that ostensibly he came on business. He was sent by the Emperor of Delhi, the Great Mogul, to plead his cause in one of the crowded streets of the city of London, in Leadenhall Street, in the gloomy East-India House, before the Court of Directors of the now extinct East-India Company. But his real business was very different. The supreme and all-absorbing interest of Râmmohun Roy's life was religion. Remember the first lines on his tombstone, "He was a conscientious and steadfast believer in the Unity of the Godhead, and consecrated his life with entire devotion to the worship of the Divine Spirit alone." He was a Brâhman by birth, and though his mind had been opened by contact with English society in India, and had been widened, purified, and liberalized by a conscientious study of the Sacred Books of the great religions of the world, yet he remained a Brâhman to the end. No doubt he admired Christianity more than any other religion; I think we may truly say he admired it more than his own; yet, for all that, he remained a Brâhman, and was therefore in the eyes of most of the people who received him in England, a non-Christian, or a heathen.

And yet we have only to ascend again to a higher elevation, as we did before under the guidance of the Science of Language, and we shall meet with a new guide, the Science of Religion, which will lead us to a higher historical standpoint, and will open before our eyes a wider panorama, where the past history of the religions of the world seems almost present again, and where we can see the ancestors of that so-called heathen, worshipping the same gods and the same God whom some of our own ancestors still worshipped in their sacred groves not more than ten centuries ago. There was a time when the fathers of the Aryan race, that noble race to which we ourselves belong, which has since been divided into Greeks and Romans, Celts and Slaves on one side, and Indians and Persians on the other, invoked with the same names the gods of the sky, and the air, and the earth, the gods whose real presence was felt in the thunder, and the storm, and the rain, whose abode was looked for in the clouds or on the inaccessible crests of the mountains, — but chiefly the God, who was seen and yet not seen in the sun, who was revealed every morning in the brightness of the dawn, and who himself revealed, far away in the golden East, that infinite Beyond, for which human language has no name, human thought no form, but which the eye of faith perceives, and after fashioning it into endless ideal shapes, and endowing it with all that is most beautiful in poetry, most choice in art, most sublime in philosophy, calls it — God.

The names of these ancient Aryan gods, such as the poor vocabulary of man could supply, were the same among the Saxons whom Charlemagne converted, and among the poets of India, whose sacred songs have been preserved to us, as by a miracle, in the hymns of the Veda.

In this panorama, which a comparative study of the ancient religions of mankind has enabled us to construct, we can still see the Aryan worshippers, breaking up from their common centre, and dividing into two branches, the North-Western and the South-Eastern.

The former marched towards the home of the setting sun, till they had reached that small peninsula which we now call Europe, and which became the stage of what we are apt to call the history of the whole world.

The latter, the South-Eastern branch, set out to discover the home of the rising sun, till they reached their earthly paradise in the valleys of the land of the Five Rivers, and, further still, along the shores of the

Ganges and the Jumnah. Though these South-Eastern Aryas are seldom mentioned in our Histories of the world, we should bear in mind that India alone has more inhabitants at the present moment than the whole of Europe.

When these two streams parted, each of them preserved some of the names of their ancient common gods, but each arrived in time at the belief in a Father of all gods, in an All-father, in a God of gods. That faith, however, in the All-father, that mystery of the One God above all gods, was preserved by the few only. The North-Western Aryas at large, call them Greeks, or Romans, or Celts, or Slaves, or Germans, forgot the true meaning of the ancient names, debased the character of their ancient gods, and forgetful alike of the All-father and of the infinite Beyond in the golden East, they became more and more absorbed in the cares and pleasures of what was called political and practical life. From this there was but one escape; and we see accordingly that all the North-Western Aryas had sooner or later to surrender the ancient and corrupt religion of their Aryan forefathers, and to embrace a new religion, not of Aryan, but of Semitic descent; a religion in which the unity of the Godhead had never been forgotten; a religion founded, not only on the worship, but on the love of the All-father; a religion lastly which, in spite of the most fearful corruptions which it has suffered, has always preserved to those who have eyes to see, something of that original simplicity, purity, and true divinity which it possessed in the minds of Christ and His disciples.

Râmmohun Roy, the Arya, the Indian, the Brâhman, came to England for the sake of that new religion. He had studied Christianity before, he had seen its working among the English residents in India; but he wished to see a whole Christian country, and he was longing for free intercourse with some of the freest and most fearless thinkers in the Christian Church. And why was that?

I told you before that Râmmohun Roy was an Arya, belonging to the South-Eastern branch of the Aryan race, and that he spoke an Aryan language, the Bengâli. He had been brought up to worship the old Aryan gods, and he lived among a people most of whom had forgotten the original intention of their ancient gods, and had sunk into idolatry of the darkest hue. He himself, like many of his countrymen, possessed the old mystery of the All-father, the father of gods and men, the Pra*g*âpati, the lord of creatures, as he would call him. Nay, he knew more. He was a true Brâhman, so called because he knew the Brahman, the Supreme Spirit, or, more correctly, the Highest Self, the One without a second, the One in all, the Self behind us and the Self within. He knew all this, at least dimly, and yet he wanted to know more; and he came to England, the first Brâhman who ever crossed the sea, to see whether Europe, whether Christian Europe, would teach him something which he had looked for in vain in the Vedas and in the Upanishads, in the Bhagavadgîtâ and in the Vedânta-sûtras. He came to England, and after spending some time in London, seeing the best men he could find, and watching the outward manifestations of Christianity, wherever they showed themselves, whether in drawing-rooms or prisons, in Church or Parliament, in schools or hospitals, he at last came to Bristol to finish his search after truth, a search which only ended with his last breath.

I have thus tried to lay before you a map of the world, — a mere sketch, it is true, yet sufficiently clear, I hope, to make you see that Râmmohun Roy's visit to England was not merely a fortuitous adventure, but that it had historical antecedents, that it had an historical character, in the true sense of the word. If History is to teach us anything, it must teach us that there is a continuity which binds together the present and the past, the East and the West. And no branch of history teaches that lesson more powerfully than the history of language and the history of religion. It is under their guidance that we recognize in Râmmohun Roy's visit to England the meeting again of the two great branches of the Aryan race, after they had been separated so long that they had lost all recollection of their common origin, of their common language, of their common faith. In Râmmohun Roy you may recognize the best representative of the South-Eastern Aryas, turning deliberately North, to shake hands once more with the most advanced outposts of the other branch of the Aryan family, established in these islands. It is true that, long before his visit to England, England had visited India, first for the sake of commerce, then for the sake of self-defence and conquest. But for the sake of intellectual intercourse, for the sake of comparing notes, so to say, with his Aryan brothers, Râmmohun Roy was the first who came from East to West, the first to join hands and to complete that world-wide circle through which henceforth, like an electric current, Oriental thought could run to the West, and Western thought return to the East, making us feel once more that ancient brotherhood which unites the whole Aryan race, inspiring us with new hopes for a common faith, purer and simpler than any of the ecclesiastical religions of the world, and invigorating us for acts of nobler daring in the conquest of truth than any that are inscribed in the chronicles of our divided past. If England is to be the great Indo-European Empire of the future, Râmmohun Roy's name will hold a prominent place among the prophets and martyrs that saw her true mission, and her true greatness and glory in the distant future.

This must suffice as the historical background. Let us now look at the man who steps forward from it to do his own work in life, and to fight his own battle, trying with all his might to leave the world, and more particularly his own country, a little better than he found it.

There is little to be said about the mere life of Râmmohun Roy, and even the little we know from himself and from his friends is far from trustworthy. There is no taste for history in India, still less for biography. Home life and family life are shrouded by a veil which no one ventures to lift, while public life, in which a man's character shows itself in England, has no existence in the East. On the other hand, loose statements, gossip, rumor, legend, fable, myth — call them what you like — are marvellously busy in the East; and though Râmmohun Roy has been dead for fifty years only, several stories are told by his biographers which have clearly a mythological character.

What interests us so much in the biographies of great men, their home-life, their early friendships, their married life, all this is wanting in Râmmohun Roy's biography. We shall hear something about his feelings for his mother, but of his married life we know no more than that he had three wives. His first wife died when he was very young, and his father married him to a third wife while the second was living. His second wife was the mother of his two sons, Râdhâprasâd and Râmprasâd, and all we know of her is that she died soon after his mother's death. His eldest son died without leaving male issue, while the younger attained eminence at the bar, and was elected the first native Judge of the High Court of Fort William, though he died before taking his seat.

The real biography of Râmmohun Roy must be read in the work which he did; and in order to understand that work it will be sufficient for us to remember only a few prominent events of his life.[1]

Râmmohun Roy was born in Bengal in 1774, so that at the time of his death he was not more than fifty-nine years of age. His ancestors on both sides belonged to the Brâhman caste. His paternal ancestors, however, had been engaged in secular pursuits, while his maternal ancestors adhered to a life of religious observances and devotion. Râmmohun Roy himself was educated for practical life, and, as a boy, devoted much time to the study of Persian and Arabic, though the influence of his mother's relations seems to have induced him not to neglect altogether the study of Sanskrit, in which the main body of Hindu literature, law, and religion is composed. His doubts and misgivings as to his ancestral religion seem to have been roused at a very early age, but the statement that, at the age of sixteen, he composed in

[1] Miss Collet, who is collecting materials for a complete life of the Râjah, remarks that even the date of his birth is doubtful. The Râjah's younger brother placed it in 1772.

Persian a treatise against the idolatry of all religions[1] — a bold subject for a man of sixty, much more for a boy of sixteen — rests on authority that may be doubted.[2]

What seems certain is that, owing to some misunderstandings with his father on religious subjects, he left his paternal home when he was about sixteen, and travelled over a considerable part of India, proceeding even beyond the frontiers of his country, if report speaks true, and spending some time in Tibet.

That he studied the language and literature of Tibet, and became really acquainted with the Sacred Canon of the Buddhists in Tibet, I doubt for various reasons; still the impressions he received on these wanderings may have told on his future career, by opening his eyes to the similarity of all religious belief, hidden under a great diversity of outward form and ceremonial.

After his father's death in 1803 Râmmohun Roy first returned to Murshadâbad, the capital of the Soubah of Bengal, at whose Court his ancestors had found employment. He then served for a number of years as Dîwân (Sheristâdar) in the East-India Company's service. This was the highest post to which at that time a native could aspire, and a special clause had to be inserted in his Agreement that he should not be kept standing in the presence of his employer. At that time Dîwân meant often *de facto* magistrate, *de facto* collector, *de facto* judge. While holding this office at Rungpore, under Mr. John Digby, his knowl-

1 The book here referred to is probably the one mentioned on p. 33 as *Present to Monotheists*, of which, as Miss Collet informs me, one printed copy exists in the Adi Samâj Library. It was written after his father's death.

2 See note on p. 44.

edge of English was much improved, and he succeeded at last in writing and speaking it with considerable accuracy.

After having secured an independent fortune[1] — according to some amounting to ten thousand rupees a year — he went in 1814 to settle in Calcutta. He bought a house, built in the European style, and a garden, and in 1818 we first hear of meetings held there by his friends. We catch a glimpse of his life at that time through Mr. Arnot, who visited him at his garden-house near Calcutta, and found him one evening, about seven o'clock, closing a dispute with one of the followers of Buddha who denied the existence of a Deity. The Râjah had spent the whole day in the controversy, without stopping for food, rest, or refreshment, rejoicing more in confuting one atheist than in triumphing over a hundred idolaters. The credulity of the one he despised, the skepticism of the other he thought pernicious, being "deeply impressed with the importance of religion to the virtue and happiness of mankind."

Râmmohun Roy, however, was equally outspoken

[1] Remarks have been made on the sudden wealth which Râmmohun Roy was supposed to have accumulated during his Dîwânship. It is stated that he inherited next to nothing from his father, but that does not prove that other ancestral property did not come to him. Mr. Sandford Arnot states that "the death of relatives enabled him to retire from active life." Dr. Carpenter states that his father divided his property amongst his sons two years before his death, while Mr. Arnot declares that Râmmohun Roy was disinherited by his father. Certain it is that in an action instituted against Râmmohun Roy in the Calcutta Provincial Court in 1823, by the Râjah of Burdwan, Tej Chand, for a balance due from his father on a Kistbundy bond, Râmmohun Roy stated that, so far from inheriting the property of his deceased father, he had, during his life-time, separated himself from him and the rest of his family in consequence of his altered habits of life and change of opinions, and that, inheriting no part of his father's property, he was not legally responsible for his father's debts (*Biogr. Acc.*, p. 197). His brother, Jugmohun Roy, died in 1811.

against his co-religionists as against Buddhists and unbelievers. At first it seems to have been his contact with Mohammedans which made him a believer in One God. Afterwards, however, when his early hatred of everything English had been changed into a feeling of sincere respect,[1] and when his knowledge of the English language enabled him to become intimately acquainted, not only with some members of the Civil Service, but also with the master-works of English literature, his mind became more and more impregnated and invigorated by European thought and by Christian sentiment.

The social intercourse between English and Indian gentlemen was at that time much more cordial than it is at present, and religious, social, and literary questions were freely discussed on both sides. Religion has always been the principal subject of thought, and a favorite subject for discussion with the people of India, and Râmmohun Roy, in answering the questions or repelling the taunts of his English friends, seems to have felt no hesitation in expressing openly his contempt for that idolatrous worship which by others was taken to be the true and only religion of the country.

He appealed to the Sacred Books, written in Sanskrit, as bearing witness against the idolatry of the priest-ridden masses.

At that time, however, thanks to the labors of such men as Sir William Jones, Wilkins, and Colebrooke, Sanskrit MSS. were no longer sealed books, and it was easy to retort on Râmmohun Roy that his

[1] "He saw the selfish, cruel, and almost insane errors of the English in governing India, but he also saw that their system of government and policy had redeeming qualities, not to be found in the native government." Adam, *Lecture*, p. 26.

own Purâ*n*as and even the Mahâbhârata and Râmâ-ya*n*a, sanctioned idolatry, polytheism, caste, burning of widows, and many other abominations.

It was then that Râmmohun Roy took his stand on *the Veda*, as the true Bible of India. The Veda, he declared, sanctioned no idolatry, taught monotheism, ignored caste, prohibited the burning of widows; contained in fact a religion as true, as pure, and as perfect as Christianity itself, nay, free from some of the blemishes which offended him and many of his countrymen in the teaching of the missionaries.

This was a bold assertion, half true, half false, as we know now, but an assertion which at that time no one could venture to criticise or contradict.

Although there existed MSS. of the Veda, these MSS. were religiously guarded. No Englishman was allowed to see or to touch them. Even at a much later time, when Professor Wilson by accident put his hand on some Vedic MSS. in a native library, he told me that people rushed at him with threatening and ominous gestures. Of course, the Veda had never been printed or published, and it existed in fact, as it had existed for three thousand years, chiefly in the memory of the priests. We can hardly form an idea of the power wielded by the priests, when they were the only depositaries of Vedas or Bibles, and when there was no possible appeal from what they laid down as the catholic faith. In India their position was stronger even than in Italy, because the priest did not read the Veda from MSS., but had to learn it entirely from oral tradition, and teach it again to his pupils in the same way. No one therefore could contradict him except those who did not wish to contradict him.

Now it may sound strange, but I feel convinced that Râmmohun Roy himself, when, in his controversies with his English friends, he fortified himself behind the rampart of the Veda, had no idea of what the Veda really was. Vedic learning was then at a low ebb in Bengal, and Râmmohun Roy had never passed through a regular training in Sanskrit.

In the West and South of India the comparatively pure form of Hinduism which Râmmohun Roy endeavored to introduce into Bengal had never become extinct, and one of his native opponents, Sankara Sastri, while fully admitting the facts contended for by Râmmohun Roy, insisted strongly on this, that the latter had no claim to be considered the discoverer of a doctrine well known to all students of Sanskrit, and particularly of the Veda.[1]

Veda is the name for the oldest sacred literature of the Brâhmans. There are really four Vedas, but the most ancient and most important is the Rig-Veda. A Veda consists of two portions, a poetical and a prose portion. The poetical portion comprises hymns addressed to numerous deities, deities of the sky, the air, tho sun, the earth, fire and water, mountains and rivers. The prose portions, the so-called Brâhma*n*as, contain treatises on the various sacrifices, mixed up with a great deal of relevant and irrelevant, interesting and uninteresting matter.

The prose portions presuppose the hymns, and to judge from the utter inability of the authors of the Brâhma*n*as to understand the antiquated language of the hymns, these Brâhma*n*as must be ascribed to a much later period than that which gave birth to the hymns.

[1] W. Adam, *Lecture on Râmmohun Roy*, p. 7.

At the end of some of the Brâhma*n*as we find philosophical treatises, best known by the name of Upanishads[1] or Vedânta, literally, "End of the Veda." These contain the elements of that Vedânta philosophy which was reduced to a system in the Vedânta-Sûtras and may still be called the national philosophy of India.

When Râmmohun Roy speaks of the Vedas and of the monotheism taught by them, he almost invariably means the Upanishads, not the Brâhma*n*as, not the Mantras or hymns of the Veda. Both the Brâhma*n*as and the hymns teach a polytheistic, or, more accurately, a henotheistic, but not a monotheistic religion; yet they form the great bulk of what is called Veda, while the Upanishads form only a kind of appendix.

Râmmohun Roy had been brought up in the belief that the Veda was the word of God, that it contained a primeval revelation, that it was free from all the defects of human authorship. When therefore his friends or the missionaries pressed on him the claims of the Bible, as likewise an infallible book, he found himself between two infallible authorities, and naturally preferred his own.

And here he had a great advantage. While his English friends had simply to accept whatever he told them about the Veda, without being able to check his statements, he himself set to work to study the Bible in the original. It is extremely creditable to him that he did so; that he actually learned Greek and Hebrew in order to form his own independent opinion of the Old and New Testaments — very dif-

1 Translations of the principal Upanishads are contained in vols. i. and xv., of the "Sacred Books of the East."

ferent from many who carry on heated controversies about the Bible, who shrink from no terms of condemnation against all who differ from them, and yet shrink from the simple task of learning Greek and Hebrew.

After having studied the Old Testament with a Jewish Rabbi, the New Testament with an English clergyman, Râmmohun Roy in 1820 published his celebrated work, "The Precepts of Jesus, the guide to peace and happiness." This book consists chiefly of extracts from the Gospels, and in the Preface the author says: —

"This simple code of religion and morality is so admirably calculated to elevate man's ideas to high and liberal notions of One God, who has equally subjected all living creatures, without distinction of caste, rank, or wealth, to change, disappointment, pain, and death, and has equally admitted all to be partakers of the bountiful mercies which He has lavished over nature; and is also so well fitted to regulate the conduct of the human race in the discharge of their various duties to God, to themselves, and society, that I cannot but hope the best effects from its promulgation in the present form."

This publication brought upon him a fierce attack and a long controversy, not with the champions of the national religion of India, who might have suspected him of undermining their faith, but with the Christian missionaries of Serampore. Instead of welcoming him, on the principle that "he that is not against us is for us," they blamed him for the exercise of his private judgment, in selecting from the New Testament whatever *he* thought most likely to be beneficial to his own countrymen. He left out, for instance, most of the so-called miracles, because he felt that his countrymen, who were able without any effort to believe that a mere saint could swallow the whole ocean, and many of whom were convinced that they had seen a man throwing a rope into the air and ascending by it into the sky, were not likely to be much impressed by a change of water into wine, or by the miracle of the ascension.

And as the whole battle of his life had been to convince the people of India that there was, and that there could be, one God only, not two, not three, not many, we can well understand his anxiety that those whom he wished to bring nearer unto Christ, should on no account be led to believe that Trinitarianism was part of Christ's own teaching. As then taught by many of the missionaries in India, the doctrine of the three Persons, that is the three aspects or manifestations of the Godhead, had been hardened into mere Tritheism, the very doctrine against which Râmmohun Roy had been protesting from his earliest youth with all his might and main. It is well known that in India one of the most damaging charges brought against modern Christianity is that it admits three Gods, and it was against Mohammedan scoffers quite as much as against Christian missionaries that Râmmohun Roy argued in maintaining that Christ Himself, as we knew Him from the Gospels, believed in one God only, that He was in fact a Unitarian in the highest sense of that word. What Râmmohun Roy wanted for India was a Christianity, purified of all mere miracles, and relieved of all theological rust and dust, whether it dated from the first council or from the last.

That Christianity he was willing to preach, but no

other, and in preaching that Christianity, he might still, he thought, remain a Brâhman, and a follower of the religion of the Veda. He was engaged with two missionaries, William Yates and William Adam, in a Bengâli translation of the four Gospels, but this undertaking seems to have failed.[1]

There is an interesting story told by Mr. William Adam in his lecture on Râmmohun Roy which he gave many years ago in America, and which has lately been published at Calcutta.[2] Dr. Middleton, the first Bishop of Calcutta, thought it his duty to endeavor to convert Râmmohun Roy to Christianity, and in doing so, he dwelt not only on the truth and excellence of his own religion, but spoke of the honor and repute, the influence and usefulness he would acquire by becoming the Apostle of India. Râmmohun Roy expressed his bitter indignation that he should have been deemed capable of being influenced by any consideration but the love of truth and goodness, and he never afterwards visited the Bishop again. The same Mr. W. Adam, who had gone to India as a Protestant missionary, became a Unitarian, chiefly through the influence of Râmmohun Roy. He lived to a considerable age. I had some letters from him, but was unfortunately prevented from seeing him at Beaconsfield, where he died last year (1883).

Râmmohun Roy's influence grew rapidly. Some of the best, the most cultivated, and most enlightened among his countrymen, now joined him openly. Meetings were held on Saturdays[3] at his house, and

[1] *Lecture on Râmmohun Roy*, by W. Adam, p. 9.

[2] Calcutta, 1879, p. 24.

[3] They were held on Saturdays, as Miss Collet informs me, from November, 1828, to January, 1830. After the opening of the new Hall, in January, 1830, the day was changed to Wednesday.

these, as they became more largely attended and acquired greater regularity, formed the foundation of that movement which is known to you all as the Brâhma-Samâj, at first called also Brâhma Sabhâ.[1] I call it a movement, because it seems to me that, even at present, more than fifty years after its first beginning, the Brâhma-Samâj is still a movement only, an emotion, an aspiration, if you like, a religion; but not a settlement, a sect, or a church. At the weekly meetings of the Brâhma-Samâj extracts were read from the Vedas, discourses were delivered chiefly in Bengâli, hymns were sung, mostly composed by Râmmohun Roy himself. Great care, however, was taken not to wound national feeling more than could be helped. The Vedas, for instance, were chanted by Brâhmans only, from an adjoining room, where people of the lower castes were not allowed to enter.

Brâhma-Samâj means "Society of the believers in Brahman, the Supreme Spirit."[2]

In opposition to it, the orthodox and conservative party started the Dharma-sabhâ, the society or church of Dharma, the law. What was meant by law may be gathered from the fact that one of the first acts of the Dharma-sabhâ was to petition Government against the abolition of Suttee, that is, in favor of the continuance of the burning of widows. Râmmohun Roy had published, as early as 1818, a treatise entitled "A Conference between an Advocate for and an Opponent of the Practice of Burning

[1] See W. Adam, *Lecture*, p. 8.

[2] I write throughout Brâhma-Samâj. The various spellings, Brahmo Somaj, Brahmo Sumâj, etc., represent the various pronunciations of the word. Brahmo has almost become a new Anglo-Indian word, and, when used by others, it has sometimes been allowed to stand. Brâhma is meant as an adjective, derived from Brahman.

Widows alive." He lived to witness the triumph of his cause, but not till his arrival in England, when the last appeal of the members of the Dharma-sabhâ against the abolition of the burning of widows was heard in the Privy Council, and rejected.

This was in 1831 — not so very long ago, after all. It was the year of the Reform Bill; and a shudder comes over one, if one realizes the fact that up to that time, in a country governed by some of the greatest English statesmen, women were burnt wholesale, even in the immediate neighborhood of Calcutta. The official returns of the Bengal Government for the year 1823 show that the number of widows burnt during *one* year, in the Bengal Presidency only, amounted to 575; 310 widows perished within the limits of the Calcutta Court of Circuit. Their ages give a still more ghastly reality to that holocaust. We read that 109 were old women about sixty; 226 were from forty to sixty; 208 were from twenty to forty; and 32 were actually young girls under twenty years of age! We always say, "Such things would be impossible now!" Let us hope that the future may not say the same of us. I cannot help thinking, nay, I cannot help hoping, that some pages in "The Bitter Cry of London" will sound as ghastly to future generations as widow-burnings did to us.

Râmmohun Roy, however, by no means restricted his activity to controversial publications. He built schoolhouses, and established schools in which useful knowledge was gratuitously taught through the medium both of the English and native languages. He gave ardent and most zealous support to the missionaries of the Scotch Presbyterian Church in establishing in Calcutta a seminary in which Christian as well as general knowledge was daily and gratuitously taught to five or six hundred native youths by missionary instructors; and, following his example, one of his wealthiest friends and adherents gave still more liberal pecuniary encouragement to a similar school established by the same missionaries in the interior of the Jessore District in Bengal.[1]

In 1830 a Prayer Hall was opened in Calcutta by Râmmohun Roy, in which meetings were held every Wednesday. The foundation of the Brâhma-Samâj is dated from that year.[2]

This was almost the last public act of Râmmohun Roy before his departure for England. He sailed for

[1] Adam, *Lecture*, p. 18.

[2] The following extracts are taken from the Trust Deed of that Institution: "The Hall is to be used as a place of public meeting of all sorts and descriptions of people, without distinction, as shall behave and conduct themselves in an orderly, sober, religious, and devout manner, for the worship and adoration of the eternal, unsearchable, and immutable Being who is the Author and Preserver of the Universe; but not under or by any other name, designation, or title peculiarly used for and applied to any particular being or beings by any man or set of men whatsoever; and that no graven image, statue, or sculpture, carving, painting, picture, portrait, or the likeness of anything shall be admitted within the said messuage, building, land, tenements, hereditaments and premises, and that no sacrifice, offering, or oblation of any kind or thing shall ever be permitted therein; and that no animal or living creature shall, within or on the said messuage, building, land, tenements, hereditaments and premises, be deprived of life either for religious purposes or food; and that no eating or drinking (except such as shall be necessary by any accident for the preservation of life), feasting or rioting be permitted therein or thereon; and that in conducting the said worship and adoration, no object, animate or inanimate, that has been, or is or shall hereafter become, or be recognized as an object of worship by any man or set of men, shall be reviled or slightingly or contemptuously spoken of or alluded to either in preaching, or in the hymns or other mode of worship that may be delivered or used in the said messuage or building; and that no sermon, preaching, discourse, prayer, or hymns be delivered, made, or used in such worship, but such as have a tendency to the promotion of the contemplation of the Author and Preserver of the Universe, to the promotion of charity, morality, piety, benevolence, virtue, and the strengthening of the bonds of union between men of all religious persuasions and creeds," etc.

England on the 15th of November, 1830, as envoy of the Emperor of Delhi, the Great Mogul, who had bestowed on him the title of Râjah. He arrived at Liverpool on the 8th of April, 1831, and, after a short stay, proceeded by Manchester to London. You may read, in most of the biographical accounts of the Râjah, how he was received, how he was the lion of the season, how he was presented to the King, called on by dukes and duchesses, feasted by aldermen and the directors of the East India Company; how he went to Paris, and dined twice with the king, Louis Philippe, and elsewhere, how in the end his health gave way, and he returned to England weary in body and mind. We have no time to dwell on these items of fashionable intelligence. We have hardly time to do more than to point out the few really important events during his stay in England, — how, when at Liverpool, he was invited by William Roscoe to shake hands with him on his death-bed; how William Bentham, the utilitarian philosopher, who had secluded himself from all the world, was the first to call on the Râjah, of whom he used to say, "He has cast off three hundred and thirty millions of gods, and has learnt from us to embrace reason in the all-important field of religion;" how he knew Henry Brougham, not yet banished to the House of Lords; how he gave important evidence before several Parliamentary Committees at the time of the renewal of the Charter of the East India Company; how, lastly, as soon as he could free himself, he carried out his long-cherished wish of going to Bristol, a city famous at that time as the home of Dr. Carpenter, John Foster, Dr. Jerrard, Dr. Symonds, Mr. Estlin, Dr. Prichard, and others — men known not only for their learning, but for their liberal spirit, their wide sympathies, and their true charity towards men of the most opposite convictions in religion and theology. Here, in the house of Miss Castle, at Stapleton Grove, he thought he would find rest and repose. Here he hoped for help in solving those honest doubts which never forsake the heart of an honest man. But it was too late. He was attacked by fever, and in a few days his weakened brain succumbed. Dreaming of distant lands, of distant hopes, and distant friends, the Eastern philosopher, the believer in the religion of the Veda, the sincere admirer of the religion of Christ, expired.

Such was Râmmohun Roy, to my mind a truly great man, a man who did a truly great work, and whose name, if it is right to prophesy, will be remembered for ever, with some of his fellow-laborers and followers, as one of the great benefactors of mankind.

I know that this opinion is not shared by those who think that nothing great and nothing good can ever come out of India. What difference, they say, is there between Râmmohun Roy and many of those highly-educated, polished, liberal-minded gentlemen from Bengal whom we often see now in England, who laugh at idols, are horrified at the idea of burning widows, and speak patronizingly of the religion of Christ?

Surely the difference is very great. We know even in England how easy it *now* is to express opinions and support reforms for which men were executed three hundred years ago, excommunicated two hundred years ago, execrated one hundred years ago, and called ugly names within the recollection of some of the older members of this assembly.

The German name for prince is *Fürst*, in English *first*, he who is always to the fore, he who courts the place of danger, the first place in fight, the last in flight. Such a Fürst was Râmmohun Roy, a true prince, a real Râjah, if *Rájah* also, like *Rex*, meant originally the steersman, the man at the helm.[1]

If, however, I was wrong in calling Râmmohun Roy a really great man, I wish that those who seem so jealous of greatness would at least explain on what grounds *they* would bestow that ancient title.

An attempt was lately made in America to find out the Hundred Greatest Men of the world. The process was a very simple one. Greatness was settled by a majority of votes. Lists of names were printed and sent round to men of eminence in America and Europe, and whoever received the largest number of votes was admitted as one of the Hundred Greatest Men. The result was afterwards published in a splendid series of portraits, each portrait followed by a biography. It is astonishing to see what names were put forward, and what names were forgotten. Of course you see Napoleon the Great, and who could doubt that in one sense, as a clever soldier, as a bold diplomatist, he was great; but read the memoirs of his Court, and you will call him the smallest, the meanest, the most wretched of men. Or take another case. Perhaps the greatest revolution in Europe was produced by the invention of printing. Would you call the inventor of printing a great man? He did no more than what any carpenter might do — cutting an engraved block into smaller blocks, each containing one letter. You may call that clever, you may even take a patent for it; but surely there is nothing

1 See E. C. Clark, *Practical Jurisprudence*, p. 82.

great in it. In fact, that title of Great Man has been used so recklessly that to most people it conveys no longer any meaning at all.

And yet I like to call Râmmohun Roy a great man, using that word, not as a cheap, unmeaning title, but as conveying three essential elements of manly greatness, namely, *unselfishness*, *honesty*, and *boldness*. Let us see whether Râmmohun Roy possessed in a high degree these three essentials.

You know he gave up idolatry. This may seem to us a very easy performance ; but in India, as well as in Europe, nothing is more sacred to a child than the objects which he sees his father worship, nothing dearer than the prayers which he has been taught by his mother to repeat with uplifted hands, long before he could repeat anything else. There is nothing so happy as the creed of childhood, nothing so difficult to part with. And do not suppose that idol-worship is more easily surrendered. Idol is an ugly name, but it meant originally no more than an image. At first the image of a deity, like the image of a distant or departed friend, is only gazed at with a mixture of sadness and joy ; afterwards something like a real presence is felt, and good resolutions are sometimes formed from merely looking at the familiar features of a beloved face. And if at any time those who value such an image as their dearest treasure, pour out their sorrows before it, or implore it to fulfill some anxious prayer, and if such a prayer is fulfilled once, or twice, or, it may be, a hundred times out of two hundred, need we wonder that the very image is believed to be endowed with miraculous power, nay, that such faith remains unshaken, even if it be decreed that it is better for us that certain prayers should not be fulfilled? We must remember what sacred images are to millions of human beings even in Christian countries, and we shall then be better able to appreciate the unselfishness, the honesty, and the boldness of a boy of sixteen, who could bring himself to say, "I will not worship what my father worships, I will not pray as my mother prays; I will look out for a new God and for new prayers, if haply I may find them."

There was everything to induce Râmmohun Roy to retain the religion of his fathers. It was an ancient religion, a national religion, and allowed an independent thinker greater freedom than almost any other religion. But openly to condemn and reject that religion, or at least its present form, involved more serious consequences in India than almost anywhere else. It entailed not only censure and punishment, and the loss of the love of his parents; it entailed loss of caste, expulsion from society, loss of property. All this Râmmohun Roy was prepared to face; and he had to face it. He was banished from his father's house once or twice; he was insulted by his friends; his life was threatened, and even in the streets of Calcutta he had to walk about armed. Later in life his relations (his own mother) tried to deprive him of his caste, and indirectly of his property, and it was a mere accident that the law decided in his favor.

And remember that during all these struggles, and when he was left almost alone, he did not join any other community where, as a convert, he might have been received with open arms and warm hearts. He never became a Mohammedan, he never became a Christian, but he remained to the end a Brâhman, a believer in the Veda, and in the One God who, as he maintained, had been revealed in the Veda, and especially in the Vedânta, long before He revealed himself in the Bible or in the Korân.

He wished to reform his religion, not to reject it. His mother, we are told, was for a time broken-hearted about her son. It was she who, after the death of her eldest son (Ramtanu Roy), brought an action against Râmmohun Roy to disinherit him as an apostate and infidel.[1] But her son had the satisfaction, later in life, to hear from her own loving lips words which must have consoled him for many sorrows. "Son," she said to him, a year before her death, "you are right. But I am a weak woman, and am grown too old to give up those observances which are a comfort to me." This was said by her, before she set out on her last pilgrimage to Juggernaut, where she died.

With such self-denying devotion did she conform to the rites of the Hindu religion, that she would not allow a female servant to accompany her to Juggernaut, or any other provision to be made for her comfort or support during the journey. When at Puri, she occupied herself in sweeping the temple of the uncouth idol! Her son knew all this, and he bore with her, as she had borne with him. Perhaps he knew that the hideous idol which she worshipped in the fetid air of his temple, Juggernaut, as we call it, was originally called Jagannâtha, which means "Lord of the World;" and that He, the Lord of the World, the true Jagannâtha, would hear her prayers, even though addressed to Juggernaut, the uncouth image.

In all these trials Râmmohun Roy had nothing to

[1] *Lecture on Râmmohun Roy*, by W. Adam, Calcutta, 1879, p. 6.

support him but his belief in the Veda, and that very still, that very small voice within, which is better than the Veda, better than any written book. And I say again, a man who is ready to sacrifice everything for the voice of truth, who submits to be called a skeptic, a heretic, an atheist, even by his dearest friends, is an unselfish, an honest, a bold man,—is a great man, in the best sense of the word.

There is a quiet courage, a simple straightforwardness in all Râmmohun Roy's acts. Some of his friends have misunderstood him, and claimed him for a Mohammedan, or a Christian. He said himself, just before he set out for Europe, that on his death each sect, the Christian, the Hindu, and the Mohammedan, would claim him as their own, but that he belonged to none of them. His real religious sentiments are embodied in a pamphlet, written and printed in his life-time, but, according to his injunction, not published till after his death. This work discloses his belief in the unity of the Deity, his infinite power, his infinite goodness, and in the immortality of the soul.[1]

With such a faith nothing would have been easier for him than to do what so many of his countrymen, even the most enlightened, are still content to do,—to remain silent on doctrines which do not concern them; to shrug their shoulders at miracles and legends; and to submit to observances which, though distasteful to themselves, may be looked upon as possibly useful to others.

With such an attitude towards religion, he might have led a happy, quiet, respectable, useful life, and

[1] *Calcutta Review*, December, 1845, pp. 387-389. The title of the work as there given is, *Tuhfatu'l-Muwahhidin*, or "*Present to Monotheists.*"

his conscience need not have smitten him more than it seems to have smitten many others. But he would not. He might part with his old mother in silent love and pity, but towards the rest of the world he wished to appear as what he was. He would not say that he believed in three gods, when he believed in One God only; he would not call idols symbols of the Godhead; he would not have ritual, because it helped the weak; he would not allow Suttee because it was a time-hallowed custom, springing from the true love of a wife for a dead husband. He would have no compromising, no economizing, no playing with words, no shifting of responsibility from his own shoulders to others. And therefore, whatever narrow-minded critics may say, I say once more that Râmmohun Roy was an unselfish, an honest, a bold man—a great man in the highest sense of the word.

And mind, I do not say that the world is poor in men as great as Râmmohun Roy, and I know full well that many of them pass away unheeded, and leave behind them no name, no fame, no monument. But what is that? It only shows that the world is richer in good and great men than we thought it was.

But why should we grudge their greatness and their fame to those whom the world likes to honor? Go into a great library if you wish to know the meaning of the immortality of a name. Go into Westminster Abbey if you wish to know the value of a crumbling monument. True immortality is the immortality of the work done by man, which nothing can make undone, which lives, works on, grows on for ever.

It does good to *ourselves* to remember and to honor the names of our ancestors and benefactors, but to them, depend upon it, the highest reward was not the hope of fame, but their faith in themselves, their faith in their work, their faith that nothing really good can ever perish, and that Right and Reason must in the end prevail.

I have no doubt that when Râmmohun Roy muttered his last prayer and drew his last breath at Stapleton Grove, he knew that, happen what may, his work would live, and idolatry would die. That was the chief object of his life, and small as the results which he achieved might seem to others, he knew full well that all living seeds are small.

I am more doubtful about his belief in the divine origin of the Veda. It seems to me as if he chiefly used his arguments in support of the revealed character of the Veda as an answer to his opponents, fighting them, so to say, with their own weapons. But however that may be, it is quite clear that this very dogma, this little want of honesty or thoroughness of thought, retarded more than anything else the natural growth of his work.

After the Râjah's death the Church which he had founded, the so-called Brâhma-Samâj, languished for want of new interests and for want of a real head. During the next seven or eight years, its chief representative was Pandit Râm Chandra Vidyâbagîsh, one of Râmmohun Roy's earliest disciples; while its material wants were supplied by the generosity of Dvârkânâth Tagore, the same who erected the monument to the memory of Râmmohun Roy in the Arno's Vale Cemetery at Bristol, and who himself lies buried in Kensal Green. I knew him well while he was staying at Paris, and living there in good royal style. He was an enlightened, liberal-minded man, but a man of this world rather than of the next.

Dvârkânâth Tagore, however, became a still greater benefactor of the Brâhma-Samâj, though indirectly, through his son, Debendranâth Tagore, who is still alive, though he has for many years left the world, preferring to live by himself in perfect solitude, and devoted to meditation, and to the contemplation of the Divine Spirit, within and without. He, being a young man of considerable wealth, suddenly, at the age of twenty, saw the vanity of all earthly pleasures, and determined to devote the rest of his life to a search after truth, to a constant meditation on the things which are not seen, and chiefly to the discovery and recovery of his own true self in the Divine Self. He started a Society called the Truth-teaching Society, the Tattva-bodhinî Sabhâ, which lasted from 1839 to 1859, while its journal, the "Tattva-bodhinî Pâtrikâ," still continues to appear.

He was soon attracted towards the Brâhma-Samâj,[1] and his accession gave fresh life to it. In 1843 a new covenant was introduced, by which each member of the Brâhma-Samâj bound himself to give up idolatry altogether, and to cultivate daily prayer, addressed to the One God whose attributes were now more clearly defined.[2]

1 According to Sivanâth Sâstri, *New Dispensation*, p. 4, Debendranâth joined the Brâhma-Samâj in 1838; according to a statement made by Debendranâth himself, he did not really join the society till 1841. The foundation of the Tattva-bodhinî Sabhâ is dated by some in 1842, instead of 1839.

2 Extracts from the Brahmaic Covenant of the year 1843 (see *A Brief History of the Calcutta Brâhma-Samâj* from January, 1830, to December, 1867, Calcutta, 1868, pp. 8 seq.; and Pandit Sivanâth Sâstri, *New Dispensation*, p. 12: —

"First Vow: By loving God and by performing the works which He loves, I will worship God the Creator, the Preserver, and the Destroyer, the Giver of salvation, the Omniscient, the Omnipresent, the Blissful, the Good, the Formless, the one only without a second.

But a still more important step was soon to follow. Debendranâth Tagore's fervent soul was not satisfied with the Veda, or with any book that was to tell him once for all what to believe, and what not to believe. Doubts also seem to have arisen in his mind as to the grounds on which human beings could ever take upon themselves the right to ascribe a divine origin, in the miraculous sense of that word, to any book whatsoever. Nor have I the least doubt that here, for the first time, the learning of the West began to tell on the religion of the East. The Vedas, as I remarked before, were little studied in Bengal, yet in all controversies with Europeans these unknown Vedas were always quoted as the highest authority in all matters of faith. Thus, when the burning of widows was to be abolished, the Brâhmans simply quoted a verse from the Rig-Vega in support of it. This, they thought, was enough, and so it was indeed in the eyes of the law, which had promised protection to all established religious practices of the Hindus. We know now that the lines quoted from the Rig-Veda were garbled, and that, so far from enjoining the burning of widows, the Veda presupposes the opposite custom.

I tried to explain to you why it was so difficult for European scholars to gain a knowledge of the Veda.

"Second Vow: I will worship no created object as the Creator.

"Third Vow: Except the day of sickness or tribulation, every day, the mind being undisturbed, I will engage it in love and veneration of God.

"Fourth Vow: I will exert myself to perform righteous deeds.

"Fifth Vow: I will be careful to keep myself from vicious deeds.

"Sixth Vow: If, through the influence of passion, I have committed any vice, I will, wishing redemption from it, be careful not to do it again.

"Seventh Vow: Every year, and on the occasion of every happy domestic event, I will bestow gifts upon the Brâhma-Samâj.

"Grant me, O God, power to observe the duties of this great faith."

All other Sanskrit MSS. were freely communicated to Englishmen resident in India, but not the MSS. of the Veda. And even in cases where such MSS. had fallen into the hands of barbarians, the Pandits declined to translate them for them. Colebrooke alone seems to have overcome all these difficulties, and his Essays "On the Vedas, or the Sacred Writings of the Hindus," though published in 1805, are still extremely valuable.

When Râmmohun Roy was in London, he saw at the British Museum a young German scholar, Friedrich Rosen, busily engaged in copying MSS. of the Rig-Veda. The Râjah was surprised, but he told Rosen that he ought not to waste his time on the Hymns, but that he should study the text of the Upanishads.

Rosen, however, knew better. He published a specimen of the Hymns of the Rig-Veda in 1830, which gave European scholars the first idea of what these ancient hymns really were. Unfortunately he died soon after, and only the first book of the Rig-Veda was finished by him, and published after his death in 1838.

When Dvârkânâth Tagore came to Paris, he found me there in 1845 copying the text and commentary of the Rig-Veda, and there can be little doubt that his son Debendranâth heard from his father that European scholars had begun in good earnest the study of the Veda, and that its halo of unapproachable sanctity would soon disappear. Debendranâth Tagore, not knowing much of Vedic literature, in order to satisfy his own mind, sent four young Brâhmans to Benares about 1845 or 1846, to study the Vedas under some of the most learned theologians of that Indian seat of learning.

Interesting as the Vedas are to us, as historical documents, for they date from at least 1500 B. C., and give us an insight into the origin and growth of religion unsurpassed by any other literature, no one in his senses would for one moment claim for them a superhuman origin. After the report made by the four students after their return from Benares to Calcutta, Debendranâth Tagore did not hesitate, and in 1850 the Brâhma-Samâj solemnly pronounced the dethronement of the Veda.

There is nothing analogous to this in the whole history of religion, but this bold step, far from endangering the Brâhma-Samâj, really put new life into its members. The Brâhma-Samâj was now a Church without a Bible, and Debendranâth Tagore, its leader, felt inspired with new hopes and higher aspirations. There was nothing now between him and his God, and in this state of mind, not of despair, but of fervent faith, he revised the Brâhmaic Covenant, and wrote and published his "Brâhma-dharma,"[1] or

[1] In the *Brâhmadharma*, published in 1850 (third ed., Calcutta, 1869,) we find the Brâhmadharmavîga, Confession of Faith, as follows: —

(1) Om, Brahma vâ ekam idam agra âsît, nânyat kim*k*anâsît, tad ida*m* sarvam as*rig*at.

(2) Tad eva nitya*m* g*n*ânam ananta*m* *s*iva*m* svatantra*m* niravayavam ekam evâdvitîya*m* sarvavyâpi sarvaniyant*ri* sarvâsraya*m* sarvavit sarvasaktimad dharu*n*am pûr*n*am apratimam iti.

(3) Ekasya tasyaivopâsanayâ pâratrikam aihika*m* *k*a *s*ubham bhavati.

(4) Tasmin pritis tasya priyakâryasâdhana*m* *k*a tadupâsanam eva.

After that follows the Brâhmadharmagraha*n*a, i. e. the covenant to be signed by new members: —

Asmin Brâhmadharmavîge visvasya Brâhmadharmavîga*m* g*ri*h*n*âmi.

(1) God alone existed in the beginning, and He created this universe.

(2) He is intelligent, infinite, benevolent, eternal, governor of the universe, all-knowing, omnipotent, refuge of all, devoid of limbs, immutable, alone, without a second, all-powerful, self-existent, and beyond comparison.

(3) By worshipping Him and Him alone we can attain the highest good in this life and in the next.

(4) To love Him and to do the works He loves constitutes this worship.

By declaring my belief in the above combined four fundamental princi-

the religion of the one true God. After finishing this work, the young Saint retired for a time to the solitude of the mountains, to be alone with himself and with his God.

You see here how among all the books which are supposed to be held sacred by the people of India, it was the *Veda* alone, not the Bhâgavata Purâ*n*a or any other Purâ*n*a, that troubled the mind of these religious reformers. For them the Purâ*n*as had no such interest. They knew what stuff they were made of. They might be useful for women and children, they might contain grains of truth which every Brâhma would value,[1] but their childish legends could never stand in the way of men like Debendranâth Tagore. Does that show that the Veda was dead and forgotten, and that the true religion of modern India must be studied in the Purâ*n*as or Tantras?

Even after the fall of the Veda, do not suppose that the religious reformers of India discarded it altogether. They deprived it of its Divine Right, but they seemed to value it all the more, and they preserved all that they thought worth preserving in it, particularly the Upanishads.

When challenged by the Rev. J. Mullens, a missionary of the London Missionary Society, as to the new principles of the belief of the Brâhmas, Debendranâth replied: "The doctrines of the Brâhmas, or spiritual worshippers of God, whom I suppose you mean by modern Vedântists, are founded upon a broader and more unexceptionable basis than the

ples of Brahmaism I accept it as my faith. See Pandit Sivanâth Sâstri, *New Dispensation*, p. 12.

1 "The Purans and the Tantras are Shastras, because they also proclaim the unity of God." Râmmohun Roy, Bengâli translation of the Ishopanishad.

scriptures of a single religious denomination on earth. The volume of Nature is open to all, and that volume contains a revelation clearly teaching, in strong and legible characters, the great truths of religion and morality; and giving us as much knowledge of our state after death as is necessary for the attainment of future blessedness, yet adapted to the present state of our mental faculties. Now, as the Hindu religion contains notions of God and human duty which coincide with that revelation, we have availed ourselves of works which are the great depositaries of the national faith, and which have the advantage of national association on their side, for disseminating the principles of pure religion among our countrymen." [1]

The time will come, I hope, when scholars in India will study the Veda, as we study it in Europe, namely as an historical record of the highest value in the history of religion; but even then I trust that in India the Veda will always retain its peculiar position as the oldest book which, for the first time, told the inhabitants of that country of a world beyond this world, of a law beyond human laws, and of a Divine Being in whom we live, and move, and have our being.

If we may judge of Sacred Books by their fruits, then the life of such a man as Râmmohun Roy, who professed to be entirely guided by the Veda, would bear high testimony indeed to the intrinsic value of that oldest among all Sacred Books of the Aryan race, however crude, childish, unscientific it may seem to us.

Still more interesting, however, will it be to study and examine the lives of his disciples and followers, who no longer looked upon the Veda or any other

[1] *Brief History of the Calcutta Brâhma-Samâj*, 1868, p. 13.

book as divinely or miraculously revealed, and to whom the Veda had become simply a venerable book by the side of other venerable books, in order to find out whether a kind of heavenly halo is really indispensable in order to secure to Eternal Truth an entrance into the heart and an influence on the acts of man; or whether, as some believe, Truth, Eternal Truth, requires no credentials, but is to rule the world in her own right, nay, is to be welcomed all the more warmly when she appeals to the human heart, unadorned by priestly hands, and clad only in her own simplicity, beauty, and majesty.

To Râmmohun Roy the Veda was true, because it was divine; to his followers it was divine, because it was true. And which of the two showed the greater faith?

I have thus tried, and I hope not quite in vain, to enlist your sympathy, your real respect and love, for that great religious reformer of India, Râmmohun Roy. In India his name has been enrolled in the book of the prophets; and I hope that in future some at least of those who have kindly listened to me tonight will allow to this true Aryan nobleman a place among those who deserve to be called great and good.

APPENDIX.

THERE is a letter, supposed to have been written by Râmmohun Roy shortly before he left England for France, and addressed to Mr. Gordon of Calcutta. It was first published after the Râjah's death, in the

"Athenæum," October 5, 1833, by Mr. Sandford Arnot, who had acted as the Râjah's secretary during his stay in England. It was republished by Miss Mary Carpenter in "The Last Days of the Râjah Râmmohun Roy," London, 1866, p. 249. Although the relations between the Râjah and his secretary were not very friendly towards the end of the Râjah's visit to England, there is nothing in that letter to betray any unfriendly feeling. Whether the Râjah wrote or dictated the whole of it may be doubted, but to reject the whole as a fabrication would be going much too far. See letters from John Hare in "Times," October 28, 1833; from S. Arnot, November 23, 1833; from J. Hare, December 11, 1833. Mr. Arnot states that after the Râjah's return from Paris, both his mind and body seemed to be losing their tone and vigor, that his manners were changed, and his language became violent and coarse. His friends at Bristol, however, perceived nothing of this.

"My dear Friend,

"In conformity with the wish you have frequently expressed, that I should give you an outline of my life, I have now the pleasure to give you the following very brief sketch.

"My ancestors were Brahmins of a high order, and, from time immemorial, were devoted to the religious duties of their race, down to my fifth progenitor, who about one hundred and forty years ago gave up spiritual exercises for worldly pursuits and aggrandizement. His descendants ever since have followed his example, and, according to the usual fate of courtiers, with various success, sometimes rising to honor, and sometimes falling; sometimes rich and sometimes poor; sometimes excelling in success, sometimes miserable through disappointment.[1]

"But my maternal ancestors, being of the sacerdotal order by profession as well as by birth, and of a family than which none holds a higher rank in that profession, have up to the present day uniformly adhered to a life of religious observances and devotion, preferring peace and tranquillity of mind to the excitements of ambition and all the allurements of worldly grandeur.

"In conformity with the usage of my paternal race, and the wish of my father,[2] I studied the Persian and Arabic languages — these being indispensable to those who attached themselves to the courts of the Mohammedan princes; and agreeably to the usage of my maternal relations, I devoted myself to the study of the Sanskrit and the theological works written in it, which contain the body of Hindoo literature, law, and religion.

"When about the age of sixteen,[3] I composed a manuscript calling in question the validity of the idolatrous system of the Hindoos. This, together with my known sentiments on that subject, having produced a coolness between me and my immediate kindred, I proceeded on my travels, and passed through different countries, chiefly within, but some beyond, the bounds of Hindostan, with a feeling of great aversion to the establishment of the British power. When I had reached the age of twenty, my father

[1] Râmmohun's grandfather filled posts of importance at the Court of Murshadabad, the capital of the Soubah of Bengal. His father, Râmkânt Roy, left Murshadabad and lived at Râdhânagore, in the district of Burdwan, where he had landed property, the patrimony of the family.

[2] Râmkânt Roy.

[3] A. D. 1790.

recalled me, and restored me to his favor; after which I first saw and began to associate with Europeans, and soon after made myself tolerably acquainted with their laws and form of government. Finding them generally more intelligent, more steady, and moderate in their conduct, I gave up my prejudice against them, and became inclined in their favor, feeling persuaded that their rule, though a foreign yoke, would lead more speedily and surely to the amelioration of the native inhabitants; and I enjoyed the confidence of several of them even in their public capacity. My continued controversies with the Brahmins on the subject of their idolatry and superstition, and my interference with their custom of burning widows and other pernicious practices, revived and increased their animosity against me; and through their influence with my family, my father was again obliged to withdraw his countenance openly, though his limited pecuniary support was still continued to me.

"After my father's death, I opposed the advocates of idolatry with still greater boldness. Availing myself of the art of printing, I published various works and pamphlets against their errors, in the native and foreign languages. This raised such a feeling against me, that I was at last deserted by every person except two or three Scotch friends, to whom, and the nation to which they belong, I always feel grateful.

"The ground which I took in all my controversies was, not that of opposition to Brahminism, but to the perversion of it; and I endeavored to show that the idolatry of the Brahmins was contrary to the practice of their ancestors, and the principles of the ancient books and authorities which they profess to revere and obey. Notwithstanding the violence of the opposition and the resistance to my opinions, several highly respectable persons, both among my own relations and others, began to adopt the same sentiments.

"I now felt a strong wish to visit Europe, and obtain, by personal observation, a more thorough insight into its manners, customs, religion, and political institutions. I refrained, however, from carrying this intention into effect until the friends who coincided in my sentiments should be increased in number and strength. My expectations having been at length realized, in November, 1830, I embarked for England, as the discussion of the East-India Company's Charter was expected to come on, by which the treatment of the natives of India, and its future government, would be determined for many years to come; and an appeal to the King in Council, against the abolition of the practice of burning widows, was to be heard before the Privy Council; and His Majesty the Emperor of Delhi had likewise commissioned me to bring before the authorities in England certain encroachments on his rights by the East-India Company. I accordingly arrived in England in April, 1831."

KESHUB CHUNDER SEN.

(1838–1884.)

I HAD just said what I wished to say about Râjah Râmmohun Roy, when I received the news of the death of Keshub Chunder Sen, his devoted follower and successor. Whereas I knew Râmmohun Roy in the spirit only, I knew Keshub Chunder Sen both in the spirit and in the flesh. We were true friends through good and evil days, and I little expected that he would leave this busy world before me. The time to give a full account of Keshub Chunder Sen's life and life-work has hardly come as yet. Many little things must be forgotten before his true greatness can be realized. But there are certain impressions which he has left on our memories which, if not recorded at once, may fade away and be lost. Of his life, in the ordinary sense of the word, I know little, and the little I know, I know from his Indian friends only, with whom all responsibility for dates and facts must rest. But there are some hidden phases of his inner life which I know better perhaps than even his best friends in India. In his very last letter, which he wrote at Simla on the 20th June, 1883, he said: "Our affinity is not only ethnic, but in the highest degree spiritual, which often draws you into my heart and makes me enjoy the pleasures of friendly intercourse. I forget the distance, and feel we are very near each other. These Himâlayas ablaze with India's ancient glory constantly remind me of you, and as I read your Lectures on "*India, what can it teach us?*" in the veranda of my little house in the morning, I feel so intensely the presence of your spirit in me that it seems I am not reading your book, but talking to you and you are talking to me in deep spirit-intercourse."

However, before I can give a few records of our spirit-intercourse, I must try to give a slight sketch of the outward life of my friend, at least so far as it bears on his spiritual growth. I have no doubt we shall soon have a long biography, telling us of his ancestors, of his childhood, his youth, his manhood, full of dates, full of facts, full of anecdotes. I do not wish to anticipate these chroniclers, who so often tell us the very things that ought to be forgotten; and not always the things which it is right to remember. All I feel inclined to do is to give some slight frame to hold the portrait of the man.

Keshub Chunder Sen, in Sanskrit Kesava *K*andra Sena, died on the 8th of January, 1884, at the age of 46, having been born on the 19th of November, 1838. Though sprung from one of the orthodox Vaidya families in Bengal, European influences had reached and permeated his home for at least two generations before his birth. His grandfather, Râm Comul Sen, is known to Sanskrit scholars as the friend of Horace Hayman Wilson, and as the author of a useful Bengâli Dictionary. Râm Comul Sen had four sons, the second being Peary Mohun Sen, for some time Dîwân of the Calcutta Mint. This Peary Mohun Sen had three sons, and the second of them was Keshub Chunder Sen. The grandfather, Râm Comul Sen, was evidently on really intimate terms with Professor

H. H. Wilson, and the latter often spoke of his old friend in terms of affection such as one seldom hears now from the mouths of old Indian Civil Servants when speaking of their native subordinates. But Râm Comul Sen remained through life a thorough Hindu, strictly orthodox and minutely conscientious in the discharge of his religious duties; nor was Wilson the man to force his own theological opinions on his friend, so long as he knew that he could trust him as an honest man. He, being Director of the Mint, appointed Râm Comul Sen to the responsible office of Bullion Keeper. He afterwards became Dîwân of the Mint, Cashier of the Bank, and Native Secretary of the Asiatic Society. In his office of Dîwân he was succeeded by his son, Peary Mohun Sen. The office became almost hereditary in the family, devolving, after the father's death, on a younger brother, and after his death on Babu Jadunâth Sen, a cousin of Keshub Chunder Sen. When his cousin had to resign, Keshub Chunder Sen was prevailed upon to officiate for a time as Dîwân of the Mint until the Dîwânship was transferred to the family of the Dutts of Rambagun.

We thus see how in Keshub Chunder Sen's family European enlightenment and English principles of morality were united with strong Hindu patriotism and orthodoxy. He was brought up as a Bhakta, that is as a boy who would bathe every morning, put on a silk dhoti, and have his body anointed with sandal-wood powder. When he was ten, his father died, and Keshub was brought up by his uncle, though he had also the benefit of retaining through life the loving care of a mother who still survives him. She stood at his death-bed, lamenting that she, poor sinner, should be left behind while the dearest jewel of her heart was being plucked away from her. "Don't say so, dear mother," he replied. "Where can there be another mother like you? All that is good in me I have inherited from you; all that I call my own is yours." So saying he took the dust of her feet and put it upon his head.

As a boy Keshub Chunder Sen was admitted into the Bengâli Patshala (pâ*th*a*s*âla), an elementary school, from which he proceeded to the Hindu College, and afterwards to the Hindu Metropolitan College under Captain Richardson. His success at school seems to have been varying, his weak point being throughout mathematics. When he joined the Presidency College he does not seem to have distinguished himself, though he remained in the College as an ex-student, devoting his attention to history, logic, psychology, and zoölogy. His favorite books were Shakespeare, Milton, and Bacon; and so ardent was his devotion to his studies that those who knew him, after he had left the College and when he went to Bombay in 1864, described him as a pale, tall, and slender youth.

He developed at an early time a strong taste for acting. We are told that he acted Hamlet in his native village (Garifa, now Gouripore), the part of Laertes being taken by his young friend, now his probable successor, Protap Chunder Mozumdar. He also was a clever juggler, and occasionally performed in that capacity, passing himself off as an Englishman. But he soon began his career of public usefulness. In 1855 he established an Evening School for the children of working men, and this was continued with great success till 1858.

In 1856 he was married to a very young girl, the marriage being celebrated with the usual pomp. He himself disapproved of all extravagance, and he tells us how his thoughts began at that time to turn into a new direction. "I entered the world," he says, "with ascetic ideas, and my honeymoon was spent amid austerities in the house of the Lord." This continued for three or four years, during which time he became an ardent student of the Bible, helped by the Rev. T. H. Burne, Domestic Chaplain to Bishop Cotton. If any one could have persuaded Keshub Chunder Sen to become a Christian, it would have been the large-hearted Bishop Cotton. But this was not to be, and we may well believe that Keshub Chunder Sen, struggling all his life after truth, was a more impressive lesson to his countrymen than he would have been if he had been received and kept within the fold of the English Church.

Keshub Chunder Sen soon became attracted by the Brâhma-Samâj, the Society founded by Râmmohun Roy, the early history of which I have tried to describe before. The exact date of his joining that Society has been much discussed. It was supposed to be 1859,[1] but in a letter to Miss Collet, dated November 23, 1872, he wrote, "I became a Brâhma in 1857, when Debendranâth Tagore was in the Hills." This was from *S*aka 1778 to *S*aka 1780, A. D. 1856–1859, during the time of the mutiny. Debendranâth retired to the Himâlayas in 1855, and after three years of solitary contemplation returned to Calcutta.[2]

[1] *The New Dispensation and the Sâdhâran Brâhmâ-Samâj*, by Pandit Sivanâth Sâstri, M. A., Madras, 1881, pp. 6, 15 ; *Liberal*, March, 16, 23, 1884.

[2] See *Faith and Progress of the Brâhma-Samâj*, by P. C. Mozumdar, Calcutta, 1882, p. 192.

The fact was not, however, much known to the public till after Debendranâth's return. Unfortunately the original document, written in Bengâli by his own hand, in which he declared that Brâhmaism was the only true religion in the world, and avowed his faith in the holy Brâhma Dharma, is lost. But the date is of less consequence than the cause of his joining the Brâhma-Samâj.

The time had come for him to be formally initiated in the mysteries of his ancestral religion, but Keshub Chunder Sen declined to submit to any idolatrous rites, and it was the persecution of his own family which at that time drove him to seek refuge and advice with Debendranâth Tagore. Their first meeting was the beginning of a long friendship between the man of fifty and the young disciple of twenty, a friendship which, though outwardly severed for a time, lasted in their hearts till it was severed at last by Keshub Chunder Sen's death. Debendranâth Tagore was a rich man, and he enabled Keshub Chunder Sen to maintain himself at Calcutta, and to work for the cause they both had at heart. We soon hear of the young convert at the head of a Brâhma school, which was finally established on the second floor of the Brâhma-Samâj. Here two lectures were given every week, one in Bengâli by Debendranâth Tagore, the other in English by Keshub Chunder Sen.

About the same time we find Keshub Chunder Sen superintending the performance of a Bengâli play, written by Umesh Chundra Mitra, and called Bidhaba Bibaha Natak, "The Marriage of the Widow." This play had a great success at the time, being intended to influence public opinion in favor of widow-marriages.

In the same year, November 1, 1859, Keshub Chunder Sen was appointed to a clerkship in the Bank of Bengal, at a salary of £36 a year, which was soon raised to £60. His appointment left him sufficient leisure to pursue his favorite studies, to write, and even to lecture in public. His first tract, which appeared in 1860, was called, "Young Bengal, this is for you." In 1860 we hear of his meeting Mr. Dyson at Krishnaghur, in a public disputation on the merits of Christianity and the Brâhma religion. In the same year he accompanied Debendranâth Tagore and his son Satyendranâth to Ceylon.

In 1861 Keshub Chunder Sen gave up his post in the Bank of Bengal, having now determined to devote his life to the religious regeneration of his country. Speaking of that period of his life, he says:[1] "I do not believe in an absentee Lord. God is unto us all an ever-present Deity. As I saw my God, I naturally asked him where I should go to find means of subsistence and satisfy my hunger and thirst. To the Bank? To a mercantile office? No. The Lord told me, in plain and unmistakable language, to give up secular work altogether. But I said, 'Lord, will not my family starve, if all means of subsistence are thus deliberately cut off?' 'Talk not as an infidel,' was the reply. I was ashamed of my skepticism. I was assured that 'all things shall be added unto you.'" He and Debendranâth Tagore were at that time like two souls and one thought. Debendranâth Tagore wished his young friend to assume the ministership of the Brâhma-Samâj, and Keshub Chunder Sen, who had till then been tolerated as a member of a thoroughly orthodox family, resolved to enter with

1 *Lectures in India*, p. 268.

his wife the house of Debendranâth Tagore, and to dine with a man looked upon as a heretic and as excommunicated. Upon this he himself was expelled from his family, and had to live under the protection of his old friend, till in December, 1862, he obtained re-admission to his ancestral house. In the same month his eldest son was born. On the death of his father Keshub Chunder Sen received his share of the ancestral property.

Being now less hampered in his public career, Keshub Chunder Sen became more and more recognized as the champion of the Brâhma-Samâj. In his lecture, delivered 8th of April, 1863, "The Brâhma-Samâj vindicated," he clearly defined his position, both as against native opponents and Christian missionaries. An association, called the Sangat, or Sangata-Sabhâ, served as a centre for religious and moral discussions between him and his followers. Rules were agreed upon, pledges were taken, and the society became more strictly organized. Idolatrous rites were entirely put down.

The first Brâhma marriage, which of course was considered by native opinion as no marriage at all, was celebrated as early as 1861, Debendranâth Tagore himself setting the bold example of allowing his daughter to be married without the customary rites. Other reforms followed. The birth-festivals, the naming-festivals, initiations, and funerals were all conducted according to Brâhmic rites. Even the sacred thread was thrown off, and Debendranâth again set the first example. We have no idea how hard this surrender of cherished national customs appeared to many of the Brâhmas, and how deeply it afflicted those who had wished not to break openly with their Brâhma friends. Still nothing could restrain the ardor of Keshub Chunder Sen. In 1864, on the 9th of February, he started for Madras. It was his first great missionary enterprise, and he succeeded in planting a Brâhma-Samâj in the Madras Presidency. From thence he proceeded to Bombay, where he won many hearts, both English and native, and then returned to Calcutta with greater determination than ever to carry out his great social and religious reform. Opposition only roused his enthusiasm, friction only called out brighter sparks of eloquence. His old friend, Debendranâth Tagore, continued for a long time the friend and fellow-worker of Keshub Chunder Sen. We know that he gave up the Sacred Thread, that ancient and harmless religious symbol which even Râmmohun Roy would never part with, and which was found on his breast after his death.

But at last even Debendranâth became frightened, or allowed himself to be frightened by his more conservative friends. He and his friends were prepared to give up all that was idolatrous and pernicious, but they would not part with all their ancient national customs, they would not have their religion denationalized. They found all they wanted in their own ancient literature, and in the book of nature, open before their eyes, while Keshub Chunder Sen was looking more and more beyond the narrow frontiers of India, and seeking for spiritual food in the Christian Bible, and also, though in a less degree, in the Korân and other sacred books.

The celebration of a marriage between persons of different castes in August, 1864, produced a strong commotion. It must not be forgotten that Keshub Chunder Sen himself was not of Brâhmanic descent.

His appointment as Minister had hurt the feelings of other Brâhmas who, however much they might strive to be free from prejudice, could not altogether forget that all religious functions belonged by right to Brâhmans and to Brâhmans only. When therefore Keshub Chunder Sen insisted on making the removal of the Sacred Thread a *sine quâ non* of Brâhma fellowship, they rebelled. Debendranâth Tagore, who was by age and position the recognized head of the Brâhmas, and who had lifted Keshub Chunder Sen to the high office which he held as Minister, suddenly dismissed his young friend and his most active companions from all posts of trust and influence in the Samâj.[1]

Keshub Chunder Sen felt this deeply, but he was not to be discouraged. The separation took place in February, 1865, and as early as the 11th of November, 1866, he and his friends had founded a new society, still called the Brâhma-Samâj, but the Brâhma-Samâj of India, while the conservative Samâj now went by the name of the Âdi Brâhma-Samâj, *i. e.*, the First or Original Brâma-Samâj.

There was naturally more activity in the new than in the old Church. Debendranâth Tagore was tired of the world, and often spent many years in succession in the recesses of the Himalayan mountains in undisturbed communion with God, while the affairs of the Samâj were managed by Râjanarâyan Bose and a Committee.

Keshub Chunder Sen, on the contrary, after he had once come to the front, never left his place. He and many of his followers gave up all secular employment, and became preachers, teachers, and missionaries. "From comfortable and easy circumstances several

[1] See the correspondence in the *Tattvabodhinî Patrikâ*, No. 264.

came down to want and poverty, and had, on many occasions, to go without even the bare necessaries of life." They published books of theistic texts from all the Sacred Books of the world ; they built a new Prayer Hall in 1869, and Keshub Chunder Sen, by his marvellous eloquence not only in Bengâli but in English, won thousands of hearts for his cause. New journals were started, new schools opened, and great efforts were made to raise the women of India, so as to make them fit fellow-laborers in the cause of religious and social reform.

In doctrine there was little that divided Debendranâth from Keshub. "The fatherhood of God and the brotherhood of men" formed the common ground of their faith and their work. Their opinions also on the true character of the Veda were the same. Both had surrendered their faith in the revealed character of the Veda, both looked to other scriptures as well as the Veda for light and guidance.

The following is an authoritative summary of the doctrines of the old Brâhma-Samâj as accepted by Debendranâth Tagore. The same doctrines were embraced from the first by Keshub Chunder Sen, and with slight modifications held by him to the last.[1]

I. The Book of Nature and Intuition form the basis of the Brâhmaic faith.

II. Although the Brâhmas do not consider any book, written by man, as the basis of their religion, yet they do accept, with respect and pleasure, any truth contained in any book.

III. The Brâhmas believe that the religious condition of man is progressive, like the other parts of his condition in this world.

[1] *Brief History of the Calcutta Brâhma-Samâj from 1830 to 1867*, Calcutta, 1868, p. 17.

IV. They believe that the fundamental doctrines of their religion are at the basis of every religion followed by man.

V. They believe in the existence of One Supreme God, a God endowed with a distinct personality, moral attributes equal to His nature, and intelligence befitting the Governor of the Universe, and worship Him — Him alone. They do not believe in His incarnation.

VI. They believe in the immortality and progressive state of the soul, and declare that there is a state of conscious existence succeeding life in this world, and supplementary to it, as respects the action of the universal moral government.

VII. They believe that repentance is the only way to atonement and salvation. They do not recognize any other mode of reconcilement to the offended but loving Father.

VIII. They pray for spiritual welfare, and believe in the efficacy of such prayers.

IX. They believe in the Providential care of the Divine Father.

X. They avow that love towards Him, and performing the works He loves, constitutes His worship.

XI. They recognize the necessity of public worship, but do not believe that they cannot hold communion with the Great Father without resorting to any fixed place at any fixed time. They maintain that we can adore Him at any time and at any place, provided that time and that place are calculated to compose and direct the mind towards Him.

XII. They do not believe in pilgrimages, but declare that holiness can only be attained by elevating and purifying the mind.

XIII. They do not perform any rites or ceremonies, or believe in penances as instrumental in obtaining the grace of God. They declare that moral righteousness, the gaining of wisdom, Divine contemplation, charity, and the cultivation of devotional feelings are their rites and ceremonies. They further say, — Govern and regulate your feelings, discharge your duties to God and to man, and you will gain everlasting blessedness. Purify your heart, cultivate devotional feelings, and you will see Him who is unseen.

XIV. Theoretically there is no distinction of caste among the Brâhmas. They declare that we are the children of God, and therefore must consider ourselves as brothers and sisters.

If we compare this Confession of Faith with the declaration of principles delivered by Keshub Chunder Sen at the opening of his own Church (Mandira), on August 22, 1869, we shall find little difference between the two, though in the practical carrying out of their doctrines their roads were diverging more and more.

Keshub Chunder Sen on that occasion read the following statement:[1] —

"To-day, by Divine Grace, the public worship of God is instituted in these premises for the use of the Brâhma community. Every day, at least every week, the One only God without a second, the Perfect and Infinite, the Creator of all, Omnipresent, Almighty, All-knowing, All-merciful, and All-holy, shall be worshipped in these premises. No created object shall be worshipped here. No man or inferior being or material object shall be worshipped here, as identical with

[1] *Brâhma Year Book*, 1876, p. 11.

God or like unto God; or as an incarnation of God; and no prayer or hymn shall be offered or chanted unto or in the name of any except God. No carved or painted image, no outward symbol which has been or may hereafter be used by any sect for the purpose of worship, or the remembrance of a particular event, shall be preserved here. No creature shall be sacrificed here. Neither eating, nor drinking, nor any manner of mirth or amusement shall be allowed here. No created being or object that has been or may hereafter be worshipped by any sect shall be ridiculed or contemned in the course of the Divine service to be conducted here. No book shall be acknowledged or revered as the infallible word of God; yet no book which has been or may hereafter be acknowledged by any sect to be infallible, shall be ridiculed or contemned. No sect shall be vilified, ridiculed, or hated. No prayer, hymn, sermon, or discourse to be delivered or used here shall countenance or encourage any manner of idolatry, sectarianism, or sin. Divine service shall be conducted here in such spirit and manner as may enable all men and women, irrespective of distinctions of caste, color, and condition, to unite in one family, eschew all manner of error and sin, and advance in wisdom, faith, and righteousness. The congregation of 'The Brâhma Mandira of India' shall worship God in these premises according to the rules and principles hereinbefore set forth."

What were the exact causes of the breach between Debendranâth Tagore and Keshub Chunder Sen it is difficult to say. They were hardly doctrinal, as any one may see who compares these two confessions. They were not personal, for the two friends, though outwardly separated, remained united by mutual feelings of love and veneration. They were, so far as we can judge, such as arise when practical measures have to be discussed and decisions have to be taken. Then interests seem to clash, misunderstandings become inevitable, misrepresentations are resorted to, and newspaper gossip makes retreat from untenable positions very difficult. So far as I can judge, Debendranâth and his friends were averse to unnecessary innovations, and afraid of anything likely to wound the national feelings of the great mass of the people. They wanted before all to retain the national character of their religion. "A so-called universal form," they said, "would make our religion appear grotesque and ridiculous to the nation." They pleaded for toleration for Hindu usages and customs which appeared to them innocent. "If a progressive Brâhma," they argued, "requires a conservative one to reject those portions which the former considers to be idolatrous, but the latter does not, he denies liberty of conscience to a fellow-Brâhma."

It may be that Keshub Chunder Sen's devotion to Christ also, which became more pronounced from year to year, disquieted the minds of the Brâhmas. After his lecture on "Jesus Christ, Europe and Asia," delivered in May, 1866, many people, I am told, both native and European, felt convinced that Keshub Chunder Sen would openly embrace Christianity.

Keshub Chunder Sen, however, was at that time absorbed far less in doctrinal questions than in practical measures of progress and reform. To quote the words of his friend Protap Chunder Mozumdar,[1] "The great spiritual exercises and emotional excite-

[1] *Faith and Progress*, p. 39.

ment began, and the first devotional festival was celebrated in November, 1867. Side by side with the spiritual excitement the most radical social reforms were commenced, the Native Marriage Act was passed, the Indian Reform Association with its five sections was established in 1870, and the Bharat Asram (or the Indian Hermitage) was opened in 1872. A Female Normal School was founded for training lady-teachers, and a temperance movement was supported by a special journal.

Brâhma-Samâjas began to spring up in different parts of the country as a result of this new agency. A most active missionary organization was constituted, and the preachers were sent to travel from one part of the country to the other. All this culminated in the missionary expedition of 1879. The whole movement under the influence of such manifold activities began to take a new shape. New doctrines were conceived and preached. Yoga (spiritual exercises), Bhakti (devotion and love), and Asceticism were explained from a new point of view. Great reverence was felt for Christ and other Masters; pilgrimages to saints and prophets were encouraged; sacraments and ceremonials were instituted; and at last the New Dispensation, as the highest development of the Brâhma-Samâj, was proclaimed in 1880.

Much as I sympathize with Keshub Chunder Sen, I am not prepared to say that his movement was in every respect an advance beyond the point reached by Debendranâth Tagore. In one sense it might even be called a retrogression. To those who are acquainted with Hindu philosophy I could explain the difference between the two teachers very briefly, namely as a change from pure Vedânta to Yoga. Debendranâth Tagore had fully realized the philosophic poetry of the Upanishads and the more systematic teaching of the Vedânta-sûtras. He had found rest there, and he wanted little more. Keshub Chunder Sen saw that lofty height of thought at certain moments of his life, but he never reached it. And this, though to Debendranâth it must have seemed weakness, constituted in many respects Keshub Chunder Sen's real strength. While Debendranâth was absorbed in himself, Keshub labored all his life, not for himself only, but for others. He wanted a pure but popular religion and philosophy for those who were still in the lowest stage of mythological faith, and this Debendranâth could not give them.

P. C. Mozumdar seems to have felt the same, when he said: [1] "The present generation of Brâhmas were intensely impressed through their Chief Teacher, Debendranâth Tagore, with the supreme fact that God was an indwelling Spirit, and an All-pervading Soul. But it must be confessed that for purposes of personal piety, for tender devotions such as may call sinners to repentance and give salvation to the sorrow-stricken, the exalted teaching of Debendranâth Tagore, great as it was, was not sufficient. Our conceptions required more fulness and definiteness. Though from the lips of the revered saint the strange beatitudes of his own faith fell like honey, and we drank it, and were filled with gladness and enthusiasm, yet God was to us an unknown God. . . . Keshub Chunder Sen is and always has been a man of prayer. He began his religious life by appealing to God to show him the light of His face. He always insisted upon realizing the presence of God before him, as the idola-

[1] *Theistic Review and Interpreter*, July, 1881, p. 16.

ter, who unmistakably saw his idol present near his own body. Thus one of his characteristic teachings is that of seeing God. He means of course spiritual perception, vivid realization in faith of the presence of the Supreme Spirit. But this process he describes to be exceedingly simple and natural. He says, in one of his sermons, that 'as it is easy for the body to see and hear, so it ought to be easy for the soul to see and hear. Hard struggles are not necessary for the soul to see God. Bring the soul to its natural condition, and you will succeed.'"

It is difficult to understand why all this good work should have roused so much opposition, not only among those who were opposed to all reforms, but among Keshub Chunder Sen's own friends. No doubt in some of his utterances and in some of his public acts he might have seemed extravagant. But religious reformers cannot be judged according to the ordinary rules of taste. It is sad indeed to have to confess that there is something in human nature that resents success for its own sake. Keshub Chunder Sen's success as a preacher and as a leader was, no doubt, very great. Drunkards were reclaimed, men of abandoned character were made to feel the influence of the Divine Name. Lord Lawrence invited the young reformer to Simla, and the house reserved for the reception of distinguished native visitors was placed at his disposal. We need not ascribe the violent abuse which began to be poured forth at the same time in the newspapers to the worst of all motives, mere envy. We may admit that even envy arises sometimes from a sense of justice, from a feeling that success ought to be in a certain proportion to merit. But what surprises the unprejudiced student of that painful and instructive chapter of history is the unreasonableness of the charges brought against Keshub Chunder Sen. It was his lecture on "Great Men," delivered about five months after his lecture on Christ, which supplied the chief indictment against him. While in the eyes of his orthodox countrymen he was a heretic and atheist, he was accused by some of his own followers of aspiring to the honor due to the Godhead only, and his most intimate friends were found guilty of man-worship.

Keshub Chunder Sen, though feeling perfectly guiltless, had to defend himself, but in doing so, he only incurred new blame from his adversaries, namely that of mock-humility. There is no crime which a partisan cannot defend, there is no purity which a rival cannot besmirch. It is a pity that men should not know this and should bemean themselves by defending themselves against charges of which the grand-jury of their own heart finds them innocent. These charges were continued from year to year, and it may be well to give here at least one specimen of his defence, though it dates from a later time, from a lecture delivered at the Forty-fifth Anniversary of the Brâhma-Samâj (1875). "To dwell in love," he said (p. 30), "is to dwell in heaven. Accept then the gospel of love as the gospel of universal redemption. . . . I have borne witness to the truth, and if you, friends and countrymen, accept what I have said, it will undoubtedly conduce to your spiritual welfare. . . . But I fear I may run some risk in quite another direction. I apprehend I may be accepted as a teacher by unthinking thousands among my countrymen. They may turn round to me, and pointing to the scheme of salvation I have set forth, say,—We shall accept you as our teacher, for you profess to have received from Heaven the light of our salvation. This may mean a compliment, and many are its temptations. But to me it is repulsive, and the Lord directs me to repel the offer as a snare and a danger. You know how in India religion has degenerated into hero-worship. . . . Looking upon this painful spectacle, my heart naturally shudders and recoils from the thought of setting up as a teacher. I shrink back from the awful responsibilities which attach to the position of a religious guide. Nay, without any hesitation or equivocation I can emphatically assure you I am *not* a teacher, and I will never be a teacher unto my countrymen. . . . If you believe in God, believe that He has not commissioned me to be an infallible guide unto you. . . . The very creed my mouth has preached to-day disowns me, and points to God alone as the source of all truth. If you exalt me as a teacher, and then falling down before me accept every utterance of mine as a divine message, you do so at the risk of debasing yourselves and jeopardizing your highest interests. You will perhaps say, this is nothing but humility and modesty, so common among professed preachers. I say candidly, I claim neither humility nor honor before my countrymen. I am not in the least anxious that you should credit me with extraordinary self-abasement or self-esteem. I simply state a fact. . . . All that I contend for is this, that whatever truth there may be in my teachings should be accepted and followed, not for my sake, but for the sake of the truth itself. Let not my name carry the weight of authority. . . . In the economy of Providence, opposition, far from extinguishing, sets ablaze the torch of truth by shaking it. Am I afraid of those who have conspired to resist the progress of the true gospel? Depend upon me, the Lord shall confound and discomfit them, and His truth shall prevail at last. . . . Have I not been slandered and abused, for some years past, in the cruelest manner, and has not the vilest calumny been heaped upon the men and women who have taken shelter under the present dispensation? Most scandalous charges have from time to time been brought against us, which, if true, would render us odious and detestable in the estimation of all mankind. I repudiate these unfounded and false imputations with a clear conscience. Far be it from me to attempt a personal vindication. The righteousness of the cause I advocate and the purity and sincerity of my motives will vindicate themselves in the course of time."

This language shows how deeply Keshub Chunder Sen felt the charges which envy and ignorance engendered in the hearts of his countrymen. Of course, he claimed inspiration, and no artificial, exceptional, or miraculous, but the real, natural, and only true inspiration which every one knows who knows what truth is, and who has felt his heart vibrate, if only once, in perfect unison with the voice of God. What he meant by inspiration he tries to explain again and again. Thus in his lecture at the Forty-third Anniversary of the Brâhma-Samâj (1873), he first of all explains his conception of Prayer. "Men," he says (p. 8), "had always to pray for salvation before they received it. None received it who did not ask for it. Ever since man was created, the whole spiritual world has been governed by the immutable law of prayer. The law is, Ask, and it shall be given you; Seek, and ye shall find; Knock, and it shall be opened unto you. . . .

We must assume the attitnde of prayer before God reveals His light unto us. . . . It is absurd to think that God breaks or suspends His laws or keeps them in abeyance every time He responds to our prayers. To grant a prayer is to act in accordance with fixed laws, not in opposition to them. . . . Assuredly God does speak to us in reply to every word we say unto Him. He either rebukes our hypocrisy and wickedness or He grants our requests. He either sends us away from His presence with a warning and a reprimand or heaven rings with a loud Amen to our humble prayers. . . . Only those who pray in the right spirit hear a favorable response. Those who truly ask receive; those who truly seek find. The law of prayer is immutable."

After having thus explained prayer as a conforming to the will of God, he proceeds to explain what he means by Inspiration. "Let us see now what Inspiration is. It is the thrilling and, I may add, the electrifying response which God gives to our prayers. I have already told you that prayer and inspiration are two sides of the same fact of spiritual life. Man asks and God gives. The spirit of man kneels and is quickened by the spirit of God. The cause and the effect seem hardly distinguishable, and in the reciprocal action of the human and the divine spirits there is a mysterious unity. Hardly has man opened his heart in prayer, when the tide of inspiration sets in. The moment you put your finger in contact with fire you instantly feel a burning sensation. So with prayer and the consequent inspiration. The effect is immediate, necessary, and inevitable. . . . We must not regard inspiration as God speaking by fits and starts, but as a perpetual breathing of His spirit. . . .

Whether we hear Him or not, He speaks always; whether we catch the rays of His inspiration or not, He shines eternally, and sends forth His light in all directions. . . . With the profoundest reverence be it said that it is possible for man to put on God. For then self is completely lost in conscious godliness, and you feel that you do nothing of yourself, and that all your holy thoughts, words, and actions are only the breathings of the Holy Spirit. So the great prophets of earlier times thought and felt. . . . In the highest stage man's aspiration and God's inspiration are continually exchanged with all the ease and force of natural breath. They become in fact the soul's vital breath without which it cannot breathe."

But we must not anticipate. While all this spiritual fermentation was going on, while some members of the Brâhma-Samâj were frightened by the fearless progress of their young leader, and others began to clamor that even he did not advance fast enough, Keshub Chunder Sen himself suddenly announced his intention of leaving the battle-field for a time and paying a visit to England. That resolution was carried out almost as soon as it was conceived, and in the year 1870 Keshub Chunder Sen landed in England.

His stay in England was a constant triumph. "He had many personal characteristics," as the Indian "Daily News" truly said, "which fitted him for religious work. A fine countenance, a majestic presence, and that rapt look which of itself exerts an almost irresistible fascination over impressible minds, lent wonderful force to a swift, kindling, and poetical oratory which married itself to his highly spiritual teaching as perfect music unto noble words."

I need not dwell here on the successive events of

his sojourn in London and his journeys to the principal towns. All this has been well described by Miss Collet, and many of my readers must remember his eloquent addresses and the deep impression which they produced in the widest spheres. His name has become almost a household word in England, and I have been struck, when lecturing in different places, to find that the mere mention of Keshub Chunder Sen's name elicited applause for which I was hardly prepared. I made his personal acquaintance in London at the house of my friend, Dean Stanley. He afterwards paid a visit to me at Oxford, and our friendship, which then began, has lasted to the end.

While at Oxford, I took him to see Dr. Pusey, and I regret that I did not write down at the time the deeply interesting conversation that passed between the two. I saw a short account of that meeting in the "Liberal" of June 1, 1884: "Mr. Sen paid flying visits to Oxford and Cambridge. At the latter place he saw his old friend, Mr. Cowell, and had also a friendly interview with Mr. F. Maurice, whose broad and tolerant views so well agree with those of his Eastern friend. To Oxford he went accompanied by Professor Max Müller. The most remarkable incident of this visit was his interview with Dr. Pusey. Mr. Sen and Professor Max Müller were shown into a small room upon the tables and floors of which were scattered heaps of books and papers in delightful confusion, in the midst of them all being seated the venerable figure that had stood many storms, led many controversies, and gained many trophies. A serious talk ensued, in the course of which Professor Max Müller asked if a man in the position of Mr. Sen should receive salvation. Dr.

Pusey answered with a smile, 'Yes, I think he will.' This was no small compliment and concession from the man who had no word to say in favor of Dr. Colenso."

I need hardly say that the question was not asked quite so abruptly. Dr. Pusey was at first reserved till the conversation turned on prayer. Keshub Chunder Sen, while defending his own position towards Christianity, burst out into an eloquent panegyric on prayer, which ended with the words, "I am always praying." This touched Pusey's heart, and he said, "Then you cannot be far wrong." I hesitate now to write down from memory what followed afterwards. I only know that I never heard Pusey speak with so much of truly poetical eloquence. There was an image of an evening in a village churchyard which he drew with a few graphic words, and which has remained in my memory ever since, though I should not venture to copy it here. It was meant to illustrate the affection of the people for their Church, around which they buried what was dearest to them in this life. My rather abrupt-sounding question was addressed to Dr. Pusey, after he had been expatiating on what seemed to him necessary for salvation, in answer to Keshub Chunder Sen, who had maintained that on all that was essential in Christ's teaching he was at one with the best of English divines. Dr. Pusey's remarks seemed to me to describe a form of Christianity which neither Keshub Chunder Sen nor India at large could ever accept, nay, which I thought St. Paul himself would not have accepted, and I therefore ventured to interpose the question whether, at the time of Christ, a man who believed what Keshub Chunder Sen believed would or would not have been received as a disciple.

Keshub Chunder Sen came to England to see and to learn. He saw the most distinguished statesmen, scholars, and divines, and made a real study of all the institutions intended for the improvement of the young, the succor of the sick, and the punishment of criminals. "I have come to England," he said, "to study the spirit of Christian philanthropy, of Christian charity, and honorable Christian self-denial." The Queen, knowing how great a power for good he wielded in India, granted him a private audience, which left an indelible impression on his heart.

But though Keshub Chunder Sen came to learn, he had also to teach and to preach. People of all shades of opinion wished to know what a man like him, who was believed to be thoroughly honest, really thought of the religion of Christ. Some wished to know why he believed so much, others why he did not believe all. The answers which he gave to these inquiries are extremely interesting, but it is difficult to summarize them by means of extracts. The following article from the "Indian Mirror," reprinted in "Essays, Theological and Ethical," Calcutta, 1874, p. 35, will give, I believe, a sufficiently clear and complete idea of his conception of Christ and Christianity and their importance for India: "There is an infinite diversity of opinions among Indian Theists respecting Jesus of Nazareth, ranging from intense hatred on the one hand to profound reverence and personal attachment on the other. Not a few there are who look upon him with almost the same spirit of sectarian antipathy and abhorrence as Hindus, and even go to the length of calling him an impostor. Such ideas are happily dying out. The vast majority of our brethren of the liberal school cherish respect and gratitude towards Christ, and some even accept him as a guide and master. We have no desire to enter into a theological controversy on this subject, but we think it necessary to say a few words to point out the manner in which we accept Christ, so as to make him unto us not a source of wranglings and disputes, but of life, strength, and righteousness. We Theists must take it to be foreign to our purpose to canvass the thousand theories which have been propounded about him and his creed; but surely it is our interest and duty to receive from him that healthy moral influence which he is appointed in God's economy to exercise on the world, to love him and revere him and follow his teachings and example. We must remember that there is a bodily Christ and a spiritual Christ, a local Christ and a universal Christ, a dead Christ and a living Christ. Orthodox Christians may deal with the former and seek revelation and salvation in the visible and tangible incidents of the Christ that was. But our business is with the spiritual, universal, and living Christ. What shall we do with the *body?* We want the *spirit.* Not the son of man, but the son of God in Christ is needful for our salvation. In the purely human Christ we can hardly feel any interest; but the divine elements of his character come home to every man's bosom and business, and are of the highest importance to our redemption as involving the eternal and universal principles of ethics. By Christ we mean not the person bearing that name, not his form and flesh, but the spirit he embodied, — the spirit of faith, love, righteousness, and sacrifice of which he was unquestionably a noble impersonation. We always attach to him this significance; we look upon him in this light; we try to imitate and follow him as such. He does not come to us as God, the Father, Ruler, and Saviour, in human form; he is not an advocate or intercessor striving to appease an angry deity; he does not present himself to us as an external fact to be believed on historical testimony; nor is he to us a mere good man who lived a pious life and died a noble death. Christ stands before us always as an incarnation of faith and loyalty to God, an example of self-sacrificing devotion to truth; he is to be accepted in spirit and converted into an internal fact of our life; he is to live in us perpetually as the spirit of godliness. We do not care to believe in the outward and dead Nazarene, or make a declaration of such belief in an orthodox style. But we do care to assimilate the spirit of Christ to our souls. We must eat the flesh and drink the blood of the spiritual Christ, and thus incorporate into our spiritual constitution the principles of faith and sacrifice, love and obedience, which he embodied. Thus the spirit of Christ shall constantly abide in us as the living Christ; thus instead of adoring him or praying to him, we shall ever strive to enter into deeper communion with his spirit, and to advance nearer and nearer to the Infinite Father with the spirit of that holy brother's faith and love growing within us."

After his return to India Keshub Chunder Sen set to work to apply some of the lessons which he had learnt in England. It was then that he and his followers established their Boarding House, called the Bhârata Âsrama, or the Indian Hermitage. He organized the Indian Reform Association, with its five branches for Female Improvement, Education, Cheap Literature, Temperance, and Charity. A Normal

School for training lady-teachers began to do useful work, and a special journal was started to spread the principles of temperance. Industrial schools, night schools, and other charitable experiments followed, but in the attempt to do so much at once, failure and disappointment were inevitable. Others went even beyond Keshub Chunder Sen. Against his advice, women were admitted to public seats in church and at other meetings. On the 19th of March, 1872, the Brâhma Marriage Bill was passed, which legalized marriages concluded according to the simple Brâhma ritual, prohibited polygamy among Brâhmas, and fixed the minimum age of fourteen for the bride, and eighteen for the bridegroom.

Keshub Chunder Sen was during all that time the recognized leader of the Brâhma-Samâj of India, but the greater his influence grew, the stronger grew also the spirit of opposition among his followers. His government seemed too despotic even to Oriental minds, and his frequent appeal to what he called Âdesa or Divine Command did not tend to conciliate the feelings of his adversaries. While this discontent was growing stronger and stronger, Keshub Chunder Sen suddenly announced the betrothal of his daughter to the Râjah of Cutch Behar. This was the spark that made the mine explode. His daughter was nearly, but not quite fourteen, and the young Râjah not yet sixteen. Therefore Keshub Chunder Sen was accused of having broken the Brâhma Marriage Law, which he had been chiefly instrumental in getting carried, and was considered as no longer fit to be Minister of the Samâj. Keshub Chunder Sen would not listen to any remonstrances. He simply appealed to Âdesa or the voice of conscience within, and when some members of his congregation voted his deposition, he took forcible possession of the pulpit in his own Mandira, nay, he called on the police to help him. This finished the schism. Many of his former adherents left him, and founded on the 15th of May, 1878, a new Samâj, called the Sâdhâran Brâhma Samâj, or the Catholic Samâj.

Keshub Chunder Sen seems to me never to have recovered from this blow. An insidious disease was at the same time undermining his health, making him not only irritable, but at times not quite master of his thoughts. If his friends had been more forbearing, if they had remembered his past services, and given him credit for those excellent intentions which he had so often proved by sacrifices of every kind, my impression is that Keshub Chunder Sen might have recovered his health, his intellectual balance, and his power for doing good. But we are all very exacting with men whom we love and honor, and our friend is only another instance of an idol, first worshipped and then broken.

We need not dwell at great length on this painful chapter in Keshub Chunder Sen's life, as I intend at the end of this article to publish some of the letters which passed between us, and which will contain his views and my own on the most important points at issue.

In the year 1880 Keshub Chunder Sen began to speak of what he called a New Dispensation, by which he meant no doubt a special manifestation of God's will. He says himself: "When men are hopelessly gone in the way of misery and ruin, when a thick gloom of sin settles upon society, when human eyesight is unable to discern the right path, it is then that Providence sends to the world one of those men whose life has been sold to His almighty will."

This no doubt refers to himself, but it is no more than what he had expressed already in his lecture on "Great Men." I can see no harm, nor any overweening conceit in it. It is after all our human weakness only which makes us look on a special manifestation of God's will as something higher than a general manifestation, as if before a perfect Being there could be any distinction between what is special and what is general. To Keshub Chunder Sen, the more he was deserted, the more he felt himself alone with God, and inclined to look upon himself as the recipient of a special revelation of God's goodness and wisdom. His few remaining friends used even stronger language, and spoke of him as the Heaven-appointed Missionary of the Brâhma-Samâj, and of his utterances as infallible. Keshub Chunder Sen himself might protest against this extravagance as strongly as he could, the outcry against him became only more violent, and an understanding between the two contending parties became more hopeless every day. My only hope for conciliation and peace between them lay in common practical work, and, more especially, in the organization of a large system of charity. This I recommended as strongly as I could, as far superior to new ceremonies, new doctrines, new names. But it was in vain, at least during Keshub Chunder Sen's life.

Two points only seemed to me of real importance in the teaching of his last years, first, the striving after a universal religion and the recognition of a common substance in all religions; secondly, the more open recognition of the historical superiority of

Christianity as compared with more ancient forms of faith. Keshub Chunder Sen rejoiced in the discovery that, from the first, all religions were but varying forms of one great truth. This was his pearl of great price. To him it changed the whole aspect of the world, and gave a new meaning to his life. That the principle of historical growth or natural evolution applied to religion also, as I had tried to prove in my books on the Science of Religion, was to him the solution of keenly felt difficulties, a real solace in his own perplexities. Thus he writes in his Lecture, "The Apostles of the New Dispensation:"[1] "Only science can deliver the world, and bring light and order out of the chaos and darkness of multiplied Churches. If there is science in all things, is there no science in the dispensations of God? Do these alone in God's creation stand beyond the reign of law and order? Are they the arbitrary and erratic movements of chance? Are they the madness and delirium of nature? . . . Sure I am that amid their apparent anomalies and contradictions there is a logical unity of idea and method, and an unbroken continuity of sequence. All these Dispensations are connected with each other in the economy of Providence. They are linked together in one continuous chain, which may be traced to the earliest ages. They are a concatenated series of ideas, which show a systematic evolution of thought and development of religious life."

And again (p. 380): "Such is the New Dispensation. It is the harmony of all scriptures and prophets and dispensations. It is not an isolated creed, but the science which finds and explains and harmo-

[1] *Lectures in India*, p. 356.

nizes all religions. It gives to history a meaning, to the action of Providence a consistency, to quarrelling Churches a common bond, and to successive dispensations a continuity. It shows by a marvellous synthesis how the different rainbow colors are one in the light of heaven. The New Dispensation is the sweet music of divers instruments. It is the precious necklace in which are strung together the rubies and pearls of all ages and climes. It is the celestial Court where around enthroned Divinity shine the lights of all heavenly saints and prophets. It is the wonderful solvent which fuses all dispensations into a new chemical compound. It is the mighty absorbent which absorbs all that is true and good and beautiful in the objective world."

I could not command the fervor of feeling and the eloquent expression of these lines, but I agree entirely with the thought which Keshub Chunder Sen has tried to place before us, and I hope that in India more than anywhere else, and in the Brâhma-Samâj sooner than in any other communion, the principle of the historical evolution of all religious thought will be recognized, and if not raised into an article of faith, accepted at least as an undoubted fact.

If, as his opponents say, this is not a new theory, so much the better. And if they quote from the Bhâgavata Purâ*n*a the verse, "As the bee gathereth honey from flowers great and small, so does the really wise man gather substantial truth from the chaff of all scriptures great and small," I say again, so much the better. Truth does not spoil by growing old.

I have hitherto spoken chiefly in defence of Keshub Chunder Sen, but I am not so blinded by my friendship for him as to say that in his controversies with his friends he always was in the right. All I say is that I have never seen reason to doubt his good intentions, though I have often regretted the attitude which he assumed of late years towards his critics.

If I have sometimes tried to smooth down his anger, this has been done, not because I thought that his opponents were always in the wrong, but because I have long been afraid that not only his physical, but his mental strength also, was in imminent danger. How seldom we think of that, and how often we wish we had done so, when it is too late!

I have not a word to say against the new Sâdhâran-Samâj, and several of its leaders seem to me to act in an excellent spirit. I entirely agree with them that a Church should be constitutionally governed, and that tyranny of every kind should be resisted.

If we call the separation of the Brâhma-Samâj of India from the old Âdi Brâhma-Samâj, and again the separation of the Sâdhâran-Samâj from the Brâhma-Samâj of India, a schism, we seem to condemn them by the very word we use. But to my mind these three societies seem like three branches of one vigorous tree, the tree that was planted by Râmmohun Roy. In different ways they all serve the same purpose, they are all doing, I believe, unmixed good, in helping to realize the dream of a new religion for India, it may be for the whole world, a religion free from many corruptions of the past, call them idolatry, or caste, or verbal inspiration, or priestcraft, and firmly founded on a belief in the One God, the same in the Vedas, the same in the Old, the same in the New Testament, the same in the Korân, the same also in the hearts of those who have no longer any Vedas or Upanishads or any Sacred Books whatever between themselves and their God. The stream is small as yet, but it is a living stream. It may vanish for a time, it may change its name and follow new paths of which as yet we have no idea. But if there is ever to be a real religion in India, it will, I believe, owe its very life-blood to the large heart of Râmmohun Roy and his worthy disciples, Debendranâth Tagore and Keshub Chunder Sen.

I shall dwell no longer on the declining years of Keshub Chunder Sen. They were years of intense suffering, and full of many disappointments. His life had been an uninterrupted warfare, and some thrusts had wounded him to the very heart. Like an invalided soldier, he fought on as bravely as ever, but with an effort too great even for so stout a heart as his. His death came at last suddenly, though not unexpectedly. He died on January 8, 1884, surrounded by his nearest relations and friends. His most devoted fellow-worker, Protâp Chunder Mozumdar, was unfortunately absent. But his place was worthily filled by his old friend and guide, Debendranâth Tagore. His love for Keshub Chunder Sen had never ceased. They had been torn asunder by a torrent, but in their deepest foundation they had always remained one. After Keshub Chunder Sen had been taken from him by death, the old man addressed the following words to some friends who came to condole with him[1]: —

"When I had him near I considered myself the master of all the wealth which the kings of the world could command. When I sat up with him, often till one or two in the morning, conversing with my departed friend, I never perceived how the time passed.

[1] *The Liberal*, March 30, 1884.

The union between our souls is never to be destroyed. Like the Durbar of earthly kings, he said, the King of heaven has two Durbars. One is public, the other private. The sky and the heavens are the public Durbar of the heavenly King, and the spiritual world within our hearts is the private Durbar. God reigns supreme in both. In the spiritual world everything is spiritual, and God is revealed there in the innermost recesses of our spirit. The public are not allowed to enter there. They see their God in the outward Durbar as seated upon the glorious throne of His creation, and they are content with worshipping Him from a distance. Hence the ancient Rishis saw Him in the sun and other heavenly bodies, and bowed down before Him and paid homage. It is very difficult, he said, to acquire the privilege of entering God's private Durbar. Very great patience and long watching are required before this can be hoped for."

Debendranâth Tagore was able to come to Calcutta and see his beloved disciple once more. A few days before the last fatal symptoms of his malady appeared, Keshub said to Debendranâth that he had still a good deal to say and to do. And so he had indeed. He was engaged in a work which had grown every year, which had at last quite absorbed him, and which we know he would never have finished, even if he had reached the threescore years and ten. What he aspired to was not only the religious regeneration of India, but the religious regeneration of the whole world. What he had experienced himself in his short life, a transition from the bondage of an effete traditional religion to the perfect freedom of the spirit, was not, he thought, an impossible task for others, if only he could reach them and help them. He had often witnessed the irresistible power of his preaching; and as he had won hundreds and thousands, he did not see why he should not win millions.

But man has to do his appointed task within a short span, trusting that others will finish what is worth finishing. Hard as it is to say it, it is true nevertheless that Keshub Chunder Sen's own special work was done. What remained to be done, could better be done by others. He has died young, but not too young for what he was meant to do. A slowly darkening evening would have proved a disappointment to himself and to his friends. He will live more really now that he is dead, than he would if his life had been spared for many years. All the suspicion and obloquy that hampered him from the day he consented to his daughter's marriage with the Râjah of Cutch Behar have died with him. What could not be forgotten while he lived was forgotten and forgiven by all who gathered round his death-bed. There are good and brave soldiers ready to step into the gap which he has left. They know whither he wished to lead them, and thither, I trust, they will march, as if he himself were still in their midst.

IMPORTANT DATES IN THE HISTORY OF THE BRÂHMA-SAMÂJ.

Râmmohun Roy born	1772 or 1774
Brâhma-Samâj founded at Calcutta	January, 1830
Râmmohun Roy arrived in England	8 April, 1831
Râmmohun Roy died	27 Sept. 1833
Debendranâth Tagore (born 1817) joined the Brâhma-Samâj	1838 or 1841
Keshub Chunder Sen born	19 Nov. 1838
Tattvabodhinî Sabhâ	6 Oct. 1839 (or 1842)–59
New Brâhma covenant established	Dec. 1843
Dvârkânâth Tagore in Paris; meetings with M. M.	1845

Scholars sent to Benares to study the Vedas	1845
Veda discarded, Brâhma-dharma published	1850
Keshub Chunder Sen's School at Colootolah	1855–58
Keshub Chunder Sen married	1856
Keshub Chunder Sen joins Brâhma-Samâj	1857
Play of "Widow Marriage" acted at Calcutta . . .	1859
Brâhma School under K. Ch. Sen and Debendranâth	24 April, 1859
Journey to Ceylon	1860
First Brâhma marriage without idolatrous rites . .	26 July, 1861
Keshub Chunder Sen appointed Minister	13 April, 1862
Exclusion from family; illness; returns to his house .	Dec. 1862
Birth of his son Karuna	19 Dec. 1862
First Intermarriage of persons of different Castes . .	2 Aug. 1864
Brâhma Mission. Keshub goes to Madras and Bombay . .	1864
Secession of Progressive Brâhmas	26 Feb. 1865
Brâhma-Samâj of India established	11 Nov. 1866
Lecture on "Jesus Christ, Europe and Asia" . . .	5 May, 1866
Lecture on "Great Men"	28 Sept. 1866
Brâhma-Mandira of India, opened at Calcutta . . .	22 Aug. 1869
Keshub Chunder Sen's visit to England	1870
Native Marriage Act passed	19 March, 1872
Protest against Cutch Behar Marriage	28 Feb. 1878
Formal Marriage of Mahârâjah of Cutch Behar and daughter of Keshub Chunder Sen	6 March, 1878
Establishment of Sâdhâran Brâhma-Samâj . . .	15 May, 1878
Meeting in honor of Râmmohun Roy at Debendranâth Tagore's house	19 Jan. 1879
New Dispensation proclaimed	Jan. 1880
Real Marriage of Mahârâjah of Cutch Behar . . .	20 Oct. 1880
Death of Keshub Chunder Sen	8 Jan. 1884

LETTERS OF

KESHUB CHUNDER SEN, F. MAX MÜLLER, AND PROTAP CHUNDER MOZUMDAR.

THE following are some of the letters that passed between Keshub Chunder Sen and myself at the time when not only his friends in India, but his friends in England also, were attacking him for sanctioning the marriage of his daughter with the Mahârâjah of Cutch

Behar, and for some of the opinions put forward in his lectures. Extracts from most of these letters have been published in India, but they are here published for the first time in their complete form, and with certain additions and corrections which seemed necessary.

The beginning of our correspondence was the following article which I published in the "Times," on the 24th of November, 1880:—

Mr. Charles Voysey's statement in the "Times," of November 20 that Keshub Chunder Sen is at present almost universally repudiated by Hindu Theists will, I know, surprise and pain many of his old friends and admirers in England who during the years that have elapsed since his memorable visit here have followed his work in India with an ever-increasing interest, though at times not without serious misgivings. The new schism in his sect, the Brâhma-Samâj of India, which took place in 1878, has been widely regretted, not so much because every schism is in itself to be regretted, but because this schism seemed almost entirely due to personal causes. Though it cannot be denied that the case of the seceders, as stated with great knowledge and ability by Miss S. D. Collet, in the "Brahmo Year Book" for 1879, leaves several charges against Keshub Chunder Sen unanswered and unexplained, yet his friends ought to remember how extremely difficult it is for us, so far removed from the social and religious atmosphere of modern India, to form an impartial opinion of all the hidden motives that may have influenced those who seceded from and those who remained faithful to the great reformer. The question of marriage has been a stumbling-block to many reformers, and if Keshub

Chunder Sen has shown himself a weak father in allowing a betrothal of his daughter to the Râjah of Cutch Behar let us not forget that a man may be a weak father and yet a great and honest man. Many Brâhmas, though admitting Keshub Chunder Sen's weakness, have forgiven it, and he still commands a large number of devoted followers. Mr. Charles Voysey would probably say that these believers in Keshub Chunder Sen have forfeited the name of Theists, because this leader has more and more inclined to the doctrines of Christianity. But surely Christianity and Theism are not terms that exclude each other, and every Christian, before being anything else, must be a Theist in the received sense of that word. Keshub Chunder Sen has at no time made a secret of his feelings for Christ. His great sermon on Christ and Christianity was preached so far back as 1870 (see "Selected Essays," vol. ii. p. 82), and in the "Theistic Quarterly Review" for January, 1880, p. 58, his earliest profession of faith in Christ is referred to the year 1866, while the secession of the so-called Sâdhâran or Catholic Brâhma Samâj took place only two years ago, its chief cause, so far as we can judge, being personal feelings aroused by Keshub Chunder Sen's ascendancy, and not any fundamental difference of doctrine.

In a new society like the Bhâratavarsha Brâhma-Samâj, or, as it is now commonly called, the Brâhma-Samâj of India, founded as it was on the universality of Theism, and supported by a book containing extracts from the Scriptures of all nations, it was but natural that new ideas should spring up from year to year and acquire more or less prominence. The recognition of Christ as a great prophet was but one of these ideas, and it was never intended to exclude the duty of showing reverence to the founders and teachers of other religions. In the outward life of the Brâhma-Samâj the introduction of Utsubs (utsavas or religious festivals) and of Sankivtan (the practice of enthusiastic religious singing) produced some change and commotion; but there never was any strong pressure used to induce those who did not approve of them to take part in these functions. The idea of the Communion of Saints, as preached by Keshub Chunder Sen, was hardly more than a belief in a spiritual intercourse between the departed and the living, and his doctrine of inspiration did not go beyond the admission of a Divine impulse imparted to the soul through a devout seeking after the will of God. The most objectionable doctrine put forward by the liberal reformer of Hinduism was, no doubt, the Âdesa, the claim of being directed by an inward voice which admitted no gainsaying. This, particularly when mixed up with questions of worldly wisdom, made his position incompatible with the freedom claimed by every member of his Samâj, and, more than anything else, led to the secession of some of his former friends and followers. It is the old story over again. Nothing is so difficult for a reformer, particularly a religious reformer, as not to allow the incense offered by his followers to darken his mental vision, and not to mistake the Divine accents of truth for a voice wafted from the clouds. In this respect, no doubt, Keshub Chunder Sen has shared in the weakness of older prophets; but let us not forget that he possesses also a large share of their strength and virtue. One of his followers writes of him ("Theistic Quarterly Review," October, 1879, p. 61): —

"Babu Keshub Chunder Sen is neither our mediator nor indispensable for our acceptance with God. Only he has done the Brâhma-Samâj incalculable good, and in common gratitude we acknowledge his services and our obligations to him. But there are men in the Brâhma-Samâj who, we are sorry to say, can bear the mention of every other name but his name, who cannot bear to see the least credit given to him for anything. And hence they are fiercely angry with the Brâhmas' creed, and circulate all manner of falsehood in relation to it. Them we do not hope to convince, but to others, who want to judge correctly, we may say that we hold some of our leaders in genuine love and honor for what they have taught us, and we want that our gratitude should be shared in by every Theist, here as well as elsewhere. To Babu Keshub Chunder Sen's teaching the Brâhma-Samâj is deeply indebted; but it is also indebted to others, and among the latter we may eminently mention Babu Debendranâth Tagore, and the founder of our Church, Râjah Râmmohun Roy."

Nothing can be more instructive to the student of religion than to trace the origin and growth of the Brâhma-Samâj from Râmmohun Roy to Keshub Chunder Sen. Much may be learnt from the old conservative Âdi Brâhma-Samâj; much from the reformed branch, the Brâhma-Samâj of India, under Keshub Chunder Sen; aye, something even from the Ârya-Samâj under Dayânanda Sarasvatî, the most perverse interpreter of the Vedas. I tried in my lecture, delivered in Westminster Abbey, December 3, 1873, to give a sketch, though I am afraid a very imperfect one, of the religious movement inaugurated by Râmmohun Roy, and carried on by Debendranâth and Keshub Chunder Sen; and I see little or nothing to retract what I then said about Keshub Chunder Sen. The utterances of late have shown signs, I am sorry to say, of an over-wrought brain and an over-sensitive heart. He sometimes seems to me on the verge of the very madness of faith. But I fear for his health and his head far more than for his heart, and I should deeply regret if any harsh words from those who ought to know best how to make allowance for the difficulties and dangers of all religious reformers should embitter a noble life already full of many bitternesses.

F. MAX MÜLLER.

Oxford.

I then received the following letter from Keshub Chunder Sen: —

LILY COTTAGE,
72 UPPER CIRCULAR ROAD, CALCUTTA,
22 *Dec.* 1880.

MY DEAR SIR, — Allow me to thank you most cordially for having said a good word for us in the "Times." I have read your letter with very great interest, and thankfully appreciate your heartfelt sympathy with us in our trials and difficulties. You can hardly imagine the troubles I have had during the last two or three years and the grossly false and libellous charges brought against me week after week. Thank God, I have endured these undeserved and cruel attacks quietly and calmly, thinking it wrong to resent. Even the Police was instigated by some of my antagonists to inquire and ascertain if I was not guilty of embezzlement! And even my good wife came in for a share of wanton abuse in a vernacular dramatic work! All this I say to you privately because you have been good enough to give us your sympathy as a friend, and because you have boldly come forward, as few have done, to assert publicly that personal feelings lie at the bottom of the opposition movement. However, God's will be done! I sincerely trust an impartial public will in future give a patient hearing to the actual facts of the case and proclaim a truer verdict. Surely I can afford to wait. There is a Bengâli saying — "Heaven bears the burden of all trusting servants." I can assure you God has been very kind to us in our trials and tribulation, and all the antagonism and persecution we have suffered have greatly strengthened us and helped the progress and extension of our Church. Our influence spreads on all sides, and there is far greater enthusiasm among us now than in any previous period in the history of our Church. I think we owe it to so kind a friend and sympathizer as yourself that we should strengthen your hands by putting you in possession of facts and thereby enabling you to maintain the position you have taken. May I ask you to accept a few of my lectures and tracts which I have taken the liberty to forward to you by the present mail?

I remain, honored friend,
Yours most sincerely,
KESHUB CHUNDER SEN.

Should you require information on any particular subject, I beg you will kindly let me know.

A copy of the letter of the Brâhma Missionary Conference is herewith enclosed.

At the same time I received the following letter from the Members of the Brâhma Missionary Conference of the Brâhma-Samâj: —

Brahmo Missionary Conference,
29 *Dec.* 1880.

Sir, — I am directed by the Missionary Conference of the Brâhma-Samâj of India to convey to you their cordial thanks for having kindly contradicted in the "Times" some of the unfounded statements made by Mr. Charles Voysey and others regarding our Church. We should have passed over these misrepresentations in silence, believing and trusting that truth would triumph at last — [illegible] — and that the British nation, with its characteristic regard for truth, would not readily allow itself to be misled by interested agitators, but would ere long discover the real truth of the matter. You will no doubt admit that those whom the Lord leads and protects have nothing to fear from the shafts of calumny, and that Truth needs no human advocate to defend her. However, as you have thought it proper publicly to vindicate the Brâhma-Samâj of India from unfounded charges, it seems incumbent upon us, while gratefully acknowledging your kindness, to place before you such facts as may enable you to verify your statements and silence your critics.

In Mr. Voysey's statement that "Babu Keshub Chunder Sen is at present almost universally repudiated by Hindu Theists," one sees at once that the wish is father to the thought. No one can deny that the Bhâratavarshya Brâhma Mandira, the Church of which Mr. Sen is the Minister, continues to be as largely attended now as before the schism, and that not a single devout member of his congregation has left the Church. Nor is it possible to gainsay the fact that the congregation of our Mandir is far larger than that of any other section of the Brâmah-Samâj.

If the number of persons who are attracted to hear be any index to the personal influence of a religious leader, you may form some idea of Babu Keshub Chunder Sen's growing influence from the fact that in the course of our expeditionary movement last year he addressed, in six weeks, crowded assemblies in Calcutta and the Provinces numbering upwards of ten thousand people. In fact, since the organization of the New Dispensation our movement has excited far greater interest and sympathy, and achieved much greater success than in any previous year. Another evidence of even greater importance is to be found in the fact that all our missionaries and leading workers have remained faithful and loyal to our leader throughout the crisis. The members of the Missionary Conference desire me to say emphatically that though they have now and then differed from him in non-essential matters, their grateful reverence for him as their Heaven-appointed leader and friend continues unabated. They are his close companions, and they have had opportunities of examining closely the details of his daily life, some for ten, others for twenty years, and they have never had reasons to suspect their confidence in their trusted leader was misplaced. The only missionary who has deserted our Church since the schism is the person who charged him twelve years ago with encouraging "man-worship," but who subsequently recanted. Whatever our antagonists may say, the Brâhma-Samâj of India is, in spite of the rupture, a growing power, and it retains in itself the entire devotional and spiritual life of the community. It is still, as it was before, a mighty instrument in the hands of Providence to teach the Hindu nation faith, love and purity, prayer, communion, and inspiration. The seceders are, we may say without being uncharitable, deficient in religious life, and are given more to outward social refinement, magnifying the things of the flesh over things of the spirit. Such men cannot stand against God's Church, unless they establish their superiority on the ground of faith and godliness. That their secession is due almost entirely to personal causes cannot be disputed. The rupture began some years before the marriage controversy took place, "its chief cause being," as you rightly observe, "personal feelings aroused by Keshub Chunder Sen's ascendancy, not any fundamental differences of doctrine." The bitterness was greatly aggravated by the marriage of the Minister's daughter, chiefly because the offer of one of the leading seceders, the chief editor of their journal, to have his daughter married to the Mahârâjah of Cutch Behar was declined, the match not being approved by the State officers in Cutch Behar, who, after having seen both girls, gave decided preference to the Minister's daughter. The disappointment thus caused fomented the jealousies already existing, till they culminated in a schismatic rupture. For nearly three years we and our leader have been reviled and maligned in the most reckless manner, the arguments used being almost invariably personal invectives against our character, and not doctrinal criticisms.

With reference to the Cutch Behar marriage, I may be permitted to say that there is nothing in it which has been disapproved by the most fastidious critic which the Minister himself and his friends have not regretted, and this dissent was clearly set forth in the official statement published by the Brâhma-Samâj of India at the time. The marriage itself, or rather the match, we most devoutly believe, was providential, although we freely admit there were errors and improprieties in the *modus operandi*. The Lord directed the choice and initiated the nuptial rites. But in this, as in other cases, human agency must be distinguished from the actions of Providence. The charge of child-marriage has long ago been exploded. For the consummation of the marriage took place only the other day, October 20, in the Brâhma Mandira. The proceedings of the ceremony you will find in the "Sunday Mirror" of the 24th of October.

The doctrines of Âdesa (Inspiration) and the Communion of Saints have provoked warm controversy both here and in England, and also our attitude towards Christ and other prophets. It is a matter of regret and wonder that in these matters a Christian nation should misunderstand our position or misconstrue our views. To rationalists we are, and must continue to be, a stumbling-block. But surely to the spiritually-minded the above doctrines are intelligible. It seems to us that it is not the doctrines themselves, but the oriental and metaphorical dress in which they are presented, to which exception has been taken. Allegories and parables may not suit the Western mind, but they are the natural inheritance of all Eastern nations, and we instinctively indulge in the poetry of religion. The mysticism attributed to us is nothing but teaching by allegory and parable, of which Christ Jesus Himself furnished a preëminent example. In March last the plain meanings of most of the words we use, divested of metaphor, were published, a reference to which will convince you of the truth of what we say. One of the main causes of irritation is, as you rightly apprehend, the Minister's allegiance to Christ, which has greatly annoyed the rationalists here and in England, and especially Mr. Voysey. This cannot be helped. We believe that in the Spirit of Christ Asia and Europe shall be united in the fulness of time, and we rejoice to see that through God's grace India is drawing near to "Him crucified." If we are deserted and persecuted for this we need not complain.

Yours respectfully,
WOOMA NATH GUPTA,
Brâhma Missionary Conference.

OFFICIAL PAPER.

Marriage of the Mahârâjah of Cutch Behar.

The principal event of the year was the Râjah's marriage, which was celebrated on the 6th March, 1878, at the Raj Bari in Cutch Behar, in the presence of a large assemblage of spectators, both Native and European. The difficulty of reconciling the Hindu and Brâhma ceremonial forms was, as may be imagined, an arduous one. *It was necessary to the legality of the marriage that the rites should be Hindu in all essential features.* After much deliberation and argument, *Babu Keshub Chunder Sen was brought to see that the Râjah, not being a Brâhma, and the Brâhma Marriage Act not being in force in Cutch Behar, it was absolutely essential that the marriage, if it took place at all, should be a Hindu marriage.* Idolatrous mantras were, however, excluded, and the name of the Deity substituted wherever local custom had introduced that of any particular idol. *The best proof of the perfect orthodoxy of the marriage is that the Brâhmans consented to perform it.* They are not by any means under our thumb, and in one matter, the performance of the *Hom* ceremony, which is, strictly speaking, the adoration of fire, they refused altogether to give way or to dispense with the presence of the bride and bridegroom. Babu Keshub Chunder Sen was equally determined that his daughter should not assist at an idolatrous ceremony. The matter was ultimately arranged by the Brâhmans consenting to the removal of the bride on some pretext before they performed the mystic ceremony. As this did not come off till three A. M., and as the poor young lady had been sitting in an uncomfortable attitude for about five hours, the excuse for removing her could not be called a pretext. The Râjah remained present during the ceremony, but took no part in it. *The marriage has since been formally declared legal by the Commissioner, acting under Government as the law-giving power, and his declaration to that effect has been filed among the permanent records in the archives of Cutch Behar.* In connection with this event, I wish to record my sense of the valuable assistance rendered by Babu Kali Komul Lahiri, the Dwar Muktear, an old and faithful servant of the Râjah's family, not only in his position as principal officer of the household, but also as a Brâhman, in smoothing over difficulties which arose, and in reconciling the adverse factions of Pundits and Brâhmans. The Cutch Behar Pandit sent to Calcutta to arrange the form of ceremony had not conducted the negotiation in a very straightforward manner, and the consequence was that I and the Dewan found ourselves in a very difficult position on the very eve of the marriage. In arranging these difficulties the Dwar Muktear's influence was of the greatest assistance to us, and enabled us to discriminate between what orthodoxy really demanded and what bigotry was unwilling to give up. — *Administration Report of the Cutch Behar State, by G. T. Dalton, Esq., Deputy Commissioner.*

To these letters I sent the following reply: —

MY DEAR FRIEND, —Your letter was a real pleasure to me. Though I felt almost certain that you would take what I had written in the "Times" as words coming from a true friend, yet I was glad to hear from yourself that you had not forgotten me, and that you still counted me among your old and faithful friends. You may have wondered that I should never have written to you since you left England to return to your own country and to your own work among your own people. I have often thought of you, and whenever my memory went on a long pilgrimage to my friends who are doing good work in different parts of the world, I always lingered before your image, and wondered whether I could and ought to help you in your struggle, as it grew harder from year to year. But as our span of life grows smaller and smaller, work seems to grow thicker and thicker. If we want to do anything, to finish anything at least up to a certain point, we must learn to let many things take their own course. We must learn to trust: and I can assure you that ever since I saw you face to face, ever since I listened to you pleading your cause so powerfully before our great theologian, Dr. Pusey, and afterwards heard you unfolding to me your brightest hopes for the future of India, I have always trusted you. That does not mean that I have always approved of all that you have written and done. Far from it. But with regard to most of the matters which have been discussed between you and your opponents, what right had I to condemn the steps which you thought it right to take, or, at all events, to put my judgment against yours? I do not call that trusting our friends, if we want them always to think and speak and act exactly as we ourselves would think and speak and act. Trusting our friends means to give them credit for good and honest intentions, even when we differ from them and they from us. It is easy to trust in a Divine Providence if all goes well with us; but to trust when all goes against us, that is real trust. It is the same with our faith in men. I know that your one object in life is to do good to your countrymen, to help them to amend certain defects in their social life, and to purify their religious ideas, and I shall never believe that a man who has devoted his life to so noble a purpose can be guilty of the charges brought against you. I never shall think you infallible in your judgments, but whatever may happen, I trust, aye I know, that you will always remain true to your own noble self.

After your great success both in India and in England I was quite prepared that a reaction would set in. Success is apt to produce a certain languor and conceit in ourselves, while in others it is sure to arouse envy, the worst poison that grows in the human heart. The Buddhists say truly that a man has "left the path of envy" when he begins to lead a new life; but it is marvellous to observe how few even among the best men are quite above that wretched feeling. Besides, many of those who applauded you and patronized you before you had achieved your best successes did so because it was the fashion. They had no idea of the real nature of the work you had taken in hand, but they liked to pat you on the back and give you advice and warn you against dangers and all that. You see you were only a native — and is not every European far wiser than a Hindu? How I hate that conceit. I do not mean to say that it is general, but it exists; and what is the worst, it exists in influential quarters. Men who have been in India, men who write on India, men who profess to have studied the language and literature of India, speak even of the most learned, the best and wisest of your countrymen, of men in knowledge, manners, and character infinitely their superiors, as of so many ignorant and naughty children. Have we not conquered India, they seem to say, do we not govern India, and should we not know much better than Râmmohun Roy, or Debendranâth Tagore, or Keshub Chunder Sen what is the right course which Indian social and religious reformers ought to follow? I know of men who could not construe a line of Sanskrit, and who speak and write of your ancient literature, religion, and philosophy as if they knew a great deal more than any of your best *S*rotriyas. How often you must have smiled on reading such books! The idea that anything could come from the East equal to European thought, or even superior, never enters the mind of these writers, and hence their utter inability to understand and appreciate what is really valuable in Oriental literature. There is no problem of philosophy and religion that has not been a subject of deep and anxious thought among your ancient and modern thinkers. We in the West have done some good work too, and I do not write to depreciate the achievements of the Hellenic and Teutonic mind. But I know that on some of the highest problems of human thought the East has shed more light than the West, and by and by, depend on it, the West will have to acknowledge it. There is a very able article in the last number of the "Edinburgh Review" (January, 1881), on Dr Caird's "Philosophy of Religion." Dr. Caird is a representative man in England, and more familiar than most Englishmen with the solid work of modern German philosophers. And what is the last result at which Dr. Caird arrives, and of which even the "Edinburgh Review" approves? Almost literally the same as the doctrine of the Upanishads! Dr. Caird writes: "It is just in this renunciation of self that I truly gain myself; for whilst in one sense we give up self to live the universal and absolute life of reason, yet that to which we thus surrender ourselves is in reality our truer self." And again: "The knowledge and love of God is the giving up of all thoughts and feelings that belong to me as a mere individual self, and the identification of my thoughts and being with that which is above me, yet in me — the universal or absolute self, which is not mine or yours, but in which all intelligent beings alike find the realization and perfection of their nature" (p. 257). I need not tell you or any one who knows the Upanishads how powerfully the same doctrine, the doctrine of the Âtmâ and Paramâtmâ, was put forth by your old Rishis more than two thousand years ago.

Many years ago I ventured to show that the five-membered syllogism of the Indian Nyâya philosophy is the best form that can be given to the syllogism of inductive logic. But European logicians cannot get over the idea that there is no logic like that of our schoolmen, and that every deviation from it is a mistake.

The same conceit runs through almost all that is written on India. India may be patronized, some works of Indian poets and philosophers may be called clever and curious, but to recognize in anything the superiority of Indian thought, or the wisdom of Indian native opinion, that is out of the question.

I do not write this in order to flatter you, but in order to warn you against being disheartened by foreign criticism. Few people in Europe, very few, understand the object of your work, or have any idea of the dangers and difficulties which you have to encounter. You should look upon praise and blame as we do upon sunshine and rain. It comes and goes, we know not why. But there is one thing that serves as a parasol against conceit, and as an umbrella against despair, and that is a clear conception of the true purpose of our life. Let me quote once more from Buddha (Dhammapada, 227, 228): "This is an old saying, this is not only of to-day: they blame him who sits silent, they blame him who speaks much, they also blame him who says little; there is no one on earth who is not blamed. There never was, there never will be, nor is there now, a man who is always blamed, or a man who is always praised."

I can quite feel with you and understand that you should be disheartened by the defection of some of your friends, but you should not allow this to turn you away for one moment from the path that lies straight before you. I am particularly sorry that so true and intelligent a friend as Miss Collet should have turned against you, but I have little doubt she will in time forget the things that are behind, and look forward to the great work that is still before you. She judges you, I think, unfairly, because she forgets that you are a Hindu and a Brâhma, and not at the same time an Englishman and a Christian, in her sense of the word. She expects too much from you, and that shows after all how she respects and honors you.

If the number of your followers in India has decreased, as she maintains, though you deny it, that would influence very little my feelings for you and my hopes for your cause. I do not believe in numbers; and all through life I have but seldom found myself in a majority. If such men as Mozumdar remain true to you, that is better than a legion: but better than all is that you should remain true to yourself. People may call the separation of the Âdi Samâj, the Brâhma Samâj of India, and the Sâdhâran Brâhma Samâj a schism: to my mind they are three strong branches of one powerful stem. They all have the same root, and they all, I trust, will yet bear rich fruit.

I cannot write more to-day, but there are several points on which I hope to write, whenever I find a little leisure. You have written to me as a friend, and I have answered you as a friend, with perfect frankness. I shall always do that, and hope you will do the same.

I have received the copy of a letter in which the Brâhma Missionary Conference points out a number of misstatements made by —— in a lecture delivered before the Royal Asiatic Society; also a letter addressed to me by the same Conference. I did not feel at liberty to publish these letters. Please to convey to the Conference my best thanks and the expression of my fullest sympathy.

I remain, my dear Friend,

Yours very truly,

F. MAX MÜLLER.

P. S. — I was much interested in the publications you sent me. As you kindly offer me your assistance, might I ask you to send me the first number of the "Theistic Quarterly Review." Any information on Râmmohun Roy would be very welcome, but I must tell you that I find it difficult now to read Bengâli.

Some of the letters that passed between Keshub Chunder Sen and myself are lost, because at the time I did not consider them of importance. I only kept rough copies of my own letters, and cannot now fix their exact dates. The next letter which I wrote to him treated chiefly of the Cutch Behar marriage.

MY DEAR FRIEND, — I am truly sorry that the first subject on which I feel I must write to you should be the marriage of your daughter with the Mahârâjah of Cutch Behar. It has, however, been made the battle-field between your friends and your enemies, and as I have often declared that, if placed in your position, I should probably have acted as you have done, I feel that I owe it to myself as well as to you to explain what I feel on the subject.

I may say at once, I wish that this difficulty had never arisen. For a difficulty it was, and you must have felt it so. You were placed in a conflict of duties, the duties of a father and the duties of a public man, and out of such a conflict it is almost impossible to emerge without a wound.

Now let me tell you first where I differed from you. I think when we find ourselves in such a difficulty, we ought to take our friends into our confidence, and place the reasons which make us incline towards the right or towards the left unreservedly before them. You, so far as I remember, remained silent for a long time, and at last appealed to the inner voice, the Âdesa, which told you that you had acted rightly and for the best.

I know myself full well how hard it is to have to defend one's self against suspicions that ought never to have arisen, and to repel charges that ought never to have been brought. But the world likes to hear a man defend himself, if only for the pleasure of pronouncing a verdict of Not Guilty, and I think our friends have a certain right to hear what we say to ourselves. To appeal simply to Âdesa is not respectful, and the voice of Âdesa, however pure it may be when it enters into our ears, is never quite so pure when it passes out of our mouth. That still small voice is meant to be still: it is meant for us, and for us only, not for the loud contests of the world. I believe if you had asked your friends whether you should sacrifice the happiness of your daughter, or agree to a marriage which both you and they consider objectionable, but which till a few years ago was considered perfectly legitimate, and which even now hardly one in a million of your own countrymen would disapprove, they would probably, particularly if they had known all the more private circumstances of the case, on which I need not enlarge, have given you a bill of indemnity.

But after having said so much against you, I must say that many of your friends seem to me to have acted towards you in a most unfriendly, nay, unreasonable manner. They seem to me to have entirely forgotten that you were born in India, and not in England, and that there is no subject on which different nations entertain such different ideas as on marriage.

I have no reason to doubt that you still consider early marriages objectionable, and that you decidedly prefer your own Brâhma rite of celebrating marriage to any other ceremonial. But when, on medical advice, you have fixed the minimum of the marriageable age of women in India at fourteen, then surely the case of your daughter, who was only a few months under fourteen when she was formally married, and sixteen when she was really married, might have been passed unnoticed. I know the atmosphere in which you live. I know how from the earliest days it was considered in India the duty of a father to find a proper husband for his daughter. Manu says so, all your old lawyers and poets say so; and however good a reformer you may be, I can quite understand your feeling the disgrace which in India it is supposed to be if a father leaves a daughter unmarried; or, at all events, your hesitating to sacrifice the happiness of your daughter to your own convictions on social reform. Manu, who allows hardly any freedom to a woman at any time of her life, allows her to choose a husband for herself, if, three years after she has attained a marriageable age, her parents have failed to do so (Manu, ix. 90). Other law-givers (Vish*n*u,

xxiv. 40) allow her still greater freedom. I do not suppose you would be frightened by your old Smritikâras into doing something actually wrong, yet I can well understand that you should continue to feel their indirect pressure. And when it is considered how difficult it is to find a proper husband for a daughter, educated as yours had been, and how desirable, not only from a worldly point of view, her marriage with the young Râjah of Cutch Behar must have appeared to you, then to demand that you should have deprived your daughter of a freedom of choice that even Manu would have allowed her, seems to me going very far. Even in Europe great concessions are often made with regard to marriages, objectionable from some, desirable from other points of view. I shall not press the point that this is particularly the case in royal and princely families, where often great interests are at stake, and where the choice of husbands and wives is limited. In England, for an uncle to marry his niece would be considered intolerable; in Roman Catholic countries dispensation is granted to such unions. In England, marriage with a deceased wife's sister is illegal; in the English colonies it is allowed. The lowest savages consider marriages between members of the same clan quite shocking, and that prejudice remains even after they have been converted to Christianity; while certain missionaries tolerate even polygamy in their converts rather than allow them to cast off their old wives. In all this, I do not plead for laxity, but only for a recognition of peculiar difficulties, and for that kind of forbearance which English society has of late shown in much more extreme cases.

To call the marriage of your daughter a Child-marriage is utterly unfair, and it is hardly less so to say that you gave your consent to idolatrous marriage rites being performed. I have read nearly everything that has been written and published on that marriage, and I believe you did all that it was possible for you to do to avoid giving offence to your friends without endangering the legality of the marriage. Protestants object to mixed marriages with Roman Catholics, but if they assent to a mixed marriage, they must submit to the performance of certain superstitious rites, without which the marriage would not be legal. Besides, there are in every country old marriage customs which, no doubt, date from heathen times, but which no one calls idolatrous. If we like to use hard words, it would be easy to show up plenty of idolatry in Europe. If you had joined a Christian community, then I should fully admit that, so far as you yourself are concerned, you could have been married according to the Christian ceremonial only; but even then you could not have forced your daughter, if according to native law she is of age and free to choose, to follow your example. As you are and mean to be a Hindu, though a believer in Christ, I cannot see what right your Christian friends have to blame you for allowing your daughter to marry a countryman of hers with whom, in a native state, she could be legally married according to the ancient customs of his own country only.

I am glad, of course, that you succeeded in carrying your bill for legalizing Brâhma marriages, but I can quite understand that in the eyes of many of your friends such a marriage is much the same as what a marriage before a Registrar is in the eyes of many Englishmen. It therefore comes to this, you must either prohibit all mixed marriages between Brâhmas and Hindus, which would be acting more intolerantly than the Pope, or you must allow some of the ancient marriage customs, when one of the contracting parties is not a Brâhma. And here again to call every ancient custom, every desadharma or kuladharma, idolatry is utterly unfair. At all events there are much more dangerous idols in Europe as well as in India than the old stone images in the palace of Behar.

The difficulty which you had to solve has had to be solved again and again whenever new religions or new sects have sprung up. Zealots have always denounced marriage between members of different religions, nay even of different sects. But what did St. Paul say? "The unbelieving husband," he says, "is sanctified by the wife, and the unbelieving wife is sanctified by the husband; else were your children unclean (illegitimate), but now are they holy." And again: "For what knowest thou, O wife, whether thou shalt save thy husband? or how knowest thou, O man, whether thou shalt save thy wife?" (1 Corinth. vii. 14, 16.) Whoever knows the history of religion, knows what excellent missionaries wives have made, and I trust the time may come when those who now blame you will give you credit for pure motives, and praise you for your foresight and your trust.

With sincere wishes for the welfare of your daughter and your son-in-law, I remain, my dear friend,

Yours very truly,

F. MAX MÜLLER.

LILY COTTAGE,
72 UPPER CIRCULAR ROAD, CALCUTTA,
2 *May*, 1881.

MY DEAR FRIEND, — For your most welcome epistles and the genuine assurances of kindness and sympathy they contain, I must give you my heartfelt thanks. In writing to me you need not conceal your real feelings. Discriminating criticism cannot pain me. Even the reproaches of a true friend are acceptable, and must prove beneficial. I have read your letters with the deepest interest, and I only wish I could sit with you under one of those shady trees in Oxford which I saw during my short visit, and talk over the many important subjects referred to therein, for hours together. My heart is full. What shall I write, what can I write on those various subjects within the short compass of a letter? Regarding the Cutch Behar marriage I have yet a great deal to say. I thank you for the sympathetic view you have taken of it. In certain minor matters only you have taken exception to the course I adopted, and I have no right to quarrel, for you argue as a friend, and your remonstrance is only friendly counsel and warning. I confess I was silent when the battle was raging. My patience was repulsive and disgusting. My reticence was suspicious, and led to misrepresentation and reviling. It has always been my habit secretly to refer to my God in all matters of importance in my life and to mature my plans under His guidance, and to make them known when I was almost certain of success. There were a hundred doubts and uncertainties in connection with this marriage proposal, and every moment it seemed likely to break down. The whole thing seemed most improbable till it was a *fait accompli.* Even two hours before the marriage was actually solemnized, no one could make himself certain about the affair: on the contrary, there were new difficulties springing up which seemed insuperable. Hence my disposition to maintain silence. I was waiting to find firm ground upon which to stand and take counsel of friends in regard to details, but the time never came, the marriage question — "to be or not to be" — being itself an uncertainty till the last moment. The Âdesa in the present case was far from exceptional. I do not claim, and never claimed, supernatural inspiration. My Âdesa is a command of conscience or a providential interposition. In plain language, I should say this marriage is providential; and in this respect it is like other important incidents in my life — my renunciation of secular work, my vow of asceticism, my vegetarian habits, my declaration of faith in the New Dispensation, etc. A man who trusts God and prays daily must feel that all the events in his life, and even his daily meals, are ordered by Providence. I saw the finger of God in all the arrangements, struggles, and trials in connection with the marriage. It was very like a political marriage, such as you speak of. A whole kingdom was to be reformed, and all my individual interests were absorbed in the vastness of God's saving economy, or in what people would call public good. The Lord required my daughter for Cutch Behar, and I surrendered her. The trials and difficulties I have gone through are also, I believe, providential. They have educated and disciplined and trained me, and I owe a great deal, and my Church owes a great deal, to my antagonists. The great result of all this agitation is the New Dispensation. I thank God for it. It is a wonder, a marvel. Pray read all about it, and judge for yourself whether the Holy Spirit is not moving India in the direction of true and universal Christianity. I remember the very interesting conversation we had at the Westminster Deanery, in the course of which you, and also, I believe, the excellent Dean, suggested that the future Church of India should be altogether Oriental, only it should honor Christ. You see how this is being practically carried out. Do not think our Christ is denationalizing us. We are more popular now than in any previous period in the history of the Brâhma-Samâj. Nor is our Hinduism setting us in an attitude of hostility towards Christ or Western science. I beg you will read the "New Dispensation" paper carefully, and let me know what you think of the movement. It is the religion of "Comparative Theology." We are giving effect to the "Science of Religion," of which you are the most distinguished leader. It is the great movement of the day in India. Marvellous is this Light of Heaven!

With profound respect,
Yours very sincerely,
KESHUB CHUNDER SEN.

LILY COTTAGE,
72 UPPER CIRCULAR ROAD, CALCUTTA,
16 *May*, 1881.

MY DEAR FRIEND, — Your last letter reached me a few days after I had posted mine. What a gratifying coincidence! In both letters there is an allusion to our common friend the Dean of Westminster. It is indeed a great pleasure to be assured of the unabated kindness and continued friendship of one whom I so sincerely esteem and whose views and opinions I so greatly value. I have not yet seen the answer of ——. The manner in which he has treated us from the very beginning of the controversy is so utterly unworthy of him, and is marked with such vacillation, wavering, and duplicity, that I can have no misgivings in accepting your verdict. In the mean time allow me to thank you warmly for your kind permission to publish your letters, and the emphatic assurance you have given me of your unreserved and cordial sympathy in the cause we have at heart. Your letters cannot but strengthen our cause greatly. It seems rather strange that ——, who professes to be a devout Christian, should withhold his regard and sympathy from that section of the Brâhma community which is most allied to Jesus and makes the nearest approach to the religion founded by Him. As for his arguments, they have been smashed times beyond number. In his private letters to me he professes friendship, and I have simply warned him in the most kindly spirit to ascertain facts before rushing into print.

I forgot to ask in my last hurried note whether some attempt should not be made to promote the circulation of the "New Dispensation" in England, especially among the clergy and the leading laymen of the Broad Church party. The British public ought to know how the most advanced type of Hinduism in India is trying to absorb and assimilate the Christianity of Christ, and how it is establishing and spreading under the name of the New Dispensation a new Hinduism which combines *Yoga and Bhakti*, and also a new Christianity which blends together Apostolical faith and modern civilization and science. The article on "New Sacramental Ceremony," in the first number of the paper, seems to have created great interest among the Christian community in India, and has been variously commented upon. I should also invite your attention to "Christ in Socrates," in No. 8. Such articles cannot fail to interest the Broad and liberal school in England, and by an interchange of sentiments we may hasten the spiritual union of the East and the West in Christ. There are also hundreds, I believe, in Germany who have cast off orthodoxy and can look with favor upon Theism such as we inculcate and preach under the New Dispensation. Could you tell me the name of any liberal Christian on the Continent who could help us in securing readers in Germany and other countries, and, if possible, review the paper and the movement it represents in some continental Magazine?

Trusting you will kindly remember me to the Dean of Westminster,

Yours very truly,
KESHUB CHUNDER SEN.

MY DEAR FRIEND,—The most difficult subject of all on which I feel that a perfect understanding between you and me is absolutely necessary is the true character of Christ. It may seem strange that a son of India, one who calls himself a believer in Brahman, and who therefore, in strict theological phraseology, would be called a Non-Christian, should have given offence to men who call themselves Christians by what seems to them language of excessive veneration for Christ. Yet so it is: and I shall try to explain to you why it is so, and why, in the case of some of your critics at least, the objections to your deeply impassioned utterances about Christ arise from good and honest motives.

You know that nothing is more difficult than to draw a sharp line between the Divine and the Human. At first nothing seems easier, and in many of the old religions we should have been told that these two terms exclude each other, like right and left; that what is human is not divine, and what is divine is not human. One of the most wide-spread names for the Gods was Immortals (am*r*ita, ἄμβροτοι, immortales), while men were emphatically called Mortals (marta, βροτοί, mortales).

I cannot enter here into the origin and the growth of the words for Deity in the ancient languages and religions of mankind. I have tried to show elsewhere, in my "Hibbert Lectures" which I sent you, how such a word as *deva*, for instance, came into being among our common ancestors, how it expressed at first one only of the many attributes of deity, that of light, but how it grew and expanded its meaning from one stage to another in the religious growth of our common ancestors; and how we Christians in Europe are still using the same word (deva, deus) which was applied to Agni and Indra in the earliest hymns of the Rig-Veda. To give a definition of such a word as *deva*, God, and its various modifications in the different Aryan languages, that should be applicable to them by whomsoever they may be used, is of course impossible. That word has signified everything that man has ever thought to be divine. Its meaning has changed, as we have changed; and as long as the human mind goes on growing, that word also will grow, whether for better or for worse.

What applies to the names for God in the Aryan languages, holds good also with regard to the divine names used by the Semitic races, and particularly by the Semitic race which interests us most, the Jewish. The conception of God, as you see in the Old Testament, varied very considerably at different times in the history of the Jews. It reached its highest spiritual elevation in the utterances of some of the prophets, and it sank down to mere idol-worship even with the wisest of their kings. The history of the Jewish religion has been so often and so fully written that here, too, I may refer you to other books, and simply call your attention to the fact that, at the time when Christianity arose, the Jewish conception of Jehovah was one of a God who had created the world, who ruled the world, but who, though he might be invoked as a friend and even as a father, was yet, in his essence, entirely different from man and the works of his hand. God was immortal; man was mortal: to claim immortality for man seemed almost incompatible with the awe and reverence which the Jews felt for their immortal God. In fact the distance between God and man was perhaps never conceived as greater than it was by the people among whom Christ appeared; and yet they were the very people whom Christ came to teach that "I and my Father are one."

People who have carefully read the sacred books of other religions, and have found there almost every doctrine which they had considered as peculiarly Christian, have sometimes asked me, What then distinguishes Christianity from other religions? My answer is, that historically the distinguishing feature of Christianity lies in the new conception of the relation between God and man. Here we see the pendulum of religious thought swing back completely from left to right, from the Jewish to the Christian conception of God. Though some of the Jewish prophets had preached Jehovah as a father, and had dared even to speak of men as gods, the stream of popular religion was running in a very different channel. To a Jew, at the time of the advent of Christ, the very expression of Son of God was blasphemy. It was different with Greeks and Romans. Their idea of Deity had never been so supramundane as that of the Jews, and they had therefore less difficulty in accepting heroes and demigods, or even human beings, raised to a level with their gods. But taking the Jewish idea of Jehovah as it was preached in the synagogues, we can perfectly well understand why the orthodox Jews should have shouted, "We have a law, and by our law he ought to die, because he made himself the Son of God" (John xix. 7).

Here then is the vital difference between Judaism and Paganism too on one side, and Christianity on the other; here is the thought which in the history of the world stamps Christianity as a new religion. Christ taught many things which other religious teachers had taught before, but Christ taught a new, his own conception, and more than conception, his new intuition and realization of God. Closely connected with this was his new conception, and more than conception—the new birth of man. These two concepts of God and man are so inseparable that it is impossible to modify one without modifying the other. If, as I know many do who call themselves Christians, we leave the conception of Jehovah as we find it among the Jews, and then represent Christ as the son of God, it is surely blasphemy even now. It carries us back into Greek paganism, and it has actually produced in Christian countries forms of thought, and forms of worship paid, not only to the Son of God, but to the Mother of God (θεοτόκος) which must appear to you pure idolatry.

Christianity is Christianity by this one fundamental truth, that as God is the father of man, so truly, and not poetically or metaphorically only, man is the son of God, participating in God's very essence and nature, though separated from God by self and sin. This oneness of nature (ὁμοουσία) between the Divine and the Human does not lower the concept of God by bringing it nearer to the level of humanity; on the contrary, it raises the old concept of man and brings it nearer to its true ideal. No doubt you would find even at the present day many theologians to whom what I have just written to you would sound very strange; but that only shows how little true Christianity has as yet leavened the thoughts of men — how many who call themselves Christians are really Jews, nay, how many have not yet worked themselves free from the pagan concepts of deity. You have no doubt observed among your English friends in India how easily those who call themselves Trinitarians fall into a worship of three gods, and how often those who call themselves Unitarians are no better than Jews in their conception of deity. The true relation between God and man had been dimly foreseen by many prophets and poets, but Christ was the first to proclaim that relation in clear and simple language. He called himself the son of God, and he was the first-born son of God in the fullest sense of that word. But he never made himself equal with the Father in whom he lived and moved and had his being. He was man in the new and true sense of the word, and in the new and true sense of the word he was God. If you ask me whether I am a Trinitarian, I say No; if you ask me whether I am a Unitarian, I say No. And why? Because I believe in Christ as the son of God. To my mind man is nothing if he does not participate in the Divine; and it seems to me that the Jews, with their conception of Jehovah, were perfectly consistent in not believing in a son of God, or even in the immortality of the soul. To you, brought up in the schools of Indian thought, the participation in the Divine must be quite familiar. Your sages have expressed it in philosophical phraseology by the *Pratyag-âtmâ*, the Self that lies behind us, or the *Paramâtmâ*, the Highest Self. But we want something else, something more human, more homely, and yet more holy, to express the same thought in religious language, in language that should be intelligible to the wise and the foolish, the old and the young; and that expression has been found by Christ by calling himself and all who believe in him the sons of God.

After these remarks you will better be able to understand the danger of speaking of Christ in language which carries us back to the panegyrics addressed by pagan poets to their gods and idols. If you speak of Christ as not perfectly human, in his own sense of the word, you make a new idol of him, and you utterly destroy the very soul of his religion. Other prophets have tried to reveal to us what God is: Christ has revealed to us what Man is, and that is the greatest of all revelations which all who call themselves Christians must try to preserve in its original purity. You may say, We know so little of Christ and his original teaching, and what we know of him is what his disciples, all of them Jews, believed of him. There is some truth in it, and to some this may seem a great loss. But it had its advantages also. Out of the scattered stones of the temple which we find in the Gospels, we have each of us to build up our own Christ; and you know how different the ideal and real Christs have been which different theologians have built up for themselves. We must each of us discover our own Christ. The Apostles had to do the same. They had to discover Christ, and they often found it very hard to do so. And while they saw in him that perfection which changes or rather restores human nature to its divine original, you know how others, who had the same opportunities of judging, believed that Christ was possessed of a devil. It was then as it is now, and as it always will be. The same person whom some of us love and revere as almost perfect, whose motives we never doubt, whose words we never question, is represented by others as possessed by all the devils of selfishness, falseness, and cruelty. I quite admit that there are statements in the Gospels that lend themselves to very different interpretations: for how otherwise could we have such different "Lives of Christ?" But there is one point on which there can be no doubt, and that is the extreme humility of Christ. Christ himself objected to any approach to exaggerated language on the part of his friends and disciples. He knew both the small value of superlative language, and the dangers to which it might lead. What would seem to us less liable to the charge of exaggeration than to call Christ *Good Master?* Yet we read in the Gospel of St. Mark (x. 18) that when a rich man came and kneeled to him, and asked him, "Good Master, what shall I do that I may inherit eternal life?" Jesus said unto him, "Why callest thou me good? There is none good but one, that is God." Try to realize to yourself one who could say that, who could turn away reproachfully and sorrowfully from praise that sounds to us so simple and moderate as "Good Master." What would he have said to the outpourings of high-sounding, yet often unmeaning, praise that is sung in our churches! You are perhaps more accustomed to ecstatic poetry; but much as I admire Oriental poetry, I think its profuse display of hyperbolic imagery is one of its weakest points. If you once allow that extravagance of language, panegyric will soon outbid panegyric, and in the end you will have sounds, but no thoughts. Do we not turn away with shame from the language used in Eastern, and alas even in European courts, and yet we dare to bring the same base coin into the sanctuary of God? Do we not know how every manly soul turns away with loathing from the garbage of adulation, hungry for one dry morsel of honest truth? A true friend does not tell his dearest friend one half of what he feels for him, and that very reticence is the true test of true love. Let it be so also between us and Christ. You know how easy it is to repeat the "Thousand Names of Vis*hn*u" — and you also know by whom they are repeated most frequently and most loudly. Surely you will understand then why others should shrink from such high-flown, and, for that very reason, so often empty or unrealized language, and stand almost silent before the face of Christ, feeling that in his presence words are hardly wanted, and that one kind word, or still better one kind deed, for Christ's sake, is better than sacrifice, and praise, and long prayer.

Forgive me for having thus pointed out to you what seems to me a real danger in all religions, and more particularly in those of the East, and believe me,

Ever yours very sincerely,

F. M. M.

LILY COTTAGE,
72 UPPER CIRCULAR ROAD, CALCUTTA,
9 *July*, 1881.

MY DEAR FRIEND, — There is hardly a syllable in your last epistle which I should hesitate to endorse. You have said exactly what I should have said, only in a more learned and philosophical style, such as one would expect from you. So far as your intellectual estimate of Christ is concerned I do not think there is much difference between us. I too regard him as the Son of God, and would never give him higher honor. I see in him not merely an ethical teacher, nor a mere saint of unexampled devotion and unblemished character, but "a greater than Socrates," inasmuch as he was the Son of God. I have often said, as my published lectures and sermons will show, that the distinctive feature of Christ's doctrine and life was his divine sonship. I stand, as you do, between the orthodox Trinitarians on the one hand and the rationalistic Unitarians on the other. My position is that of a Uni-trinitarian. My explanation of the doctrine of the Trinity you will find in my lecture on "Great Men" and in the later numbers of the "New Dispensation." I am so glad and thankful that the Spirit of God has helped me to work my way through

Hinduism to the point where an enlightened Christianity has brought you. I have always disclaimed the Christian name, and will not identify myself with the Christian Church, for I set my face completely against the popular doctrine of Christ's divinity. Yet I recognize divinity in some form in Christ, in the sense in which the Son partakes of the Father's divine nature. We in India look upon the son as the father born again. The wife is called *gâyâ*, for in her the father is born in the shape of the son. Hence the Hindu, while regarding the father and the son as distinct and separate persons, connects them in thought by some kind of identity. This identity does not merge the son in the father, does not by pure fiction exalt the son to the position of the father, but leaving the absolute difference of relationship intact, maintains nevertheless a unity or likeness of nature. The son is made in the image of his father, and he partakes of the father's nature. Looking upon Christ's relation to God in this light, we can readily comprehend the divinity of Jesus as contradistinguished from his "Deity." True sonship, such as it was in Christ, must be divine. The Father was in him and he was in the Father. If this be your position, as it is mine, I do not see any material difference between us concerning Christ's sonship or his divine nature as manifested in true manhood. If intellectually there is no divergence, is there any difference in emotion or devotion? You speak of prayer and praise. "Long prayer" to Christ or any other prophet I thoroughly interdict. It is contrary to our doctrine. We pray only to God for our salvation. In regard to saints we can only hold "communion." We go on "pilgrimage" to the saints in heaven, and hold loving and reverent communion in the recesses of the heart. If we do not worship or pray unto prophets, we certainly love them fervently and praise them with intense reverence. Perhaps it is to this that you take exception. And well you may. In spirit we agree; we disagree in forms. The forms of one nation are apt to be repulsive and even shocking to another. Our Oriental nature is our apology for the "impassioned utterances," the "language of excessive veneration," "high-flown language," &c., you speak of. How can I, my friend, destroy my Asiatic nature, how can I discard the language of poetry and emotion and inspiration which is my life and nature? To adopt any other language would cost me much effort, would be artificial, mechanical, unnatural, and, I may add, hypocritical. I must speak exactly as I feel; and you know my devotion is, as a rule, always extemporaneous. Our tears during prayer, our fervent and constant apostrophizing, our ascetic habits, our very forms of devotion in which we speak of God as One whom we *see* and *hear*, may be disagreeable to European eyes and ears, but so long as they are natural and national, and not affected or borrowed, we need not be afraid of serious consequences. There is certainly great danger in unreal show and Pharisaic sanctimoniousness and superstitious mysticism, but when the doctrine is pure and the heart speaks naturally and spontaneously, from impulse and inspiration, the poetry of religion, for it is nothing more, can do no harm, but will only kindle enthusiasm and sweeten faith. In these "apostolical" days in which we live you must make some allowance for warmth of feeling, which will perhaps die away with the present generation. Accept, my dear friend, my solemn assurance that the danger before us is not superstition, but dryness and skepticism, and that they are moved by the Spirit of God who indulge in the sweet poetry of *living* and *real* faith. It is such a pleasure to read your letters. Please write to me again and again, and believe me,

Yours ever very sincerely,

KESHUB CHUNDER SEN.

When Stanley, the Dean of Westminster, died (July, 1881), Keshub Chunder Sen was anxious to know more about him. Stanley had been to the end a staunch friend of Keshub Chunder Sen. As was usual with him, the attacks on the Indian Reformer had only served to strengthen Stanley's sympathy for him, and he had several times asked me whether and how he could help him. When I began to write down some of my recollections of the Dean, which I thought might be of interest and possibly of use to Keshub Chunder Sen, they soon grew beyond the limits of a letter, and I could only send him a few of my notes from time to time. Some were written soon after the Dean's death, others later. Some have been published already, others are not quite fit for publication yet.

MY DEAR FRIEND, — You know by this time that we have lost Stanley — a true friend to me, a true friend to you, a true friend to many others. He had many friends who loved him, but the number of those whom he loved was greater still. Most men wait till they are loved and then love in return. His whole disposition towards the world was one of welcome. His heart was ever ready to believe the best of every one. His arms were always open to receive you. He was one of those who liked to shake hands with both hands. So it ought to be; so, one would think, it would be naturally. Why should man not welcome man? Alas, the heart that has been deceived, and deceived more than once, knows the answer. It is so bitter to trust and to find one's trust met by envy, cunning, ill-will. . . . Stanley too must have had his bitter experiences, but his arms were open to the last. He did not sum up the experience of his life like a famous statesman lately deceased, — "Friend is the synonym of traitor!"

There is no doubt that Stanley had many enemies. No one was so thoroughly hated, and, I believe, is so still. And how can it be otherwise?

He was a truth-loving, honest, and outspoken man, and the world would be very different from what it is, if such a man had not been hated. He was not like other people, and that is what other people are least inclined to forgive.

And how was he different from other people, you may ask. I believe, first of all, because he always looked upon this world in its true light, not as a home, but as a journey. Hence he was never entirely absorbed in the contests and controversies of the day. He had his opinions and convictions, religious and political, but his horizon was too wide ever to lose himself altogether in our small lanes and valleys. With other men every little question becomes what they call a question of life and death; the thought of the possibility of error, or of surrender, never enters their mind. They fight without looking or listening. They raise dust and smoke till they cannot see through the clouds which they themselves have raised. Stanley was always willing to listen, and even, while holding determinately to his own opinions, he could at least imagine that he might be wrong, and part from his opponents with a few kind words, as if saying, "Let us wait, the time will come when we shall both know better."

Stanley had one great advantage in starting in life, an advantage which is not sufficiently appreciated by those who possess it, because it is rightly considered very honorable if those who do not possess it surmount the difficulties of life without ever forfeiting their self-respect. Stanley belonged to a good family, and was always pecuniarily independent. He never knew the temptations of a poor struggling man, who has often to choose between sacrificing the chances of obtaining a position of usefulness and influence in the world, to which he has a good right, and making certain concessions which, however small, color his character through life. A man who has once been silent when he ought to have spoken, or who has ever spoken when he ought to have been silent, will never be the same again, not perhaps in the eyes of the world which calls speech silver and silence gold, but in his own eyes, if he has eyes to see. And these temptations are great, so great that we ought to be very lenient in judging a poor man who may see actual want, loss of influence, loss of usefulness, on one side, while one small concession to the world would lead him to the bench of Judges or Bishops, or any other place for which he is the fittest man.

Stanley had his ambition, he knew what he had a right to expect, aye, to demand; but he could afford to wait. He had not to push and to urge his claims himself or through others, and he thus remained a free man through life. He was content to be a College Tutor, a Canon of Canterbury, a Professor at Oxford, and at last a Dean of Westminster. He was content, nay he was proud of his position. Yet, if he had been a worldly and what is called a prudent man, he might have been a Bishop and an Archbishop long before others.

When I first knew him as a young Tutor at University College, I was often struck by his boldness as compared with the prudence of other friends of mine. I did not know then that he was a man who could afford to walk straight forward, without looking right or left, and I honored him all the more for what seemed to me the highest chivalry of truth. Not that I honor him less, now that I know how strong and impregnable his position was, for, after all, wealth does not always produce independence of thought and word and deed. Only I do not perhaps place him now quite so high above all his contemporaries as I did when I was first drawn into the peculiar life of Oxford, and began to watch the bold or timid steps in the careers of men who have since risen to eminence. There is one expression in English which I have always liked very much. "He has an independence," that is, he has sufficient to live without caring for frowns or favors.

There was another feature in Stanley's character which from the first attracted me strongly towards him. Not being a scheming or diplomatizing man himself, he did not look upon others as if they were always driving at something. One could speak to him unreservedly, almost thoughtlessly. One knew he believed all one said. He would forgive even a stupid, silly, or selfish remark, and interpret every man according to the best meaning of which he would admit. There was in him a serene transparency, and one felt that in speaking with him there was no necessity for weighing every word, or calculating its effect, or guarding against every possible misinterpretation. It was a treat to speak with him and to find that he really took one for better than one was — it made one better. It is one of the greatest miseries of our artificial life to have always to be on the guard against possible misunderstandings. You must have felt that when you had to clothe your Eastern thoughts in Western words. I have felt it myself very often when trying to translate my German thoughts into English idiom. There are little niceties of expression which it is difficult to learn later in life. Many times I know I have been misunderstood and have offended people simply from a certain carelessness of expression. If one has to look out for the right word and does not find it at once, one often blurts out the next best. One sees at once, even without the gift of thought-reading, that there is a peculiar taste about that word which is not quite palatable to one's friend. One might stop and explain, but that often makes matters worse, and so one leaves it and goes on, trusting to one's friend's good-nature. With Stanley I never had that feeling, even when I was a mere beginner and bungler in English. I knew always that he would understand what I really meant. After all, we are all stammerers. Even the most eloquent express but half of what they feel and mean. We must all trust to a *Lector Benevolus*, and that is what Stanley was at all times and with all men.

Another feature which was most strongly marked in Stanley's character was his indignation at any injustice or even unfairness committed against a man who, whether from weakness or other circumstances, was unable to defend himself. Again and again have I seen Stanley rushing into the fray when he suspected want of fair play. Again and again have I seen him assisting men for whom he had really no sympathy, nay defending others whom he naturally shrank from, simply because they were ill-treated by the mob, whatever that mob might be. This kind of chivalry may be carried too far, but nothing after all is so amiable and so attractive as this Quixotic character. The world would be intolerable if it were not for a few such true knights. He was opposed to the publication of "Essays and Reviews," but when they were published and attacked, as they were, with clubs and tomahawks, Stanley fought more valiantly than any of the Seven, and it was said at the time, perhaps truly, that he then forfeited his chance of a mitre. Stanley never went so far as Colenso. He did not even see the value of Colenso's criticism. He knew what ancient history meant, and to his mind many of the contradictions, worked out so laboriously by the brave Bishop, were really confirmations of the historical genuineness of the Old Testament. They were what a true historian, who knows the conditions under which the earliest literary documents are composed, collected, and preserved, would expect. The absence of such contradictions would have seemed to him suspicious. But whatever Stanley's own views and feelings might be, when the Bishops and their friends tried to crush argument by authority, he stood forth, undismayed by clamor and threats, and to the last remained true to Colenso, though equally true, as we know, to his Old Testament, as a real work of antiquity, possessing all those characteristics which an ancient history ought to possess, and none of those of a short-hand report in our modern newspapers. You owe some of his sympathy to the violent attacks that were made on you, and I can trace the origin of his friendship for me to a similar cause.

Stanley's character as a theologian, and as a politician too, in fact the whole tone of his mind, was what I must call historical. Learn how things have become what they are, and you will understand them, approve of them, or at all events bear with them for a while, till they can become or can be made to become something better. This is the key-note in every one of Stanley's books from the first to the last, and he did not wait for Evolutionism to teach him that lesson.[1]

It has sometimes been said that Stanley was not quite outspoken, that he did not say all he knew, that he submitted to many things which he could not have approved in his heart. Is there one man of whom the same might not be said? We all know a great deal more, or are working up to know a great deal more than we are prepared to say and publish to the world. What a man like Stanley puts forward, he must be prepared to defend against the whole world; and if he feels that he is unable to do that, he would rightly shrink from a step that might defeat the very object he had in view. On many points our knowledge may be sufficient to satisfy ourselves, but far from sufficient to satisfy others, and to silence all possible objections.

[1] Some of what I had written here on this side of Stanley's character, has been published in an article, "Forgotten Bibles," in the *Nineteenth Century*, June, 1884, pp. 1017, *seq*.

Again, do we not all submit to many things which we do not approve? One man may be a republican, and yet submit to a monarchical government; and another may be an imperialist, and yet submit to a republican government. Stanley certainly did not approve of the Thirty-nine Articles, but he signed them as an historical document, knowing their origin and their historical purpose, and accepting them as a compromise between the different parties that have formed the Church of England.

How could we have any religion, how could we have any Church, without a compromise? It is different in philosophy. There every man may go his own way, and speak his own language. But it is the very nature of religion to be a compromise, a compromise between the young and the old, the wise and the foolish, all of whom are to use the same language, though they must use it each in his own way. Now Stanley was a man of such strong human sympathies, and so ready to enter into the thoughts and feelings of others, that he would have been the last man to disturb the religious peace of anybody. Who would like to wake a child from its peaceful slumber? We stand by its cradle and watch the little rosebud, and hardly draw our breath for fear of breaking in upon its perfect bliss. All we can do is to be near, so that, when the child awakes, it should not be frightened at finding itself quite alone. Stanley knew that, so far as mere happiness is concerned, nothing is happier than the faith of childhood, nothing more blessed than the continuance of that faith from the cradle to the grave.

In meeting friends who had that faith, Stanley could enter into their feelings with all the truth and warmth of a man who liked nothing better than to be a child once more. Is that dishonesty? As well you might call it dishonest to say that the sun rises, instead of saying that the earth sets.

But with men who were no longer children, he was a man, and an honest man. He knew that the time comes when, whether we like it or not, the child must wake, when the man must face the world such as it is, not such as he would wish it to be.

A dear friend of Stanley's, a high dignitary in the Church, asked me soon after his death, "Tell me, did Stanley believe in miracles?" I said, "Certainly not," and he seemed quite relieved, and repeated again and again, "Certainly not, certainly not." And yet this might give you a false idea of Stanley. He certainly did not believe in miracles as they are believed in by many, as irregularities committed on purpose. He was not troubled by miracles. He knew, as every historian knows, or by this time ought to know, that there is no religion without miracles, and yet that the founders of the three highest religions have unanimously condemned miracles. Your ancient native religion is full of miracles, and it would be quite as true to call them psychologically inevitable as to call them physically impossible. But Stanley knew that certain minds cannot believe anything unless they first believe in miracles. To these men of little faith miracles are everything, and if their faith in miracles were undermined, their faith in everything else would crumble to pieces. This may seem strange to you, for I am sure you did not believe in Christ because He could change water into wine, or cast out devils, or heal the sick, or feed the hungry, or calm the storm, or walk on the water. A man may be believed to have done all that and much more, as in the case of some of your ancient Rishis, and yet you would not believe his doctrines unless they could command a very different sanction. To you, all the facts, whether historical or legendary, in the life of Christ must seem entirely outside the temple of Christian truth; and the question whether the miracles were accurately reported by contemporary witnesses would probably affect you as little as it affects millions of Christians, who either cannot read or have no time for reading. Let us only see clearly that facts can never be believed, unless we do violence to the true sense of that word. Facts may be either doubted or not, either accepted or not, either rejected or not, but they cannot be believed as we believe the existence of God, the sonship of Christ, the immortality of the soul, or the holiness of truth. If you read the words which Christ addressed to Thomas (St. John xx. 29), "Blessed are they that have not seen, and yet have believed," you will see that they have a much deeper meaning than is commonly supposed, and that Christ himself placed a faith without sight high above a faith with sight.

There is hardly a miracle in the New Testament which to a man who knows the language of other religions is startling. Buddha was called the great physician, and we have no reason to doubt that Christ too was a true physician, and could heal, not only spiritual, but also physical diseases. Which of the two gifts Christ himself placed highest, we may learn from his own words, when he sends his message to John the Baptist, saying "that the blind see, the lame walk, the lepers are cleansed, the deaf hear, the dead are raised — and to the poor the gospel is preached."

But you may say that, although most miracles performed by Christ offer no difficulties to an historical mind, such as Stanley's was, there are two miracles performed, not by, but as it were for Christ, which must have been a stumbling-block to an honest mind, such as Stanley's was, namely the miraculous birth, and what may be called the miraculous death of Christ. I cannot tell for certain what Stanley thought on these two subjects, though some of his remarks on a sermon preached in Westminster Abbey by our common friend Kingsley leave little doubt in my mind that he looked for true divinity elsewhere than in the cradle and in the grave. But to your mind these two miracles ought to be the least perplexing. You know that whenever the founder of a religion has been raised to a superhuman or divine rank, the human mind rebels against an ordinary birth and an ordinary death. It is extremely curious to observe how on this point human ingenuity tries to outbid divine wisdom. The highest wisdom, whether we call it God or Nature, conceived one kind of birth as the best for man. Man invented what he thought a more becoming birth for God. The intention was good, no doubt, but it was, to say the least, uncalled for. Is there anything more wonderful than the ordinary birth of a child? is there anything more holy? anything that can more truly be called a revelation? Does a miracle cease to be a miracle because it happens every day? Does the marvellous become common because it happens every minute? Depend upon it, no miraculous birth will ever outbid the miraculousness of the plain birth of a child. "What God hath cleansed, that call not thou common."

And as to Christ's real resurrection, is it credible that, when we are told again and again that Christ came to bring life and immortality to light, the simple words that Christ rose from the dead should have been taken in a carnal, not in a spiritual sense? How would a carnal resurrection and ascension benefit us? Does heaven still mean the clouds as it did in the Veda? Did St. Paul really mean that unless Christ's body had been carried through the clouds, his faith in Christ would be in vain? It would be fearful to think so. St. Paul did not even say, "If Christ is not raised, the dead rise not," but "If the dead rise not, then is not Christ raised." Of this I am perfectly certain, that if you had said to Stanley, "Am I a Christian if I believe only in the spiritual resurrection of Christ?" he would have said "Yes, and all the more, if you do not believe that his body was taken up to the clouds." I often regret that the Jews buried, and did not burn their dead, for in that case the Christian idea of the resurrection would have remained far more spiritual, and the conception of immortality would have become less material.

One can hardly realize what Christianity would be if such men as Stanley ever became its true representatives. We should not want Missionaries then. Instead of a few converts here and there being pressed to come in, millions would press to come in, and many like yourself would say, We have long been Christians. If you had lived in the first century, you would have been a disciple of Christ, whereas now you say truly, because I am a disciple of Christ, therefore I cannot be a Christian. However, we must not despair. I well remember your parting words in Oxford, "And if fifty years hence people should find out that I have been doing the work of Christ, what harm is there?" There are many in Europe who must be content to say the same, and Christ's best disciples are found, I believe, among those whom so-called believers call unbelievers.

If what I write to you can do any good in India, remember that I never have any secrets. If my views are wrong, they can be corrected; if they are right, the more I am abused for them, the better.

Yours very truly,

F. MAX MÜLLER.

OXFORD, 7 *May*, 1882.

MY DEAR FRIEND,—I have long wished to write to you again, and to congratulate you on the cessation of the war. I am so glad that you have left the battle-field for better fields of usefulness. You have a far too important work to do, to waste your time in personal controversy. Go on preaching, teaching, and doing as much good as you can; that is the best answer to all obloquy. You know I do not flatter you. I have openly told you when I differed from you, but I have far too high an idea of the work which you are meant to do on earth to ask any further explanations from you on matters where after all you may be right and I wrong. No, no, we must learn to trust each other even when we do not always understand each other. You are an Eastern, I am a Western. There is One who knows who is right and who is wrong, and that is the Purusha within us.

I have still many things to tell you about our friend Stanley. I miss him very much. He always remained true to you. After he had once trusted a man, he seldom dropped him again. His troubles often reminded me of your troubles. He always complained that he had achieved so little — that he had lost all influence in the Church. He little knew how much he had achieved, how great his influence really was. His death revealed his greatness. I feel sure we ought not to think so much about visible success, we ought not to be disheartened at apparent failure even. All we can do is to move on straight, and not to mind if our straight line seems crooked to the crooked. Even if you were to do nothing more, you ought to feel that you have done a great and good work, which will never be undone again. That ought to cheer you, and make you go on with your work cheerfully. I am going to Cambridge next week, having been invited by the University to give some Lectures on India. I have chosen for my subject, "What can India teach *us?*" I hope you will approve.

Believe me, yours very sincerely,

F. MAX MÜLLER.

LILY COTTAGE,
72 UPPER CIRCULAR ROAD, CALCUTTA,
5 *August*, 1882.

MY DEAR FRIEND, — I had hoped to write to you from the Himâlayas, where I went for a brief sojourn for the benefit of my health, shortly after the receipt of your very kind and cheering message. These stupendous and lofty heights are dear and sacred to us Indians, as reminders of the departed glory of our fatherland, and as a source of living inspiration amid the grovelling cares of the world. Nor are they less dear and sacred to you, whose heart is so thoroughly Eastern and Indian. Perhaps you honor our country and its ancient literature more than we natives of the soil do. And I am sure a letter from the Himâlayas you would have hailed with peculiar interest and joy. Ill-health, however, prevented my writing to you from there; and though I have since my return often wished to write, I have as often failed. The fact is I have been suffering from extreme nervous debility and other complaints since our last anniversary festival in January, and even now I am not equal to my work.

You are quite right in denouncing fruitless controversies and personal wranglings. In our Church especially these are altogether out of place. Our work at present is not destruction, but reconstruction. We have had enough of the former during the earlier periods of the Brâhma-Samâj history. There was a time when an aggressive warfare had to be kept up, and we had to put down idolatry and caste with iconoclastic fury. But the New Dispensation is a work of construction. It fulfils, does not destroy; it builds, does not demolish. Our entire literature bears testimony to this positive and pacific policy of our Church. If you know the leading principles of my life and character, you will no doubt admit that I am pledged to reconciliation and harmony. If I live for any purpose it is for this, that I will preach the union of Eastern and Western Theism, the reconciliation of Europe and Asia. The idea may seem absurd to many in the present age. It may provoke ridicule and angry reviling. But posterity will prove a better judge. My honored friend, *you* need not be told that a man must stick to the high ideal of his life regardless of consequences, and remain true to the light within in spite of obloquy and persecution.

God has given me too a work to do, and my tastes and ideas, impulses and aspirations have been moulded and shaped accordingly. One half of my heart is in sympathy with Europe, and the other half with Asia. I cannot therefore bear the thought of their separation. If one branch of the Lord's family has taken one idea from Him, and another branch another idea, why should they quarrel? Are we not both the Lord's? To take only Asiatic thought or European faith is a half-measure. It is the adoption of a fraction of divine life. That Asia and Europe, the East and the West, will always continue in a state of mutual separation, divorce, and disunion is against nature and nature's God. Let us seek the perfection of the individual and the race in the union of Eastern and Western types of thought and character. I trust and pray that all scholars and thinkers and philanthropists in different parts of the world will try to bring about this international reconciliation. Let there be no more wrangling, no more sectarian antagonism. Let the angel of peace and love reign. What you say of that noble soul, Dean Stanley, is truly refreshing and encouraging. Yes, he has done a great deal, and the influence he has left behind will do infinitely more to widen and deepen the Church in Europe, and vastly help to bring about the reconciliation of the Eastern and the Western Churches. May his soul rest in peace in the bosom of God!

Believe me,

Yours more sincerely,

KESHUB CHUNDER SEN.

TARA VIEW, SIMLA,
20 *July*, 1883.

MY DEAR FRIEND,—The papers report the death of your good mother. Allow me to send you a line of condolence from the distant Himâlaya. As a Hindu I feel the deepest sympathy in your grief. For who on earth so good as the mother? We in India regard our parents, and especially the mother, as "sâkshât pratyakshadevatâ,"[1] and we have no doubt you have the same Aryan feeling and instinct in you. A mother's love who can repay? A mother's memory no loyal son can forget. Alive or dead, we honor and revere her spirit, not merely on account of our earthly obligations, but because motherly tenderness represents so truly and so beautifully the loving kindness of the Supreme Mother. May the soul of your dear mother rest in peace in the world above!

I am sorry I cannot write to you so often as I could wish. But of this I can assure you, that you are often present in my thoughts. The affinity is not only ethnic, but in the highest degree spiritual, which often draws you into my heart and makes me enjoy the pleasures of friendly intercourse. I forget the distance, and feel we are very near each other. These Himâlayas ablaze with India's ancient glory constantly remind me of you, and as I read your Lectures on "India, what can it teach us?" in the veranda of my little house in the morning, I feel so intensely the presence of your spirit in me that it seems I am not reading your book, but talking to you and you are talking to me in deep spirit-intercouse. How ardently you love India that book has made clear. Surely you honor our "fatherland" more than any of my own

[1] "A present visible deity."

countrymen, and the glowing terms in which you speak of India, her people, her religion, and her ancient greatness put to shame the enthusiasm of even the most warm-hearted patriot among us. And what you write in your book I see with my own eyes and realize in my own heart on these Himâlayan heights. Every word you say of the Rishis, their faith and devotion, is so true. Their transcendental spirituality, their unearthly asceticism, as distinguished from the busy life of the West, you justly appreciate and admire. Alas! these blessed Rishis are dead and gone. On the plains of Bengal, where I live, I miss them: I see an entirely different generation, by no means loyal to their venerable forefathers. But I do not miss them here. On these hills the ancient Rishis seem yet to live and move. I feel that they are with me and in me. Everything recalls these saintly spirits to my mind, and I see before me not the agnostic's godless earth and sky, but the ancient Aryan devotee's Sûrya, Vâyu, Varu*n*a, and Indra. How I wish to see you in this my humble hermitage, and talk together about the deeper mysteries of Rishi life in the very abode of the ancient Rishis, the Himâlaya! You say I follow the Rita of the Vedic Rishis. I wish I could always do so; in fact this is the great ambition of my life. These twenty-five years the Holy Ghost has been to me not only my teacher and guide, but also my guardian and protector. He has given me the bread of inspiration; and to His directions too I owe my daily bread. I never knew any Guru or priest, but in all matters affecting the higher life I have always sought and found light in the direct counsels of the Holy Spirit. Nor could I ever count upon a definite income for my large family, and yet through darkness and uncertainty the Holy Ghost has led me on, feeding me, my wife and ten children, and even giving us the comforts of life. From how many perils, dangers, and temptations has He delivered me! How many times has He shown me the light of heaven! or I would have perished. To so good a Spirit I look as to a personal Friend and a daily Companion, and I have made up my mind never to turn away from Him to whom I owe all that I prize in my temporal and my spiritual life. The applause of man pleases me not, if the Monitor within rebukes me. And when the world stands against me, as it often does, my Comforter comforts me as no man can. When everything fails, I find joy and strength in the cheering voice of the Holy Ghost. May I always prove faithful to Him!

Not long ago the Editor of the "Contemporary Review" wrote to me a kind note asking me to contribute an article on some Indian subject. I promised to accede to his request, but wanted time as I was unwell. Since writing to him I got worse and worse, and I have not yet found time or energy sufficient for the task. I hope to redeem my promise so soon as health permits. It is a wasting disease from which I am suffering, and it brings on terrible weakness and exhaustion at times. If convenient I beg you will do me the favor to write a line to the Editor requesting his indulgence and forbearance.

Yours most sincerely,

KESHUB CHUNDER SEN.

LETTERS FROM PROTAP CHUNDER MOZUMDAR.

PEACE COTTAGE,
73 UPPER CIRCULAR ROAD, CALCUTTA,
14 *February*, 1881.

MY DEAR SIR, — Perhaps you do not remember me. I had the great pleasure of spending an afternoon with you in autumn, 1874. Since my return home I have always thought of writing to you; but with the Hindu's indecision I have always hesitated. Yet I always felt most gratefully that your interest in the Brâhma-Samâj, of which I have been a worker nearly for the last twenty years, was unabated. When you put me into the train at the railway station you said, "Send me every information, every paper, every scrap; you will not find me speaking always, but when the time comes — here I am!" The time *has* come, and you have spoken. But, alas! we have not kept you well furnished with facts about our movement. You have watched the agitation on the Cutch Behar marriage. That agitation began from deeper causes, and ended in deeper opposition than a mere protest against the marriage. Keshub Chunder Sen's genius is too Western for his own countrymen, and too Eastern for yours. His mind is so independent and original, so far above conventional proprieties of every sort, that long before the marriage he had begun to make enemies both inside and outside the Brâhma-Samâj. They were seeking for an opportunity to crush him, they found it in the marriage, they used it to an extent of unmercifulness of which you can form no idea. But Keshub is one of those men who cannot be crushed. His spiritual vitality, his moral vigor are simply immortal. Among his opponents those perhaps have done him most harm who were his friends. Miss Collet, the compiler of the Brahmo Year Book, has tried to do him the most lasting harm. This lady's idolization of Keshub was as singular, as her present violent and unreasoning antipathy. Not a little there was in the Cutch Behar marriage to which an honest man might take objection. Some of the forms and figures subsequently used by our friend might also startle any European, perhaps even a Hindu. For my own part I am not an advocate of sensational figures of speech. But I know how absolutely beyond sober speech is every impulse of deep and genuine spirituality. Are not the original perceptions of genius obscure to the finest intellects? Deliberate obscurity is dishonesty. It may be a foible in which great souls have occasionally indulged; but to a man laboring in the awful and agonizing solitude of genius perhaps it may be found restful to indulge in expressions which he alone can fully fathom.

But I maintain a man of real and acknowledged power is entitled to some amount of public trust. If every act and every expression of his that is not understood were put down to the score of moral corruptness, all forms of organization would soon cease to exist. And this is what Keshub's opponents both in England and India have done. In not treating him with the charity to which much inferior men are entitled, they have driven him deeper and deeper into his exceedingly sensitive individuality, till he has altogether ceased to be understood. Hardheartedness produces its worst effects upon the intellect. And these people have lost the sense by which very plain words and actions can be properly construed. Except to friends, to persons disposed to treat you charitably and justly, it is often wrong to offer any explanation at all. Explanations require so often to be explained that one turns from the whole task in despair. I wonder if there can be any justice, in the proper sense of that word, apart from charity. You, sir, have shown him that charity, and hence, even in the absence of such facts as you ought to have received, you have been more *just* to him than many others, who *knew* more, have been able to be. The Cutch Behar marriage is now a thing of the past. I believe before long Keshub will have to publish more facts to clear his own conduct in regard to that affair. He has not done so because he shrank from exposing the conduct of some high officials of the Bengal Government.

The Brâhma-Samâj has come to occupy a position which may be considered apart from its relations to the Cutch Behar marriage. This doctrine of the New Dispensation promises to excite great hostility. I will by next mail post the "Theistic Review," in which some of our leading ideas on the subject are explained. The New Dispensation seems to me to be nothing more than the spiritual counterpart of your idea of a Science of Comparative Theology. What you are doing as a philosopher and a philologist we are trying to do as men of devotion and faith. It is the same universal recognition of all truths, and all prophets. It is the same war against exclusiveness and bigotry. I grant we are doing it in a Hindu style, perhaps in a Bengâli style. But there is no question that the future religion of the world must acknowledge the reign of law, order, harmony, and development in the religious records of mankind. The Fatherhood of God is a meaningless abstraction unless the unity of truth in all lands and nations is admitted. And the Brotherhood of man is impossible, if there is no recognition of the services which the great peoples of the earth have rendered unto each other. I must not take up more of your time. It will be nothing short of delight if I can ever hear from you in reply. I and my friends look upon you as an interpreter, as a mediator between ourselves and Europe. And I have no doubt you reciprocate the cordiality and confidence with which the Brâhma-Samâj regards you. With very warm and kind regards,

I remain, dear sir,

Yours very faithfully,

Prof. Max Müller. P. C. MOZUMDAR.

SIMLA,
20 *August*, 1881.

MY DEAR SIR, — Simla, as you know, is in the midst of the Himâlayas. It is the summer seat of the Government of India, and the Lieutenant-Governor of the Punjab also comes here, because it is within the province he rules, and also because he has to consult with the head of the Supreme Government on questions relating to the many frontier difficulties that have started up since the unfortunate Afghan war. Being in continued bad health for some time, I have been here for a change for the last three months. It was here I received your kind and valuable present of the translation of the Dhammapada, for which allow me to offer you my very hearty thanks. It was here also I got your card desiring me to send you certain Bengâli books, which I hope have by this time reached you. I presume you have now commenced to write the life of Râjah Râmmohun Roy, as you wished. It is my sincere desire that you get a perfect insight into the internal workings of the Brâhma-Samâj of the present day, which is so essentially different from the institution which the Râjah founded in 1830. There is no doubt the Râjah meant it to be a monotheistic church, though he gave it a purely Vedantic character. As you know very well, this monotheism was developed and formulated by Devendranâth Tagore. He has always kept strictly true to the ancient cult of the authors of the Upanishads, to the rigid and deliberate exclusion of those Christian influences which Râmmohun Roy carefully sought and cultivated. It is certain, however, that he was the first to introduce into the Samâj genuine piety and spirituality. Into the constitution of this piety a good deal of the mysticism of Hafiz and the idealism of Victor Cousin entered. I remember how intensely fond Devendranâth was of chanting the Gazels of the Persian Sufis, and reading the works of Cousin, Kant, and Fichte. So if any Christian influence can be said to have entered into his system it was indirectly through these thinkers. But for the Bible, for the character of Jesus and of His disciples, the Pradhân Âchârya of the Brâmah-Samâj has always had an unfeigned dislike. Indeed from this point of view the teachings of Devendranâth Tagore are understood without much difficulty.

With the advent of Keshub Chunder Sen the principles of the Brâhma-Samâj assumed the form of a *religion*, and that institution took the character of a *Church*. Keshub cannot be considered as a well-read man. Even his quotations from the Bible, which are pretty frequent, are made at random, and got up for the occasions on which they are meant to give point and emphasis to his own sentiments. But he deserves the credit of uprearing the whole structure of Brâhma doctrines by the unaided efforts of his religious genius. If he has been aided by anything, he has been aided only by his singular devotions, which are long, deep, and sweet. Doctrinally his teachings may be said generally to have embraced the following subjects: Existence and attributes of God as a personality; Providence, general and special; the soul of man as an immortal spirit; Conscience; Prayer; Inspiration; our relations to Christ; to Sâkya, Chaitanya, etc.; the Brâhma-Samâj as a revealed dispensation of God, including all previous dispensations, and setting forth the religion of the future. His spiritual precepts may be said to have generally embraced the following subjects: Upâsana, worship; Yoga, asceticism; Bhakti, devotion; Vairâgya, passionlessness; Sâdhana, which I would translate as self-discipline. He has besides said a good deal on domestic, social, and apostolical organization. Now his doctrinal and other precepts have been so amplified and complicated by frequent references to and applications of Hindu Puraric conceptions, as well as Christian dogmas and observances, that they have swelled to an enormous extent, until to many the primitive simplicity of their theistic character has been all but lost. And while some accuse him of relapsing into Hindu idolatry and Pantheism, others charge him with merging into Christian orthodoxy. I cannot say these misconceptions are unnatural, and they have been aggravated by certain rhetorical peculiarities and personal incidents, principal among which is the Cutch Behar marriage. His interpretations of Hindu and Christian ideas may or may not be right, but I believe no slur can be cast upon the soundness of his theistic teaching. It has long been my desire to explain some of his principles from a simple and rational theistic ground. But I sometimes feel that I should wait for a further development of his views. In this endeavor I should greatly prize the benefit of your ideas and suggestions. Keshub is continually becoming more and more metaphysical and mystical. Sometimes I am afraid he may completely elude popular understanding, and that is why I am the more anxious to explain him. Recently he has very much given himself up to symbolism. There has been a good deal of flags, flowers, fires, and sacraments of all kinds. Of course misunderstanding is in consequence on the increase. Yet Keshub's uncommon penetration, sagacity, and common sense are as clear and strong as ever. The suggestions of a friendly critic like you will be most welcome at this juncture, the more especially as the different parties in the Brâhma-Samâj seem to have lost all mutual respect and confidence. Devendranâth Tagore has retired into the hills. The other day I received a most significant letter from him. I will translate it, and publish it some day. In the meanwhile permit me to send my little "Theistic Review and Interpreter." Hoping to have the pleasure of hearing from you some day,

I remain,

Very sincerely yours,

Prof. Max Müller. P. C. MOZUMDAR.

OXFORD, 3 *August*, 1881.

MY DEAR MR. PROTAP CHUNDER MOZUMDAR,—If I have not written to you before, you may believe me that it was time and leisure only that were wanting, and that I have often longed for a quiet hour to thank you for your letters, and to exchange some thoughts with you on subjects very near to your heart and to mine. I have many kind friends in different parts of the world, and I must tell them all what I told you when we parted at Oxford, "If you *really* want me, I shall always be ready." But the day has only eight or ten hours of work in it, and often not even that; and there is much still left to do, which I feel I ought to do. Yet, as I watch the sun of my life going down, I feel I shall never be able to do even half of what I wished to do in this life. I must therefore ask you and my other friends to have patience with me. I have watched your struggles in India for many years, and I have often pleaded your cause in England with friends who were frightened by what they heard about Keshub Chunder Sen. Yet I trusted in you and in the goodness of your cause, and remained silent, at least in public. But when I saw our friend Keshub Chunder Sen pressed on all sides, attacked not only by his natural enemies, but by his natural friends, I thought I ought to come to his succor, or at all events to show him that some of his friends were able to make allowance for his difficulties, and though they might differ from him, had not lost their confidence in him. That Cutch Behar marriage was a misfortune, but what has it to do with the great work that Keshub Chunder Sen has been carrying on? Suppose even he was to be blamed, can no one be allowed to carry on a great religious reform, unless he is himself entirely blameless? Nothing I admire more in the writers of our Gospels than the open way in which they sometimes speak of the failings of the Apostles. In their eyes nothing could have been more grievous than St. Peter's denial of Christ. Yet they make no secret of it, and without any public confession, recantation, or penance, Peter, after he has wept bitterly, is as great an Apostle as all the others, nay, even greater. Surely these are passing clouds only, and what we ought to look to is the bright sky behind.

At the present moment many of Keshub Chunder Sen's old friends in England, and some particularly of his most generous and liberal-minded friends, are in despair about some of the outward religious ceremonies which he has sanctioned. His asceticism, his shaving his hair, his carrying a flag and singing in the streets, his pilgrimages — all are considered quite shocking! To tell you the truth, I am not fond of such things; but every religion is a compromise, must and always will be a compromise, between men and children; and there is no religion in which men like you and me, who care for better things, have not often to say that they are not fond of "such things," yet have to bear with them. Think of our ritualists at home. Silly children, naughty children, if you like; but, for all that, many of them very good boys. There is no real harm in shaving one's hair. A man must either shave his hair or let it grow, and who shall say which of the two is best? Buddha was called a "shaveling" (mu*nd*a), because in order to abolish all outward signs of caste or rank, he cut off his hair. But there is an old Sanskrit verse which says: —

Pañkavimsatitattvagño yatra tatrâ-srame vaset, *Gaṭî*, muṇḍî, sikhî vâpi mukyate nâtra samsayah.	"Whether a man wear matted hair, or a top-knot, or shave his hair, if he knows the twenty-five truths, he will be saved."

As to leading an ascetic life, what harm is there in that? India is the very country for leading an ascetic life, and a man does not there banish himself from society by it, as he would do in Europe. Pilgrimages too, singing in the open air and carrying flags, seem all so natural to those who know the true Indian life — not the life of Calcutta or Bombay — that I cannot see why people in England should be so shocked by what they call Keshub Chunder Sen's vagaries. Because he carries a flag, which was the recognized custom among ancient religious leaders, he is accused of worshipping a flag. I am sure he does not pay half the worship to his flag which every English soldier does to his. It often becomes to him a real fetish; and yet a soldier, when he dies for his flag, is honored by the very people who now cry out against Keshub Chunder Sen, because he honors his flag, as a symbol of his cause.

If Keshub Chunder Sen insisted on other people doing exactly as he does, the case would be different. But he does not, and whatever you and I and others may feel about the importance of "such things," there never has been and there never will be a religion "without a flag." I wish it were not so; you probably wish it were not so; but man cannot live on oxygen — he requires bread.

These, however, were not the matters I wished to speak about, when writing to you. Not the playthings of religion, but the very life and marrow of religion I wanted to discuss with you, chiefly with reference to that excellent article of yours, published in the "Theistic Quarterly Review," October, 1879. Of all the reviews which my "Hibbert Lectures" have elicited, I liked yours the best, because it went to the very core of the matter which I undertook to treat. Now there are many people who are quite as much shocked at our going to the very core of religion, as others are with our playing with the playthings of religion; and if we were to count hands, not heads, what a small minority we should be! I sometimes wonder that we are allowed to speak and to live at all, for the great mass of good and honest people in the world consider every one who, what they call, shakes their faith (what we should call, strengthens our faith), as an enemy to society, as a danger to their happiness here and hereafter, as a man to be silenced by any means. Where would your small flock be, if everybody in India were allowed to do with you what he thinks right? Remember what the majority against you consists of. First, all children up to fifteen years of age; secondly, all women, with few exceptions; thirdly, most old and infirm people; lastly, all uneducated, all timid, and all downright dishonest people. If you count up all these, I doubt whether you can reckon on one in a hundred to stand up openly for you, while the other ninety-nine would all combine against you.

And mind, with the exception of the last class of "downright dishonest people," who from motives of prudence or selfishness either do not say what they do believe, or do say what they do not believe, we have no right to complain of our antagonists. They have a right to be what they are, and many of them are sorely troubled by our supposed antagonism to them and to the views which they hold with regard to religion. Now we know from our own experience that we too were sorely troubled in our youth, and in our later years also, when we found that many things dear, aye sacred to us, had to be surrendered to a truer voice and a higher will. Then what I feel and what I say is, that if we want the majority to bear with us, — a most minute minority, — we ought to bear with them, and understand that what are to us but outward things, playthings, nothings, may be to them the only comfort they can find in this world. One thing I know, that some of these so-called ascetics, or ritualists, or bigoted and narrow-minded people, lead the most devoted, unselfish, pure, and noble lives; and every tree which can bear such fruit — whether it be the religion of Jews or Christians, or Mohammedans or Brâhmans, or Parsis or Buddhists — cannot be so entirely rotten to the core as many of our friends, in Europe as well as in India, will have it.

But now, after having pleaded the cause of those happy people who know nothing and want nothing but faith and good works, let me stand up also for those whose deepest religion makes it impossible for them to be satisfied with that kind of outward religion, whether they are Jews or Christians, or Mohammedans or Brâhmans, or Parsis or Buddhists. They seem to me to have as much right on their side as the others on theirs, and if you think that I have made "too great concessions to the rampant scientists of the time," you place me in a position which I could not accept. We have no concessions to make to rampant scientists. They have as much right on their side, if they are but honest, as anybody else, and the fact that they are again a very small minority, decides nothing as to the truth or untruth of their opinions. Depend on it, there are as good people among these rampant scientists as among the most devout ascetics.

You have seen better than anybody else that the problem which I wished to discuss in my "Hibbert Lectures," and to illustrate through the history of religion in India, was the *possibility of religion in the light of modern science.* I might define my object even more accurately by saying that it was a reconsideration of the problem, left unsolved by Kant in his "Critique of Pure Reason," after a full analysis of the powers of our knowledge and the limits of their application, "Can we have any knowledge of the Transcendent or Supernatural?" In Europe all true philosophy must reckon with Kant. Though his greatest work, the "Critique of Pure Reason," was published just one hundred years ago, no step in advance has been made since with regard to determining the limits, *i. e.*, the true powers, of human knowledge. Other fields of philosophy have been cultivated with great success by other observers and thinkers, but the problem of all problems, How do we know? stands to-day exactly as Kant left it. No one has been able to show that Kant was wrong when he showed that what we call knowledge has for its material nothing but what is supplied by the senses. It is we who digest that material, it is we who change impressions into percepts, percepts into concepts, and concepts into ideals; but even in our most abstract concepts the material is always sensuous, just as our very life-blood is made up of the food which comes to us from without.

Why should we shrink from that? Why should

we despise sensuous knowledge? Is it not the most wonderful thing we know that we should be able to see and hear and feel? We may understand, *i. e.*, be able to account for our concepts, because they are more or less our own work; but our percepts pass all understanding. They are the true miracle, the truest revelation. But men are not satisfied with the true miracles of nature and the true revelation of God; they must have little miracles of their own, and they place those miracles of man far above the miracles of God. So it is with our knowledge. Instead of seeing the light of God in every ray of light, hearing His voice in every note of music, and feeling His presence in the touch of every loving hand, our wise philosophers turn round and say that what *they* want is what cannot be seen and cannot be heard and cannot be touched, and that until they have that, their knowledge is not worth having.

Now on this point Kant, too, seems to me to be under the influence of the old philosophical prejudices. He thinks that the knowledge supplied to us by the senses is finite only, and that there is no sensuous foundation for our ideas of the Infinite or the Unconditioned. He does not indeed surrender these ideas, but he tries to justify them on practical and moral grounds, not on the grounds on which he justifies all other knowledge, namely perception.

My chief object in my "Hibbert Lectures" was to show that we have a perfect right to make one step beyond Kant, namely, to show that our senses bring us into actual contact with the Infinite, and that in that sensation of the Infinite lies the living germ of all religion. Of course, I do not mean that this perception gives us a knowledge of the Infinite as it is in itself. This can be said of our perception of the Infinite as little as of our perception of the Finite. Kant shows again and again that our perception can never give us a knowledge of things in themselves (this is really a *contradictio in adjecto*), but that all our knowledge applies to the pressure or impressions on our senses only.

But though we cannot know things finite, as they are in themselves, we know at all events that they are. And this is what applies to our perception of the Infinite also. We do not know through our senses what it is, but we know through our very senses that it is. We feel the pressure of the Infinite in the Finite, and unless we had that feeling, we should have no true and safe foundation for whatever we may afterwards believe of the Infinite.

Some critics of mine have urged that what I here call the Infinite is not the Infinite, but the Indefinite only. Of course it is, and it was my chief object to show that it is. We can know the Infinite as the Indefinite only, or as the partially defined. We try to define it and to know it more and more, but we never finish it. The whole history of religion represents in fact the continuous progress of the human definition of the Infinite, but however far that definition may advance, it will never exhaust the Infinite. Could we define it all, it would cease to be the Infinite, it would cease to be the Unknown, it would cease to be the Inconceivable or the Divine.

But how, I have been asked, are we able to define the Infinite even in this indefinite way? My answer is, Look at the history of mankind. From the very beginning of history to the present day man has been engaged in defining the Infinite. He has ascribed to it whatever was known to him as the best from time to time, and has named it accordingly. And as he advanced in his knowledge of what is good and best, he has rejected the old names and invented new ones. That process of naming the Infinite was the process of defining it, at first affirmatively, then negatively — saying at least what the Infinite is not, when human reason discovered more and more her inability of saying what the Infinite is. If these names, from first to last, are not names of the Infinite, of what are they the names? Of the Indefinite? There is no Indefinite *per se*, but only in relation to us. Of the Finite? Certainly not, for even the lowest names of the lowest religion exclude the idea of the Finite. Then what remains? They are names of what we mean by the Infinite, the Unknown; and if we are told that this Infinite or this Unknown is mere assumption, let it be so, so long as it is the only possible assumption, the only possible name. You ask me (p. 50) how with this view of the Infinite I can say that "the outward eye, the mere organ, apprehends the Infinite, because the Infinite has neither form nor dimension?" When I used the expression "to apprehend the Infinite," I surely explained what I meant by it. Yes, I maintain — and I do so as going beyond Kant's philosophy — that the eye is brought in actual contact with the Infinite, and that what we feel through the pressure on all our senses is the presence of the Infinite. Our senses, if I may say so, feel nothing but the Infinite, and out of that plenitude they apprehend the Finite. To apprehend the Finite is the same as to define the Infinite, whether in space or time or under any other conditions of sensuous perception. You speak of "the outward eye, the *mere* organ." Is there an outward eye and a *mere* organ? Is not the simplest perception of a ray of light the most wonderful act of knowledge, which "the *mere* organ" is as little able to explain as the whole apparatus of all our so-called faculties of knowledge. Yes, to me the first ray of light perceived is the perception of the Infinite, a revelation more wonderful than any that followed afterwards. We may afterwards define the light, we may count the vibrations that produce different forms or colors of light, we may analyze the nerves that convey the vibrations to the nerve-centres in the brain, and yet with all that we want to-day, as much as the ancient prophets thousands of years ago, some Will, some Infinite Being, saying and willing, Let there be light!

You say that you agree with me so far as to think that sensuous perceptions *suggest* the Infinite (p. 53). I do not quarrel about words, and am quite willing to accept that mode of expression. But if the senses can suggest the Infinite, why then do you want, as you say, another special faculty in the soul to apprehend the Infinite? If the senses can suggest the Infinite, then let what we call the understanding or reason or faith more fully develop that suggestion; but the important step is the first suggestion. I do not object to a division of the faculties of the soul for the purpose of scientific treatment. But as the five senses are only five modifications of perception, so, in its true essence, all the so-called faculties of the soul are but different modifications or degrees of cognition. Sensuous knowledge is the first knowledge, and therefore often considered as the lowest. But as, without it, no knowledge whatever is possible to human beings, surely we are wrong in degrading it, and in not recognizing that, as the beautiful flower is impossible without the ugly root, so the highest flights of speculations would be impossible without what you call "the *mere* material organ of the eye."

Then, you ask, Why, if faith is but a development of that faculty of knowledge the first manifestations of which appear in sensuous knowledge, have not the animals arrived at the same development? Why has no animal faith in the Infinite? My answer is, Every being is not what it is, but what it can become. There are stages in the growth of the animal and of the man where both seem alike; there are stages where the animal seems even more perfect than the man. But, as a matter of fact, the animal stops at a certain stage and cannot get beyond, while man grows on to reach his full development. When we see a baby and a young monkey, we have no reason to suppose that the one will develop into a speaking and thinking animal, the other not. But so it is, and we must simply accept the facts. It is language that marks the line which no animal can cross, it is language that enables man to develop his percepts into concepts, and his concepts into ideals. The highest of these ideals is the Infinite recognized through the Finite, as, at first, the Finite was recognized through the Infinite. I have always held, and I still hold, even against the greatest of all modern philosophers, that the material out of which this ideal is constructed is, in the first instance, supplied by the senses, that it is not a mere postulate of reason or aspiration of faith, but shares with all our other knowledge the same firm foundation, namely, the evidence of the senses.

So you see my letter has grown into a long epistle,

and if you like you may publish it in the same Journal in which your review of my "Hibbert Lectures" appeared. Your friends will then see, as I hope you may see yourself, that though we may differ in the wording of our thoughts, our thoughts spring from the same source, and tend in their various ways towards the same distant goal.

Yours very truly,

F. MAX MÜLLER.

DAYÂNANDA SARASVATÎ.

(1827–1883.)

THE Indian newspapers contain the announcement of the death of Dayânanda Sarasvatî. Most English readers, even some old Indians, will ask, Who was Dayânanda Sarasvatî? — a question that betrays as great a want of familiarity with the social and religious life of India as if among us any one were to ask, Who was Dr. Pusey? Dayânanda Sarasvatî was the founder and leader of the Ârya-Samâj, one of the most influential of the modern sects in India. He was a curious mixture, in some respects not unlike Dr. Pusey. He was a scholar, to begin with, deeply read in the theological literature of his country. Up to a certain point he was a reformer, and was in consequence exposed to much obloquy and persecution during his life, so much so that it is hinted in the papers that his death was due to poison administered by his enemies. He was opposed to many of the abuses that had crept in, as he well knew, during the later periods of the religious growth of India, and of which, as is known now, no trace can be found in the ancient sacred books of the Brâhmans, the Vedas. He was opposed to idol worship, he repudiated caste, and advocated female education and widow marriage, at least under certain conditions. In his public disputations with the most learned Pandits at Benares and elsewhere, he was generally supposed to have been victorious, though often the aid of the police had to be called in to protect him from the blows of his conquered foes. He took his stand on the Vedas. Whatever was not to be found in the Vedas he declared to be false or useless; whatever was found in the Vedas was to him beyond the reach of controversy. Like all the ancient theologians of India, he looked upon the Vedas as divine revelation. That idea seems to have taken such complete possession of his mind that no argument could ever touch it.

It is here where Dayânanda Sarasvatî's movement took a totally different direction from that of Râmmohun Roy. Râmmohun Roy also and his followers held for a time to the revealed character of the Vedas, and in all their early controversies with Christian missionaries they maintained that there was no argument in favor of the divine inspiration of the Bible which did not apply with the same or even greater force to the Vedas. As the Vedas at that time were almost inaccessible, it was difficult for the missionaries to attack such a position. But when at a later time it became known that the text of the Vedas, and even their ancient commentaries, were being studied in Europe, and were at last actually printed in England, the friends of Râmmohun Roy, honest and fearless as they have always proved themselves to be, sent some young scholars to Benares to study the Vedas and to report on their contents. As soon as their report was received, Debendranâth Tagore, the head of the Brâhma-Samâj, saw at once that, venerable as the Vedas might be as relics of a former age, they contained so much that was childish, erroneous, and impossible as to make their descent from a divine source utterly untenable. Even he could hardly be expected to perceive the real interest of the Vedas, and their perfectly unique character in the literature of the world, as throwing light on a period in the growth of religion of which we find no traces anywhere else.

But Dayânanda, owing chiefly to his ignorance of English, and, in consequence, his lack of acquaintance with other sacred books, and his total ignorance of the results obtained by a comparative study of religions, saw no alternative between either complete surrender of all religion or an unwavering belief in every word and letter of the Vedas. To those who know the Vedas such a position would seem hardly compatible with honesty; but, to judge from Dayânanda's writings, we cannot say that he was consciously dishonest. The fundamental idea of his religion was revelation. That revelation had come to him in the Vedas. He knew the Vedas by heart; his whole mind was saturated with them. He published bulky commentaries on two of them, the Rig-Veda and Ya*g*ur-Veda. One might almost say that he was possessed by the Vedas. He considered the Vedas not only as divinely inspired, or rather expired, but as prehistoric or prehuman. Indian casuists do not understand how Christian divines can be satisfied with maintaining the divine origin of their revelation, because they hold that, though a revelation may be divine in its origin, it is liable to every kind of accident if the recipient is merely human. To obviate this difficulty, they admit a number of intermediate beings, neither quite divine nor quite human, through whom the truth, as breathed forth from God, was safely handed down to human beings. If any historical or geographical names occur in the Vedas.

they are all explained away, because, if taken in their natural sense, they would impart to the Vedas an historical or temporal taint. In fact, the very character which we in Europe most appreciate in the Vedas — namely, the historical — would be scouted by the orthodox theologians of India, most of all by Dayânanda Sarasvatî. In his commentary on the Rig-Veda, written in Sanskrit, he has often been very hard on me and my own interpretation of Vedic hymns, though I am told that he never travelled without my edition of the Rig-Veda. He could not understand why I should care for the Veda at all, if I did not consider it as divinely revealed. While I valued most whatever indicated human sentiment in the Vedic hymns, whatever gave evidence of historical growth, or reflected geographical surroundings, he was bent on hearing in it nothing but the voice of Brahman. To him not only was everything contained in the Vedas perfect truth, but he went a step further, and by the most incredible interpretations succeeded in persuading himself and others that everything worth knowing, even the most recent inventions of modern science, were alluded to in the Vedas. Steam-engines, railways, and steam-boats, all were shown to have been known, at least in their germs, to the poets of the Vedas, for Veda, he argued, means Divine Knowledge, and how could anything have been hid from that? Such views may seem strange to us, though, after all, it is not so very long ago that an historical and critical interpretation of the Bible would have roused the same opposition in England as my own free and independent interpretation of the Rig-Veda has roused in the breast of Dayânanda Sarasvatî.

There is a curious autobiographical sketch of his life, which was published some time ago in an Indian journal. Some doubts, however, have been thrown on the correctness of the English rendering of that paper, and we may hope that Dayânanda's pupil, Pandit Shyâmaji K*ri*sh*n*avarmâ, now a B. A. of Balliol College, will soon give us a more perfect account of that remarkable man.

In the mean time an abstract of what Dayânanda has told us himself of his life [1] may be interesting, as introducing us into an intellectual and religious atmosphere of which even those who live in India and are in frequent contact with the Hindus know very little.

Dayânanda writes: "I was born in a family of Udîchya (Northern) Brâhmans, in a town belonging to the Râjah of Morvi, in the province of Kâthiâwâr. If I refrain from naming my parents, it is because my duty forbids me. If my relations knew of me, they would call me back, and then, once more face to face with them, I should have to remain with them, attend to their wants, and touch money. Thus the holy work of the reform to which I have dedicated my life would be jeopardized.

"I was hardly five years of age when I began to study the Devanâgarî alphabet. According to the custom of my family and caste, I was made to learn by rote a large number of mantras or hymns with commentaries. I was but eight when I was invested with the sacred Brâhmanic thread, and taught the Gâyatrî hymn, the Sandhyâ (morning and evening)

[1] Dayânanda Sarasvatî's autobiography, translated from Hindi into English, and published in the *Theosophist*. I have to thank the editor of that journal for her kindness in sending it to me.

ceremony, and the Yagur-veda-samhitâ, beginning with the Rudrâdhyâya.[1] As my father belonged to the Siva-sect, I was early taught to worship the uncouth piece of clay representing Siva, known as the Pârthiva Linga. My mother, fearing for my health, opposed my observing the daily fasts enjoined on the worshippers of Siva, and as my father sternly insisted on them, frequent quarrels arose between my parents. Meanwhile I studied Sanskrit grammar, learnt the Vedas by heart, and accompanied my father in his visits to the shrines and temples of Siva. My father looked upon the worship of Siva as the most divine of all religions. Before I was fourteen I had learnt by heart the whole of the Yagur-veda-samhitâ, parts of the other Vedas, and of the Sabdarûpâvali (an elementary Sanskrit grammar), so that my education was considered as finished.

"My father being a banker and Jamâdâr (Town revenue collector and magistrate) we lived comfortably. My difficulties began when my father insisted on initiating me in the worship of the Pârthiva Linga. As a preparation for this solemn act I was made to fast, and I had then to follow my father for a night's vigil in the temple of Siva. The vigil is divided into four parts of praharas, consisting of three hours each. When I had watched six hours I observed about midnight that the Pûjâris, the temple-servants, and some of the devotees, after having left the inner temple, had fallen asleep. Knowing that this would destroy all the good effects of the service, I kept awake myself, when I observed that even my father had fallen asleep. While I was thus left alone I began to meditate. Is it possible, I asked myself,

[1] See *Catalogus Cod. Manuscr. Sanscrit. Bibl. Bodl.* vol. i., p. 74[b].

that this idol I see bestriding his bull before me, and who, according to all accounts, walks about, eats, sleeps, drinks, holds a trident in his hand, beats the drum, and can pronounce curses on men, can be the great Deity, the Mahâdeva, the Supreme Being? Unable to resist such thoughts any longer I roused my father, asking him to tell me whether this hideous idol was the great god of the scriptures. 'Why do you ask?' said my father. 'Because,' I answered, 'I feel it impossible to reconcile the idea of an omnipotent living God with this idol, which allows the mice to run over his body and thus suffers himself to be polluted without the slightest protest.' Then my father tried to explain to me that this stone image of the Mahâdeva, having been consecrated by the holy Brâhmans, became, in consequence, the god himself, adding that as *S*iva cannot be perceived personally in this Kali-yuga, we have the idol in which the Mahâdeva is imagined by his votaries. I was not satisfied in my mind, but feeling faint with hunger and fatigue, I begged to be allowed to go home. Though warned by my father not to break my fast, I could not help eating the food which my mother gave me, and then fell asleep.

"When my father returned he tried to impress me with the enormity of the sin I had committed in breaking my fast. But my faith in the idol was gone, and all I could do was to try to conceal my lack of faith, and devote all my time to study. I studied at that time the Nigha*n*tu and Nirukta (Vedic glossaries), the Pûrvamîmâ*m*sâ (Vedic philosophy), and Karmakâ*nd*a or the Vedic ritual.

"There were besides me in our family two younger sisters and two brothers, the youngest of them being born when I was sixteen. On one memorable night one of my sisters, a girl of fourteen, died quite suddenly. It was my first bereavement, and the shock to my heart was very great. While friends and relations were sobbing and lamenting around me, I stood like one petrified, and plunged in a profound dream. 'Not one of the beings that ever lived in this world could escape the cold hand of death,' I thought; 'I too may be snatched away at any time, and die. Whither then shall I turn to alleviate this human misery? Where shall I find the assurance of, and means of attaining Moksha, the final bliss?' It was then and there that I came to the determination that I *would* find it, cost whatever it might, and thus save myself from the untold miseries of the dying moments of an unbeliever. I now broke for ever with the mummeries of fasting and penance, but I kept my innermost thoughts a secret from everybody. Soon after, an uncle, a very learned man, who had shown me great kindness, died also, his death leaving me with a still profounder conviction that there was nothing stable, nothing worth living for in this world.

"At this time my parents wished to betroth me. The idea of married life had always been repulsive to me, and with great difficulty I persuaded my father to postpone my betrothal till the end of the year. Though I wished to go to Benares to carry on my study of Sanskrit, I was not allowed to do so, but was sent to an old priest, a learned Pandit, who resided about six miles from our town. There I remained for some time, till I was summoned home to find everything ready for my marriage. I was then twenty-one, and as I saw no other escape, I resolved to place an eternal bar between myself and marriage.

"Soon after I secretly left my home, and succeeded in escaping from a party of horsemen whom my father had sent after me. While travelling on foot, I was robbed by a party of begging Brâhmans of all I possessed, being told by them that the more I gave away in charities, the more my self-denial would benefit me in the next life. After some time I arrived at the town of Sayla, where I knew of a learned scholar named Lâlâ Bhagat, and with another Brahma*k*ârin, I determined to join his order.

"On my initiation I received the name of *S*uddha *K*aitanya (pure thought), and had to wear a reddish-yellow garment. In this new attire I went to the small principality of Kouthagangad, near Ahmadabad, where to my misfortune I met with a Bairâgi (Vairâgin, hermit), well acquainted with my family. Having found out that I was on my way to a Mella (religious fair) held at Sidhpur, he informed my father; and while I was staying in the temple of Mahâdeva at Nîlaka*nth*a with Darâdi Svâmi and other students, I was suddenly confronted by my father. In spite of all my entreaties he handed me over as a prisoner to some Sepoys whom he had brought with him on purpose. However, I succeeded in escaping once more, and making my way back to Ahmadabad, I proceeded to Baroda. There I settled for some time, and at Chetan Math (a temple) held several discourses with Brahmânanda and a number of Brahma*k*ârins and Sannyâsins, on the Vedânta philosophy. From Brahmânanda I learnt clearly that I am Brahman, the *g*îva (soul) and Brahman being one.

"I then repaired to Benares and made the acquaintance of some of the best scholars there, particularly that of Sa*kk*idânanda Paramaha*m*sa. On his advice I afterwards proceeded to Chânoda Kanyâli on the banks of the Narbada (Narmadâ), and met there for the first time with real Dîkshitas, initiated in the Yoga-philosophy. I was placed under the tuition of Paramânanda Paramaha*m*sa, studying such books as the Vedânta-sâra, Vedânta-paribhâshâ,[1] etc. I then felt anxious to be initiated in the order of the Dîkshitas and to become a Sannyâsin, and though I was very young, I was with some difficulty consecrated, and received the staff of the Sannyâsin. My name was then changed into Dayânanda Sarasvatî.

"After some time I left Chânoda and proceeded to Vyâsâsrama to study Yoga, ascetic philosophy, under Yogânanda. I then spent some more time in practicing Yoga, but in order to acquire the highest perfection in Yoga I had to return to the neighborhood of Ahmadabad, where two Yogins imparted to me the final secrets of Yoga-vidyâ. I then travelled to the mountain of Abu in Râjputân, to acquire some new modes of Yoga, and in 1855 joined a great meeting at Hardwâr,[2] where many sages and philosophers meet for the study and practice of Yoga.[3]

"At Tidee, where I spent some time, I was horrified at meeting with meat-eating Brâhmans, still more at reading some of their sacred books, the Tantras, which sanction every kind of immorality.

1 These are not Yoga books, but very elementary treatises on Vedânta philosophy.

2 Every twelfth year, when the planet Jupiter is in Aquarius, a great feast takes place at Hardwâr, called Kumbha-melâ. About 300,000 people are said to attend the festival. See Hunter, *Imperial Gazeteer*, s. v. Hardwâr.

3 This practice of Yoga is described in the Yoga-sûtras. Much of it consists in abstemiousness and regulation and suspension of breath. From this arises tranquillity of mind, supernatural knowledge, and different states of ecstasy called Samâdhi.

"I then proceeded to *S*rînagar, and taking up my abode at a temple on Kedár Ghât,[1] I made the acquaintance of an excellent Sâdhu, called Gangâgiri, with whom I studied and discussed philosophical books. After two months I, in company with other ascetics, travelled further to Rudra Prayâga, till we reached the shrine of Agastya Muni. Still further north is *S*ivapura, where I spent four months of the cold season, returning afterwards alone to Kedár Ghât, and to Gupta Kâ*s*i (hidden Benares)."[2]

After this follows a description of various journeys to the north, where in the recesses of the Himâlaya mountains Dayânanda hoped to find the sages who are called Mahâtmas, and are supposed to be in possession of the highest wisdom. These journeys are described very graphically, but their details have been called in question, and may therefore be passed over. That there are hermits living in the Himâlaya forests, that some of them are extremely learned, and that others are able to perform extraordinary acts of austerity, is well known. But equally well known are the books which they study, and the acts of Yoga which they perform, and there is really no kind of mystery about them. They themselves would be the last to claim any mysterious knowledge beyond what the *S*âstras supply. Nor are such Mahâtmas to be found in the Himalayan recesses only. India is full of men who seek retirement, dwell in a small cell or cave, sleep on the skin of a tiger or stag, abstain from flesh, fish, and wine, never touch salt, and live entirely on fruits and roots.[3]

1 Was not this meant for Kedarnâth?

2 A sacred spot where the old town of Kâsi is supposed to lie buried.

3 See N. C. Paul, in the *Theosophist*, February, 1882, p. 133.

It is a pity that the rest of Dayânanda's autobiography has never been published. It breaks off with his various travels, and is full of accounts of his intense sufferings and strange adventures. He seems in the end to have lived on rice and milk, finally on milk only, but he indulged for a time in the use of bhang, hemp, which put him into a state of reverie from which he found it difficult to rouse himself. Here and there we catch a curious glimpse of the religious feelings of the people. "One day," he writes, "when recovering from such a day-dream, I took shelter on the veranda opposite the chief entrance to the temple, where stood the huge statue of the Bull-god, Nandi. Placing my clothes and books on its back I sat and meditated, when suddenly, happening to throw a look inside the statue, which was empty, I saw a man concealed inside. I extended my hand towards him, and must have terrified him, as, jumping out of his hiding-place, he took to his heels in the direction of the village. Then I crept into the statue in my turn and slept there for the rest of the night. In the morning an old woman came and worshipped the Bull-god with myself inside. Later on she returned with offerings of Gur (molasses) and a pot of Dahi (curd milk), which, making obeisance to me, whom she evidently mistook for the god himself, she offered and desired me to accept and eat. I did not disabuse her, but, being hungry, ate it all. The curd being very sour proved a good antidote for the bhang, and dispelled all signs of intoxication, which relieved me very much. I then continued my journey towards the hills and that place where the Narmadâ takes its rise."

We should like very much to have a trustworthy

account of Dayânanda's studies from 1856, when we leave him in his autobiography, to 1880, when we find him again at Mirut ("Theosophist," December, 1880). In 1881 we read of his public disputations in every part of India ("Theosophist," March, 1881). At a large convocation in Calcutta, about 300 Pandits from Gau*d*a, Navadîpa, and Kâsi discussed the orthodoxy of his opinions. Dayânanda Sarasvatî had somewhat modified his opinions as to the divine character of the Veda. He now held that, of the whole Vedic literature, the Mantras or hymns only should be considered as divinely inspired. The Brâhma*n*as seemed to him to contain too many things which were clearly of human origin, and in order to be consistent he admitted of the Upanishads also those only as of superhuman origin which formed part of the Sa*m*hitâs.

Such opinions, and others of a similar character, were considered dangerous, and at the meeting in question the following resolutions were carried against him: —

(1.) That the Brâhma*n*as are as valid and authoritative as the Mantras, and that the other Sm*ri*tis or law-books are as valid and authoritative as Manu.

(2.) That the worship of Vish*n*u, *S*iva, Durgâ, and other Hindu deities, the performance of the *S*râddha ceremonies after death, and bathing in the Ganges, are sanctioned by the *S*âstras.

(3.) That in the first hymn of the Rig-Veda, addressed to Agni, the primary meaning of Agni is fire, and its secondary meaning is God.

(4.) That sacrifices are performed to secure salvation.

But although the decisions were adverse to Dayânanda, the writer of the report adds: "The mass of young Hindus are not Sanskrit scholars, and it is no wonder that they should be won over by hundreds to Dayânanda's views, enforced as they are by an oratorical power of the highest order and a determined will-force that breaks down all opposition."

In his later years he was not only a teacher and lecturer, but devoted his time to the publication of Sanskrit texts also. He published the hymns of the Rig-Veda and Ya*g*ur-Veda, with a commentary of his own, the strange character of which has been touched upon before. He also published controversial papers, all showing the same curious mixture of orthodoxy and free-thought. He believed to the end in the inspiration of the Veda, though not of the whole of the Veda, but of certain portions only. These portions he thought he was competent to select himself, but by what authority he could not tell.

He died at the age of fifty-nine, at Ajmere, at 6 P. M. on Tuesday, the 30th of October last. There was a large funeral procession, the followers of Dayânanda chanting hymns from the Vedas. The body was burned on a large pile. Two maunds of sandal-wood, eight maunds of common fuel, four maunds of ghee (clarified butter), and two and a half seers of camphor were used for the cremation.

Whether Dayânanda's sect will last is difficult to say. The life-blood of what there is of national religion in India still flows from the Veda. As in ancient times every new sect, every new system of philosophy was tested by the simple question, Do you believe in the superhuman (apaurusheya) origin of the Veda? so all the modern religious and philosophical movements, if they profess to be orthodox, are weighed in the same balance. The Brâhma-Samâj, after its surrender of the Veda, became *ipso facto* heterodox. The Ârya-Samâj, though looked upon with suspicion, remains orthodox, at least so long as it upholds with Dayânanda Sarasvatî the divine character of the Veda.

Those who are ignorant of what is going on beneath the mere surface, have often declared that the Vedas have ceased to be the Sacred Books of India, that they have been supplanted by Purâ*n*as and Tantras, and that they are hardly understood now by any native scholar. The last assertion may be true in a certain sense, but for all the rest, those who know anything of the real issues of religion in India know, or ought to know, that they depend to-day, as three thousand years ago, on the Veda.

The leader of the orthodox Ârya-Samâj, Dayânanda Sarasvatî, the determined champion of the literal inspiration of the Veda, is hardly dead before his followers flock together from all parts of India to carry on their Vedic Propaganda.[1] A meeting was held on November 8 with a view of establishing an Anglo-Vedic College. Between seven and eight thousand rupees, or, according to another statement, 38,282 rupees, were subscribed by those present. An admirer of Dayânanda, living at Amritsir, promised ten thousand rupees, and the Ferozepore Ârya-Samâj collected two thousand rupees. This Vedic College has for its object the revival of the knowledge of the ancient scriptures of the Hindus, and is to work by the side of, and in friendly accord with, Syed Ahmed Khan's Mohammedan College at Aligarh, and the numerous Christian Missionary Societies now established in India. The edition of the Ya*g*ur-veda-*sam*-

[1] See *New Dispensation*, Nov. 25, 1883.

hitâ, text, commentary, and translation, is to be continued from the manuscript left by Dayânanda. Of the Rig-veda-sa*m*hitâ, the manuscript, as prepared by him, extends to the seventh Ma*nd*ala only.

India is in a process of religious fermentation, and new cells are constantly thrown out, while old ones burst and disappear. For a time this kind of liberal orthodoxy started by Dayânanda may last; but the mere contact with Western thought, and more particularly with Western scholarship, will most likely extinguish it. It is different with the Brâhma-Samâj, under Debendranâth Tagore and Keshub Chunder Sen. They do not fear the West; on the contrary, they welcome it; and though that movement, too, may change its name and character, there is every prospect that it will in the end lead to a complete regeneration in the religious life of India.

BUNYIU NANJIO.[1]

(Born 1849.)

MR. BUNYIU NANJIO, a young Buddhist priest from Japan, on whom the University of Oxford has just conferred the degree of M. A. *honoris causa*, has been residing at Oxford since February, 1879. He had distinguished himself as a student in his monastery at Kioto by his knowledge of Chinese, which he speaks and writes like his native language. Some of his poems in Chinese are highly spoken of. He was selected therefore, with one of his fellow-students, Kenjiu Kasawara, to proceed to England in order to learn English, and afterwards to devote himself to the study of Sanskrit. Both were priests, belonging to the Shin-shiu, a sect claiming more than ten millions of the thirty-two millions of Buddhists inhabiting Japan. It is the most liberal sect of Buddhism. It traces its origin back to a Chinese priest, Hwui-yuen, who, in A. D. 381, founded a new monastery in China, in which the Buddha Amitâbha (Infinite Light) and his two great apostles, Avalokitesvara and Mahâsthâmaprâpta, were worshipped. This new school was then called the "White Lotus School," and has since spread far and wide. Some of the friars belonging to it were sent to India to collect Sanskrit MSS., and several of these, containing sacred texts of Buddhism, particularly descriptions of Sukhâvatî, or the Land of

[1] See the *Times*, March, 1884.

Bliss, in which the believers in the Buddha Amitâbha hope to be born again, were translated from Sanskrit into Chinese. They form to the present day the sacred books of the White Lotus sect in China, Tibet, and Japan.

The fundamental doctrines of that sect may be traced back to the famous Patriarch Nâgâr*g*una, who is supposed to have lived about the beginning of the Christian era. They differ from those of other Buddhist sects by preaching a simple faith in the Buddha of Infinite Light as the shortest and safest road to salvation. "There are innumerable gates," Nâgâr*g*una says, "of the Law of Buddha, just as there are many paths in the world, either difficult or easy. To travel by land on foot is painful, but to cross the water by ship is pleasant. It is the same with the paths of the disciples. Some practice diligently religious austerities with pain and suffering, others are able to attain the state of 'Never returning again,' by easy practice, by faith in Buddha Amitâbha."

After this doctrine of the White Lotus School had reached Japan in the seventh century, it branched off into different sects. The Shin-shiu, to which Mr. Bunyiu Nanjio belongs, dates from A. D. 1174. It was founded by Gen-ku (Honen), and became powerful and influential under his famous successor, Shinran (died 1262 A. D.), who gave to it the name of Shin-shiu or "True Sect."

The Sacred Books of the Buddhists in Japan are all, or nearly all, Chinese translations of Sanskrit originals. Many of these translations, however, are known to be very imperfect, either because the Chinese translators misapprehended the peculiar Sanskrit of the originals, or because the Indian translators were not able to express themselves correctly in Chinese. Hence the same texts had often to be translated again and again, and of one of the principal sacred texts used in Japan, the Sukhâvatî-vyûha, "the Description of the Land of Bliss," there are no less than twelve Chinese translations. These translations differ from each other, each succeeding one claiming to be more correct than its predecessors.

In former days Japan possessed some Sanskrit scholars who, whenever a theological difficulty arose, could consult the original Sanskrit texts. But of late the study of Sanskrit has become completely extinct in that country as well as in China, and it was in order to revive it in their island that these young priests, Bunyiu Nanjio and Kenjiu Kasawara, were sent to Europe. After spending some years in London learning English, they came to me at Oxford with letters from the Japanese Minister and the late Dean of Westminster, and explained to me their wish to learn Sanskrit and more particularly that peculiar Sanskrit and its various dialects in which the works forming the Buddhist Canon are composed. I promised to help them as much as I could, and advised them, first of all, to learn the ordinary Sanskrit in which such books as the Hitopadesa and *S*akuntalâ are written. This they did with the help of a very able young Sanskrit scholar, Mr. A. Macdonell of Corpus Christi College. After they had acquired a sufficient knowledge of the grammar, they came to me during the last four years, two or three times every week, reading the more difficult Sanskrit authors, and particularly Buddhist texts, most of which exist as yet in MSS. only, and are written in various dialects as spoken in India at the time of the rise and spreading of Buddhism.

These MSS. were brought to England by Mr. B. H. Hodgson, a marvellous man, whose name is known in every country of Europe as one of the greatest discoverers and benefactors in Oriental scholarship, and not in Oriental scholarship only, but in zoölogy, botany, and ethnology likewise, but is almost unknown in England, and not to be found even in the last edition of "Men of the Time." He may, however, console himself in his happy old age (his article on the Languages of Nepal was published in 1828) with the conviction that he is one of the few Oriental scholars who are not Men of the Time only.

Unfortunately the number and bulk of the Sanskrit MSS., constituting the Sacred Canon of the Buddhists, is enormous. Burnouf in his great work, which he modestly called an Introduction to the History of Buddhism, had made ample use of Mr. Hodgson's MSS., and my two pupils set to work determinately to copy what seemed most valuable in the libraries at Oxford, Cambridge, London, and Paris. Though these Sanskrit originals exist as yet, with few exceptions, in MS. only, the Chinese translations of the enormous Canon of the Sacred Books of the Buddhists have been published several times both in China and Japan, though it is doubtful whether any single scholar during a lifetime could ever read the whole of them. In some of the Buddhist temples the volumes forming the Sacred Canon stand arranged on an enormous revolving book-case, like those which have lately been introduced from America into this country, and by giving it a push and making it revolve a man who enters the temple is supposed to acquire the merit of having perused the whole Canon. Mr. Bunyiu Nanjio, among other useful works which he did during his stay at Oxford, compiled a complete catalogue of the gigantic Canon, called the Tripiṭaka or the Three Baskets. It contains 1662 separate works, some small, some immense. In each case the original Sanskrit title has been restored, the date of the translations, and indirectly the minimum dates of the originals also, have been fixed. This has led to a discovery which, as I tried to show in my Lectures, "India, what can it teach us?" has revolutionized nearly the whole of the history of Sanskrit literature. We know now that between the Vedic and the later Renaissance literature there lies a period of Buddhist literature, both sacred and profane, extending from about the first century before to the fifth century after Christ. Whoever wishes to study the growth of the Sanskrit language historically, must in future begin with the Veda, then work his way through the Tripiṭaka, and finish with Manu, Śakuntalâ, and other works of the Renaissance period.

The Catalogue prepared by Mr. Bunyiu Nanjio at the request of the Secretary of State for India, and printed at the Oxford University Press, is a work of permanent utility, a *magnum opus*, and has been welcomed in every country where Sanskrit is studied.

Besides this work, which took a great deal of time, Mr. Bunyiu Nanjio and his friend Kenjiu Kasawara have prepared several Sanskrit texts for publication which we may hope will in time appear at Kioto in Japan. Unfortunately, Mr. Kenjiu Kasawara, who returned to Japan last year, died there soon after his arrival. Mr. Bunyiu Nanjio, who has been suddenly summoned to return to his monastery at Kioto, hopes to establish a Sanskrit Printing Press, unless the Chinese system of wood-engraving should prove more advantageous even for publishing large Sanskrit texts. Some of the shorter and more popular sacred texts have been published already by Mr. Bunyiu Nanjio and myself in the "Anecdota Oxoniensia," such as the Va*grakkh*edikâ, the Diamond-Cutter, the Sukhâvatî-vyûha, the Description of the Land of Bliss. There is every reason to expect that his return to his native country will lead to a revival of Sanskrit scholarship, perhaps to a "Revised Version," and certainly to a more critical and truly historical study of Buddhism in the numerous monasteries, colleges, and temples of Japan.

Mr. Bunyiu Nanjio has gained the respect and friendship of all who knew him in England, and, if his life be spared, he may still exercise a most beneficial influence at home. He is a sincere Buddhist, and, as such, a sincere admirer of true Christianity. I shall miss him very much. But instead of singing the praises of my own pupil and friend, I prefer to give a few extracts from a letter written by a missionary who had made the acquaintance of these two Japanese students at Oxford, and who wrote to me from Formosa to express his grief on reading the obituary notice of Kasawara which I had sent to the "Times."

"My intercourse with Kasawara," he writes, "did not extend beyond half a year, but even in so short a time his pure character and gentle disposition drew me to him with an affection which I could hardly deem possible between men whose experience and faith differed so widely.

"I found him and his friend, Bunyiu Nanjio, extremely sensitive to everything that had the shadow of immorality on it. They were not blind to some things of this kind among a class of students at Oxford, and their hatred to everything of the kind was very keen.

"We often conversed on religious matters, but they evidently disliked controversy, and would rather admit Christ to an equal place with Buddha than quarrel with a Christian friend. I remember that one day I said to them, when dining with me in my room in Oxford, 'Is it not strange to see us three together here — you two about to go forth as missionaries of Buddhism, and I as a missionary of Christianity?' I remember well how Kasawara smiled and said, 'Yes, but the two religions have much in common — they are very similar.' They were evidently grieved that I could not look so complacently on the difference between us.

"When taking leave of them, I well remember their little presents, their kind wishes for a good journey to China, and for success in what they always called 'my holy work.'"

I have little doubt that we shall hear more of Mr. Bunyiu Nanjio after his return to Japan, and that he will reflect honor not only on his native country and his own monastery, but also on the University that has so generously adopted him among its honorary members.

I asked my friend Bunyiu Nanjio before he left England to write down the principal events of his life, and as I believe that what he has written for me will be interesting to others also, allowing them an insight into the working of a singularly good and amiable mind, I subjoin them here, with but few alterations and omissions.

A SHORT ACCOUNT OF THE LIFE OF BUNYIU NANJIO, BY HIMSELF.

(1849–1884.)

I was born on the 12th day of the 5th Lunar month of the second year of the Kayei period, 1849 A. D., in a town called Ôgaki, in the province of Mino, Japan. My father was a priest of the Shin-shiu, who died in Kioto on the 19th Octber, 1883. He had four sons and a daughter; I was the third of his sons. My great-grandfather, Tani Monjun by name, my grandfather Gijun, and my father Yeijun were in succession the possessors of a small temple, called Sei-un-*zi*. This temple now belongs to my eldest brother Riôjun, who will be succeeded by his eldest son, Kiôjun. In our sect, the Shin-shiu, the priesthood is hereditary, and each priestly family possesses a temple, which generally belongs to the eldest son. The younger sons are often adopted by other priestly families which have no sons. The same custom prevails widely among the laity also. My elder brother, myself, and younger brother were all adopted by three different priestly families.

My mother is the eldest daughter of a priest of the Shin-shiu sect. My father was a good Chinese scholar and poet, and so is my eldest brother. My knowledge of Chinese I owe almost entirely to their kind instruction at home from my first childhood to my fifteenth year. After that I read many Chinese books by myself, and also began to lecture on the Chinese classics and historical works, as far as I could understand them.

The following dates of some events in my life are present to my memory: —

In my sixth year, 1854, I could recite the "Thirty Verses" composed by Shinran, the founder of the Shin-shiu sect (who died in 1262 A. D.), and likewise Kumâra*g*îva's Chinese translation of the Smaller Sukhâvatîvyûha. These are the first books which the boys of the Shin-shiu priests have to learn to read and recite.

In my seventh year, 1855, I could read two more Chinese versions of the longer Sûtras, one of them being that of the Larger Sukhâvatîvyûha. In the same year I began to go to the private school which belonged to a learned Chinese scholar named Hishida Seiji. He was called by the people at large "Sensei" (lit. "before-born" or "elder"), i. e., Master, without mentioning even his family name. I read with him the Chinese classics, the Four Books beginning with the Dai-gaku, or the "Great Learning."

In my eighth and ninth years, 1856-57, I finished the reading of the Four Books of the Chinese classics, i. e. I had learnt how to pronounce all the Chinese characters in those books according to the Japanese way. I did not understand the meaning of the books yet. In these years I received two prizes for my reading of Chinese in the school.

In my tenth, eleventh, and twelfth years, 1858-60, I finished the reading of the Five Kings of the Chinese classics, which I learnt mostly at home. I began to compose Chinese poems, and attend to the lectures of my father and eldest brother on the Chinese classics, on history and literature.

In my thirteenth year, 1861, my father opened a private school, in which I was an assistant, for teaching younger boys to read Chinese.

In my fourteenth and fifteenth years, 1862-63, I

began to lecture on the history of China and Japan, as contained in Chinese writings.

In my sixteenth year, 1864, I was ordered to preach sermons, or rather to recite some old sermons from memory. This was the first step in my becoming a preacher.

In my seventeenth year, 1865, I accompanied a good preacher to several places and had to preach sermons before he did. This was very useful, as I could both preach myself and listen to the other preacher every day.

In my eighteenth and nineteenth years, 1866-67, there began a great change in the social condition of Japan, as the Military Government of the Tokugawa family had no longer the power to control the whole country as it had done since the beginning of the seventeenth century. As my native town, Ôgaki, was then the seat of a Daimio or feudal lord, the priests of the Shin-shiu sect under his dominion were ordered to form a priestly army. I was at once selected to become a priestly soldier, and after a short time I was made an assistant of the teachers of the army. I had to teach the recruits how to stand and how to run, how to form square or line, and how to discharge their guns. This lasted about fifteen months. The priestly army was disbanded towards the end of 1867, at the very outbreak of the Great Revolution, which was accomplished in 1868. I narrowly escaped being sent to fight at the battle at Kioto, but was soon released. One benefit I derived from my military career was that I became a very good walker and a strong man, free from all illness.

Thus ended the first period of my life.

In my twentieth year, 1868, I went to Kioto and

entered the Theological College of the Eastern Hongwanzi. There I took the first or lower degree in the summer term. I chiefly studied the principles of different schools of Buddhism.

In my twenty-first year, 1869, I was still in the College, where I was elected a leader of the students of the first degree. But I left the College after the summer term, and went back to my native town. There I began to lecture on the Chinese classics and on history and literature to the young soldiers who had just returned from the civil war in the north-eastern provinces. This tuition lasted till the end of 1870. I had daily about fifty or more hearers, with whom I spent the whole day, often even till midnight. Any other books I wished to study I could only read after midnight till the morning. Some nights I did not sleep at all. This practice of lecturing gave me a good memory of the Chinese characters at least.

In my twenty-second year, 1870, I preached a sermon every morning at the temple which belonged to my father. Through this practice of preaching during a whole year I gained a great deal of experience. I always took as my text one of the verses which had been sung in the morning-service immediately before my sermon. I sometimes found it very hard to make the congregation satisfied with my explanations, but generally I believe I was understood by the people. In the same year I continued my study of Chinese with some of my friends among the young priests of the Shin-shiu.

In my twenty-third year, 1871, I was adopted by a learned priest, Nanjio Zhingô by name, who was then a Professor at the Theological College in Kioto already alluded to. His family lived at a village in the mountains, called Kanegasu, in the Nanjio district of the province of Yechizen. He is still the possessor of a temple in that village called Oku-nen-zhi, to which he succeeded as the eldest son of a learned priest, Riôô, who was also a Professor at the same College. My adoptive father is now one of the two principal Professors at the Theological College of the Eastern Hongwanzi in Kioto, and Lecturer to the heir of the head-priest of the temple, viz., the Eastern Hongwanzi. My adoptive mother is the youngest daughter of a priest of the Shin-shiu. My parents by adoption are now living in Kioto, and my father has entrusted the charge of his temple to another young priest.[1]

In 1871 I was ordained and took the second or higher degree at my College in Kioto. I then became a lecturer at a school for young priests in that city. In the same year I lectured on both the Bud-

[1] All the monasteries of the Buddhist sects in Japan, except those of the Shin-shiu, are alike, i. e., each of them consists of a head-priest and one or more disciples or inferior priests, without family, as the name of monastery implies. But the Shin-shiu is peculiar, and while the appearance of its monasteries, viz. the building, the temple-bell, etc., is the same as with other sects, the head-priest and his family live alone in the building. Therefore in our principal monastery, the Eastern Hongwanzi, there dwells the family of our head-priest only. He is the head of our subdivision, called the Tô-ha, or the Eastern party or sect, of the Shin-shiu.

When we call ourselves the priests of the Eastern Hongwanzi, we only mean that we are the disciples or subject-priests of the head-priest of our sect who dwells in the said monastery. My friend Kanematsu is the adopted son of the present head-priest of the monastery Saihozi, so that I speak of it as his monastery.

Mr. Kasawara, Ôta, and I, are not the resident priests of the Eastern Hongwanzi, but only the disciples or subject-priests of the head-priest of that monastery. Mr. Kasawara is the son of the head-priest of the Yerinzi, in the province Ye*kk*iu, in which monastery he was born; and I am the adopted son of that of Okumenzi, in Ye*k*izen. I was born in Seiunzi, in the town of Ôgaki, in the province of Mino.

dhist and Confucianist books in my adopted province Ye*k*izen. I preached many hundreds of sermons at different places in the same province. Each sermon lasted generally half an hour.

In my twenty-fourth year, 1872, I was appointed an official priest in the Church Government of the Eastern Hongwan*z*i, and was the chief compiler of the Monthly Report, a paper which has continued to the present day. In this office I became the fellow-laborer of Kenjiu Kasawara, who has ever since remained one of my truest and most helpful friends.

In my twenty-fifth year, 1873, I went to the province of Ye*k*izen, following the Head-Priest of the Eastern Hongwan*z*i to Tôkio. In the same year I became a preacher of our sect, but was obliged to go home in the winter, on account of my adopted mother's illness.

In my twenty-sixth year, 1874, I lived with my poor sick mother in the province of Ye*k*izen, and according to her wish was married to the eldest daughter of a priest of the Shin-shiu. I lectured and preached at several places in that province during this year.

In my twenty-seventh year, 1875, I returned to the Church Government of the Eastern Hongwan*z*i in Kioto, and became a preacher of the tenth degree, receiving my appointment from the Minister of Religion in the Imperial Government.

Thus ended the second period of my life.

In my twenty-eighth year, 1876, I and my friend Kenjiu Kasawara were selected to be sent to Europe to study Sanskrit. The members of the Church Government of the Eastern Hongwan*z*i wished that the study of Sanskrit, the language in which the sacred writings of Buddhism were originally composed, should be revived in Japan, and as they had heard that that language was taught in the Universities of England, we were ordered to go to England rather than to India. The order was formally conveyed to us by the Heir of the Head-Priest of the Eastern Hongwanzi, who saw us off at Yokohama. We left Yokohama with a Japanese friend, Mr. Narinori Okoshi, on the 13th June, and arrived in London on the 11th August, 1876. At that time neither of us knew any English. We therefore stayed at first in some English families, but our progress in learning English was very slow. During our stay in London, Kasawara learnt a little of Latin and French, and I began to study Greek. We also lectured several times at the Meetings of the Society of Japanese Students in England, which are held twice every month. One of the addresses which I had delivered at that Society in Japanese was translated into English, and was read by my friend, Mr. Arthur Diósy, at a Meeting of the Liberal Social Union, held on the 28th January at St. George's Hall, Langham Place, London.

In February, 1879, I went to Oxford, and paid my first visit to Professor Max Müller, carrying with me a letter of introduction from the late Dean Stanley. He at once allowed me to become one of his pupils, and he showed me in his library a copy of a Sanskrit-Chinese-Japanese vocabulary, with which he had long been occupied, and which was afterwards mentioned by him in his writings.[1] I told him about the existence of some Sanskrit texts in Japan, and I was able afterwards to get sent to me from home at least five texts, besides several Dhâra*n*îs. The five texts are—1. Sukhâvatî-vyûha; 2. Va*g*ra*kkh*edikâ; 3. the

[1] *Selected Essays*, vol. ii., p. 338.

shorter Pra*gñ*âpâramitâ-h*ri*daya-sûtra; 4. the fuller text of the same Sûtra; and 5. Samantabhadra*k*ari-pra*n*idhâna.

According to Professor Max Müller's direction I began to study the elements of Sanskrit with Mr. Macdonell. So did Kasawara, who came to Oxford in October, 1879. We also continued our study of English with Mr. Linstead, and afterwards with Mr. Westmacott.

In the end of 1879, I brought to Professor Max Müller a copy of the text of the Smaller Sukhâvatî-vyûha, sent from Japan, and the Professor showed me in return a MS. of the text of the Larger Sukhâvatî-vyûha belonging to the Bodleian Library. This discovery was an almost inexpressible joy, not only to me and my friend Kasawara, but also to the priests and lay-people of the Pure-Land School in China and Japan. I and Kasawara copied the text, and we collated our copy with four other MSS. The result of this work was the edition of the Larger and Smaller Sukhâvatî-vyûha in the "Anecdota Oxoniensia," Aryan Series, Vol. I., Part ii., 1883, by Professor Max Müller and myself. In Part I. of the same series, the Professor edited the text of the Va*g*ra*k-kh*edikâ, from a MS. sent from Japan, in 1881. He will publish in Part III. the text of the Pra*gñ*apara-mitâ-h*ri*daya-sûtra and Ush*n*îsha-vi*g*aya-dhâra*n*î, from the ancient palm-leaves still in existence in Japan, together with the fuller text of the H*ri*daya-sûtra. I hope myself to publish the Sanskrit text of the Samantabhadra*k*ari-pra*n*idhana, with an English translation of one of its Chinese versions. We shall then have printed texts of all our sacred books, and we may hope that Professor Max Müller will soon publish the English translations of them which he dictated to us.

From 1880 to 1884, I and my friend Kasawara have constantly attended Professor Max Müller's private lectures, and read under his instruction the Sanskrit text of the Larger and Smaller Sukhâvatî-vyûha, Va*g*ra*kkh*edikâ, Lalita-vistara, Saddharmapu*n*-*d*arîka, Sânkhya-kârikâ, and several other books.

In my thirty-second year, 1880, I began to examine the Chinese translation of the Buddhist Tripi*t*aka at the India Office Library. The result of this examination was the publication of "A Catalogue of the Chinese Translation of the Buddhist Tripi*t*aka, the Sacred Canon of the Buddhists in China and Japan, compiled by order of the Secretary of State for India by Bunyiu Nanjio," printed at the Clarendon Press, Oxford, 1883. The following notice will show the nature of the work:—

"This Catalogue has been printed at the Clarendon Press with the new Chinese types cast from the matrices lately acquired in China through Professor Legge. The work was undertaken at the request of the Secretary of State for India, and is to serve, in the first instance, as a guide to the large collection of the Sacred Books of Buddhism which the Japanese Government presented to the India Office in 1875. This collection comprises the whole of the Sacred Canon of the Buddhists, translated into Chinese, and published in Japan, and consists of no less than 1662 separate works. All these works, with few exceptions, were originally written in Sanskrit, but in many cases the Sanskrit originals are now lost. After Buddhism had been introduced and recognized in China in the first century of our era, the sacred texts were translated from Sanskrit into Chinese under imperial auspices, and in later times collected, catalogued, and published. The first collection dates from the year 518 A. D., the oldest catalogue still in existence was made in 520 A. D., and the *editio princeps* of the whole Sacred Canon was published in 972 A. D. When Japan had been converted to Buddhism in the sixth century, the Chinese Canon was adopted there, and several editions of the whole collection have since been published in that island. One which is now being brought out in Japan, by subscription, may be seen in the Bodleian Library.

"Mr. Bunyiu Nanjio, who was entrusted with the compilation of this Catalogue, is a Buddhist Priest who came to England in 1876 in order to learn English and to study Sanskrit. The Sanskrit of the Buddhist texts is very ancient, and differs widely from the later Sanskrit of Manu or Kâlidâsa. Most of these texts are known as yet in MSS. only, which were brought to Europe many years ago by Mr. Hodgson, the East India Company's Resident in Nepal. Mr. Bunyiu Nanjio has not only prepared a complete catalogue of this enormous Canon, but he has restored most of the original titles in Sanskrit, a task of great difficulty, though considerably facilitated by Stanislas Julien's classical work 'Méthode pour déchiffrer les noms Sanscrits dans les livres Chinois.' He has also fixed the dates of most of the Chinese translations, and thereby rendered a lasting service to all students of Sanskrit, by enabling them to fix certain land-marks in the history of Indian literature. In this respect his Catalogue will form a new starting-point in the study of Indian history and Indian literature."

In my thirty-third year, 1881, I compiled a "Catalogue of Japanese and Chinese Books and Manuscripts lately added to the Bodleian Library." This was published at the Clarendon Press in the same year.

In September of that year, I and Kasawara accompanied Professor Max Müller, who had been sent to represent the University of Oxford at the Fifth Orientalists' Congress at Berlin. After that we went to Paris with Professor Max Müller, and copied at the *Bibliothèque Nationale* the whole of the Mahâvyutpatti, a useful Sanskrit-Tibetan-Chinese-Mongolian vocabulary, consisting of about 10,000 Buddhist technical terms and proper names. Besides this, I copied the text of the Buddha*k*aritakâvya by Asvaghosha, and afterwards collated my copy with a MS. at the University Library, Cambridge. I copied also the first half of the Suvar*n*aprabhâsa, and completed it from another MS. last year. Kasawara made extracts from the Laṅkâvatâra. Kasawara and I stayed in Paris for six weeks, and worked very hard. It was at that time that Kasawara's health began to fail. After our return to Oxford Professor Max Müller, who had been at work for some time on the Dharmasaṅgraha, a collection of Buddhist technical terms, handed over his materials to Kasawara, and advised him to prepare an edition of it. Kasawara did this in 1882, before his departure from Oxford for Japan;[1] and he also copied the whole MS. of the Abhidharma-kosavyâkhyâ.

In my thirty-fourth year, 1882, I became a member of the Royal Asiatic Society in London. I discovered

[1] I have not yet been able, owing to great pressure of work, to carry this work through the press, but I hope soon to do so with the assistance of Dr. Wenzel. It will be a worthy monument to the memory of my departed pupil. F. M. M.

a palm-leaf MS. of the Saddharmapu*nd*arîka at the British Museum, and partly copied, partly collated it. I and Kasawara copied the whole text of the same Sûtra from the Royal Asiatic Society's MS., and we collated our copy with two complete MSS. and one incomplete MS. at the University Library, Cambridge.

In August, 1882, Mr. Riogon Kanao, a Japanese priest of the Shin-shiu, came to Oxford from Japan.

In September, Kasawara, who had been suffering much, was advised by his doctor to leave Oxford for Japan.

In December, Mr. Riôhô Sugé, another Japanese priest of the same sect, came to Oxford from Japan.

In my thirty-fifth year, 1883, being now left alone at Oxford, I copied the Suvar*n*aprabhâsa and Laṅkâvatâra. During this year the printing of my Catalogue of the Chinese Tripi*t*aka took up much of my time, and I worked hard with Professor Max Müller at the edition of the Sukhâvatî-vyûha. A copy of my Catalogue was presented to the Emperors of China and Japan, to the King of Siam, and also to many scholars and learned societies in Europe and Asia.

During the years 1880 to 1883, I made literal English translations of several Chinese versions of the Buddhist works, such as the Larger and Smaller Sukhâvatî-vyûha, the Amitâyur-dhyâna-sûtra, a few chapters of the Lalita-vistara, and many others. I also translated the Chinese verses by Shinran, the founder of the Shin-shiu sect in Japan.

On the 16th day of July, 1883, Kenjiu Kasawara died, in his thirty-second year, in Tôkio. This sad news reached me in September.

On the 19th October, my real father died in his

sixty-seventh year in Kioto. This sad news reached me in December.

In my thirty-sixth year, 1884, I collated my copy of the Saddharmapu*nd*arika with the MS. lent to me by Mr. Watters, the British Consul at Formosa. This collation was finished in January last.

On the 28th February last, I received a letter from my adoptive father telling me that I should return to Japan this spring, as my adoptive mother was seriously ill and might not recover from her illness. My real mother also was anxious to have me back as soon as possible, and insisted on my leaving England. Lastly, the Head-Priest of the Eastern Hongwanzi, after Kasawara's death, had expressed his decided wish that I should return to Japan without delay.

Nothing remains for me but to obey. I should have wished to continue my study of Sanskrit till the end of 1885, and I had formerly received leave to do so. I also wished to spend some time in India before returning to Japan, and then hoped to join Kasawara at home. How changeable this world is!

I shall now leave Oxford, and be again at Yokahama next May, if there is no more change. In June next I hope to be with my relations and friends at home, after an absence of full eight years.

Thus the third period of my life as a student in a foreign country will be ended. For this most eventful and not the least fruitful period of my life I am indebted to the kindness of Professor Max Müller, and to the generous instruction and help which I have constantly received from him during the last five years in Oxford. Since my arrival in England in August, 1876, I have received much kindness from other friends also, to whom I return my best thanks.

In conclusion, I hope to be allowed to tell an anecdote concerning myself. From my earliest childhood, my mother has always told me that on my birthday there was a meeting of many friends of my father's, who were scholars and poets. When they were informed that my mother had given birth to a boy, they all said this boy would become fond of literary work, as he was born on the day of a great literary meeting. My mother always concluded this story with the following words: "Thus your father's friends are all expecting you to become a scholar, and you must be diligent therefore in your study." These tender words of my mother have always been before my mind since my childhood, and though I cannot tell whether I shall ever become such a scholar as my father's friends expected from my birthday, I wish at least to do my best so long as my life lasts and my health is not entirely broken. I shall try to follow the good words of a learned Chinese Buddhist priest, who says, 爲法不爲身 i-hô-fu-i-shin, i. e. "(I do my best) for the sake of the Law, but not for my own sake."[1]

I shall be thirty-five years old on the 12th day of May next.

BUNYIU NANJIO,
of the Eastern Hongwanzi,
Kioto, Japan.

12 March, 1884
OXFORD.

[1] See No. 1530 of my Catalogue of the Chinese Tripiṭaka.

A CHINESE POEM BY BUNYIU NANJIO.

感懷九疊韻

(1) 東人未試五天游

(2) 纔有梵書伴旅裘

(3) 道樹關心望萬里

(4) 固林絶跡送千秋

(5) 運徹皇子沒邊地

(6) 時異高僧老故州

(7) 留學於吾已過分

(8) 願無蛇尾附龍頭

TRANSLATION.

(1) "I, a man of the East, do not yet try to travel through the five (ancient) parts of India,

(2) But have only a few Sanskrit books and clothes for my journey;

(3) There is a tree of knowledge,[1] which I think of and long for even from the distance of 10,000 li;

(4) There is a forest of the "firm" trees,[2] where the foot-print of a traveller (such as Hiouenthsang [3]) might have vanished a thousand years since.

(5) Fate was so bad, that the (Japanese) prince died in a remote country region;

(6) Time was so different (from ours), that the eminent priest grew old in his own country:

(7) Now my stay and study here are already above my desert;

(8) So, I hope, that the tale of a snake will not join with the head of a dragon."

1 The famous Bodhi tree in India under which Sâkyamuni obtained Buddhahood or perfect enlightenment.

2 The Sâla trees under which Buddha obtained Nirvâna, i. e. died. Both are famous places of pilgrimage.

3 The famous Chinese pilgrim who travelled in India between 629 and 645.

NOTES ON THE POEM.

The two parallel lines (i. e. the fifth and sixth) mention two Japanese priests, who intended to go to India, but without success. The one (in the fifth line) was called Shinnyo Shinnô, or the Prince Shinnyo. He was the third son of the fifty-first Mikado (lit. "honorable (mi), gate (kado);" cf. the Porte with the Turks), Heizei Tennô (reigned A. D. 806–809); and the fourth of the ten great disciples of Kukai, better known by his posthumous title Kôbô Daishi (died A. D. 835). He, "in order to perfect his knowledge of Buddhist literature, undertook a journey, not only to China, but to India, but died before he reached that country." — "Selected Essays," vol. ii., p. 342. An account concerning his life is given in the Hon*k*io-kô-sô-den, i. e. "Memoirs of the eminent Japanese Priests," book 67, fol. 8 b.

The other priest (in the sixth line) was Hôtan by name. He is very well known among the Japanese priests. I have heard that, about two centuries ago, Hôtan ardently wished to go to India to learn Sanskrit there. With this object he sent a written petition to the military government in Yedo (the present Tôkio, or the "Eastern capital" of Japan), because this government was then so powerful that all the administration of public affairs was in its hand. But his desire was not gratified, because at that time "crossing the ocean" (i. e. a journey for a foreign country) was strictly prohibited in our country.

Hôtan was an extraordinary man. He was formerly a priest of the Tendai sect or school. He used to live at a post-town called Ôtsu, in the province of Ômi, on the Biwa lake, and studied there very hard. One day, during a thunder-storm, there came a young woman who asked him to allow her to take shelter in his house. Hôtan answered her from the inside of the door without seeing her face. But he was already unable to restrain his passion, having heard the amiable voice of the woman. Then he at once threw a handful of inflammable powder on his body and set it on fire. He cried out loudly and fell down. The young woman was very much frightened, opened the door, and found him almost breathless. She hastily sprinkled some cold water on him and put out the fire. She nursed him carefully till he came to himself again. Then he told her all the circumstances of his action. When she got home she told her parents what had happened. They admired him very much, and gave him a certain sum of money, by which he was entirely free from poverty.

While he was studying on the Hiyei mountain (where the principal temple was built in A. D. 788, and is still in existence, though it has been restored several times since), Hôtan once attended a course of lectures of his teacher on a certain book. On the first day of the course, hearers were crowded in the lecture-hall; but their number decreased every day. At length there was not a single hearer except Hôtan. Then the teacher wanted to stop his lecture, but Hôtan said to him, "Will you wait till to-morrow? I shall be able to bring some hearers here." Early on the next morning he brought with him numerous earthen images of priests, and placed them in the lecture-hall here and there. Having done this he sat down in the middle of these images and waited for the lecturer. No sooner did the teacher see this arrangement, than he blamed his pupil severely for performing such a childish trick. Then Hôtan answered him, saying, "All the priests who live in the monasteries on this mountain (formerly three thousand in number) are like these earthen images; so that there is almost no difference between the former days, when they were crowded here, and the present. During all the time there has been only one good listener, and that was I." By this answer the teacher was very much moved, and went on with his lectures till the end of the course.

At this time there seemed to exist in Japan only one

copy, either MS. or wood-cut book, of the two famous Chinese commentaries on Hiouenthsang's translation of the Abhidharmakoshasâstra (which translation was made about A. D. 650). One of these commentaries was written by Phukwang (Fukô, in Japanese), a disciple of the translator; and the other by Fapao (Hôhô, in Japanese), a rival of the former commentator: each in thirty books or thin volumes. The copy of these commentaries was then preserved in an old library belonging to a temple at Nara (formerly also called Nanto, or the "southern capital," because this place was used as the imperial capital of Japan from A. D. 710 till 861, and is situated on the south of Kioto, or Saikio, i. e. the "western capital" of Japan). The copy was so valued that no one was allowed even to look at it. But Hôtan desired not only to read the commentaries, but also to copy them. He therefore gave money to the keeper of the library, entered secretly, and was engaged in copying the rare copy day and night.

Some say that there is a poem composed by Hôtan and written in his copy of these commentaries. In this poem he says that he was so busy in making his copy that he knew nothing of worldly matters. He could only tell that it was a new year when he heard 108 sounds of temple-bells. (This number is still struck at the dawn of New Year's Day in certain temples in Japan. My father's temple is one of these in which this number is observed.)

Some also say, that when the paper which he brought into the library for his copy was all used up, Hôtan did not venture to go out to fetch more, lest he should be discovered and prevented from continuing his work. For this reason he took his long white robe off and used it instead of paper, writing on it from the collar and sleeves to the skirt without leaving any part uncovered.

By such patience he copied the whole of the two large commentaries, and afterwards published them. All who study the Abhidharmakoshasâstra in Japan have ever since been under deep obligation to him.

However, Hôtan afterwards changed his mind and became a priest of the Kegon school (i. e. the school which was founded by a Chinese priest depending on the Kegongio or the Buddhâvata*m*sakavaipulyasûtra, which school no longer exists in Japan). He then constantly criticized and refuted the tenets of his own and other schools, and wrote many books. Some people, therefore, do not consider him a safe authority.

There is a work entitled "Mio-dô-satsu," or the "Document for leading (others)," written by him. In this he refutes the principles of the Shin-shiu, or the "true sect." Soon after this work was published, there was a lecturer (i. e. the head of the college) of the Shin-shiu, *K*iku by name, who wrote a book entitled "Sesshio-hen," or the "Book for breaking or stopping a rush (of the other)," in which he answered him. Hôtan then produced his second work on the same subject, under the title of "Raifu," or the "Axe of Thunder." Then *K*iku wrote the "Shio-rô-hi," or the "Laughing at the Arms of a Praying Maniac," and ridiculed him.

Among the numerous works of Hôtan, however, there is a very useful one (in eight books) entitled "In-mio-niu-shio-ri-ron-sho-zui-gen-ki," or the "Record of the Auspicious Source of the Commentary on the Nyâyaprave*s*atârака*s*âstra" (No. 1216). It is a commentary on the famous Chinese commentary on that treatise on Logic, by Kweiki (Kiki, in Japanese), the principal disciple of Hiouenthsang, who translated the Sanskrit treatise about A. D. 650.

The above account concerning the life of Hôtan has a somewhat legendary aspect. I am not quite sure whether the whole of it is true or not. But I have written down all that I have hitherto heard of him, or have seen in his works.

BUNYIU NANJIO.

OXFORD,
12 *March*, 1881.

KENJIU KASAWARA.[1]

(1851–1883.)

THE last mail from Japan brought me the news of the death of my young friend and pupil Kenjiu Kasawara, and though his name is little known in England, his death ought not to be allowed to pass unnoticed. Does not Mr. Ruskin say quite truly that the lives we need to have written for us are of the people whom the world has not thought of — far less heard of — who are yet doing the most of its work, and of whom we may learn how it can best be done? The life of my Buddhist friend was one of the many devoted, yet unfulfilled lives, which make us wonder and grieve, as we wonder and grieve when we see the young fruit trees in our garden, which were covered with bright blossoms, stripped by a sudden frost of all their beauty and promise.

Kenjiu Kasawara was a young Buddhist priest who, with his friend Bunyiu Nanjio, was sent by his monastery in the year 1876 from Japan to England, to learn English in London, and afterwards to study Sanskrit at Oxford. They both came to me in 1879, and in spite of many difficulties they had to encounter they succeeded, by dint of hard and honest work, in mastering that language, or at least so much of it as was necessary for enabling them to read the canonical books of Buddhism in the original — that is, in San-

[1] See *Times*, Sept. 22, 1833; and *Pâli Text Society's Journal*, 1888.

skrit. At first they could hardly explain to me what their real object was in coming all the way from Japan to Oxford, and their progress was so slow that I sometimes despaired of their success. But they themselves did not, and at last they had their reward. Kasawara's life at Oxford was very monotonous. He allowed himself no pleasures of any kind, and took little exercise; he did not smoke, or drink, or read novels or newspapers. He worked on day after day, often for weeks seeing no one and talking to no one but to me and his fellow-worker, Mr. Bunyiu Nanjio. He spoke and wrote English correctly, he learnt some Latin, also a little French, and studied some of the classical English books on history and philosophy. He might have been a most useful man after his return to Japan, for he was not only able to appreciate all that was good in European civilization, but retained a certain national pride, and would never have become a mere imitator of the West. His manners were perfect — they were the natural manners of an unselfish man. As to his character, all I can say is that, though I watched him for a long time, I never found any guile in him, and I doubt whether, during the last four years, Oxford possessed a purer and nobler soul among her students than this poor Buddhist priest. Buddhism may, indeed, be proud of such a man. During the last year of his stay at Oxford I observed signs of depression in him, though he never complained. I persuaded him to see a doctor, and the doctor at once declared that my young friend was in an advanced stage of consumption, and advised him to go home. He never flinched, and I still hear the quiet tone in which he said, "Yes, many of my countrymen die of consumption." However, he was well enough to travel and to spend some time in Ceylon, seeing some of the learned Buddhist priests there and discussing with them the differences which so widely separate Southern from Northern Buddhism. But after his return to Japan his illness made rapid strides. He sent me several dear letters, complaining of nothing but his inability to work. His control over his feelings was most remarkable. When he took leave of me, his sallow face remained as calm as ever, and I could hardly read what passed within. But I know that after he had left, he paced for a long time up and down the road, looking again and again at my house, where, as he told me, he had passed the happiest hours of his life. Yet we had done so little for him. Once only, in his last letter, he complained of his loneliness in his own country. "To a sick man," he wrote, "very few remain as friends." Soon after writing this he died, and the funeral ceremonies were performed at Tokio on the 18th of July.

He has left some manuscripts behind, which I hope I shall be able to prepare for publication, particularly the "Dharmasaṅgraha," a glossary of Buddhist technical terms, ascribed to Nâgâr*g*una. But it is hard to think of the years of work which are to bear no fruit: still harder to feel how much good that one good and enlightened Buddhist priest might have done among the thirty-two millions of Buddhists in Japan. *Have, pia anima!* I well remember how last year we watched together a glorious sunset from the Malvern Hills, and how, when the Western sky was like a golden curtain, covering we knew not what, he said to me, "That is what we call the Eastern gate of our Sukhâvatî, the Land of Bliss." He looked forward to it, and he trusted he should meet there all who had loved him, and whom he had loved, and that he should gaze on the Buddha Amitâbha — i. e. "Infinite Light."

OXFORD, *Sept.* 20.

LETTERS FROM KENJIU KASAWARA.

LLANTRISSANT HOUSE, KINGSTON ROAD, OXFORD,
26 *July*, 1882.

MY DEAR SIR, — I am in receipt of your letter. I cannot adequately express my thanks for your ever unfailing kindness. It grieves me very much that I am unable to pursue my studies here as long as I hoped and was allowed to do. To lose but one year is a great loss to me, whose object it was to acquire a knowledge of that branch of literature which is vitally important for the religion I belong to, and which cannot better be obtained than through your instruction. I have passed two valuable years and a half with you. It has been no small patience on your part to watch all the time so slow a progress as I made in learning Sanskrit. I am well aware that my age — besides my inability — is passed for acquiring a new language, for which no previous knowledge, if I had any, can help. Moreover, my course of study has been more or less hindered through the want of good texts. Time alone, therefore, may have enabled me to be successful. There was a brief time for me yet to pass in Oxford, and that time is now to be cut short.

But we cannot fight against Nature. Is it not, on the other hand, a great boon of Nature that I, who am naturally weak, should have passed so long in

England without much bodily suffering? If this mischievous disease had befallen me but a year and a half earlier, all my object might have been rendered almost useless. I must be satisfied with things as they are. It remains, therefore, that I should continue what I have begun with the utmost zeal in my native land, and try by all means to make what I have gained acceptable to my friends in Japan, and to fulfil the hopes you kindly express in your letter.

Believe me, Sir,

I am your obliged pupil,

K. KASAWARA.

P. S. I am going up to London to-morrow by the four o'clock train, P. M.

HOTEL RICHEPANCE,
14 RUE RICHEPANCE, PARIS,
14 *September*, 1882.

MY DEAR SIR, — Last Saturday morning I left Oxford by the nine o'clock train for London, and took lodgings in Lancaster Road, Notting Hill. After three days' stay, I left London on Tuesday last by the 8.15 A. M. train from Charing Cross. My voyage was via Folkestone and Boulogne. The sea was calm; and the voyage would have been more pleasant if it had not rained so miserably all the while. The sky, however, gradually cleared up towards Paris. I arrived in that city a few minutes after five o'clock. I was met by two of my countrymen at the Gare du Nord, for I had written to one of them about my coming here. They are merchants, both being men from a town (in Japan) about ten miles from my native place. They are staying in the same hotel where I am now.

The sights of Paris are quite familiar to me, as if I had been here but yesterday. It is exactly one year since you, my friend Nanjio, and I came here last time. Time flies, and so do our lives. I am leaving here to-morrow morning for Marseilles, but I intend to stay a few hours at Lyon, to see Mr. Ymaïzoumi there. I shall have three Japanese companions on board the steamer Iraouaddy, a curious mixture of a noble, a soldier, a merchant, and myself a priest.

Yesterday I went to the Société Asiatique, but I found no one there. A girl came up to me and shook her head. Then I went to a bookseller's shop (which you know) in the neighborhood to make inquiries. People in the shop told me that the Society is only open on Saturday. I was puzzled, for I could not stay here till Saturday. Then I carried your manuscript to the Japanese Legation, intending to intrust it to our Minister. But on my going there I learnt he would leave Paris last night for Vienna. There I saw Mr. Oyama, an attaché whom I know well since last year, and he was quite willing to take care of the manuscript for me.

I cannot adequately express my thanks for your instruction, your liberality, and the kindness of you and your family during my long stay in Oxford. These quiet three years will ever remain in my memory as the most important epoch in my life. It is needless to say I felt very unhappy when I said farewell to you all. I lingered at your gate, and looked eagerly in the dark at your house, on the threshold of which I had stepped so often and so happily. I shall never again hear your living voice, I shall never again see the lovely city of Oxford, but I shall communicate with you as often as possible, and shall always be delighted when I hear from you.

I am, Sir, your most obliged pupil,

K. KASAWARA.

23 September, 1882. — *In the afternoon.*

MY DEAR SIR, — I wrote a letter to you from Paris, and I hope it has reached you in time. I left that city on the 15th in the morning, and arrived at Marseilles early the next day. In this place I had sufficient time to walk about and to take a drive on the coast round the town; but early on the following day I, with three other Japanese, embarked on board the steamer Iraouaddy, which left the coast a little after ten o'clock A. M.

I feel almost recovered from my recent weakness since my arrival at Marseilles, and am enjoying the voyage very much. There are about fifty passengers in the first class, forty in the second, and thirty in the third. The first and second class passengers share in common a spacious portion on the deck, where we sit on chairs, hold conversation, or walk to and fro; where some sing and some play on the piano. Food is good and ample, consisting of coffee or tea with "petit pain" in the morning, "déjeûner a la fourchette" at nine, dinner at five, and tea with biscuits at eight o'clock in the evening. I get up before six o'clock, and generally take a sea-water bath, either hot or cold, every morning.

I got an English newspaper (of Saturday last) at Naples in which I read, "The war is over in Egypt." This morning I had a walk in Port Said, where all was quiet.

From each port above mentioned I wrote a letter

to Mr. B. Nanjio. Now I am writing this to you while the steamer is passing the canal, which we entered at eleven o'clock. The heat is becoming intense day after day.

There is nothing important to describe except some trifling incidents in our society of mixed nationalities, confined within the small space the boat can afford.

This letter is to be posted from Suez, and I shall write you another from Ceylon.

I present my best compliments to your family.

I am, Sir, yours very sincerely,

K. KASAWARA.

COLOMBO, CEYLON, 22 *October*, 1882.

MY DEAR SIR,—I arrived in Ceylon on the 8th last, and remained there during a fortnight. As my intention was to see some old temples and ruins there, I spent the greater part of these days in travelling about. I visited Kandy, a town about seventy-two miles from Colombo. There is a temple in which one of Buddha's teeth is kept, but, owing to the recent death of the keeper, I could not see it. At a distance of about sixteen miles from Kandy there is a small town named Mâtale, and there I visited a rock-temple called Ala Vihâra, in which it is said the Pi*t*akas were first committed to writing. The railway does not extend any farther than this place. In going to Anurâdhapura, I was obliged to take the bull-coach which regularly leaves Mâtale once a day for Anurâdhapura. It is a sort of omnibus, but too small even for one person, as he has to pass a night in it. The distance between those places is only sixty miles, but the coach takes seventeen hours in reaching the end of the journey. During this journey, a traveller like myself finds no place to get food. But Anurâdhapura is a place worth visiting. It is full of ruins of grand buildings. I saw there that old Bo-tree which Fa-hian saw one thousand four hundred years ago. I remained there two days, sufficient for seeing all the Buddhist remains. Although I found now only three priests near the ruins of the Mahâvihâra, I have no doubt that the Vihâra had, at the time of the Chinese pilgrim, some six hundred inmates, as the enormous sizes of the granite alms-vessels, for instance, clearly show us that there were once great multitudes of priests in those Vihâras, who partook of their contents.

On my return from this journey I remained at Colombo only two or three days. I often saw the high priest Sumangala, who was passing the vassa (Lent) in a place near Colombo. He was teaching about sixty of his pupils there. He speaks, as I was told, both Sanskrit and Pâli. I presented him with a copy of the Va*g*ra*kkh*edikâ, and he read it, at the same time rendering it into English. While reading it, he said, "It is not one of the Holy Books; it is not written in pure Sanskrit." He and some other Buddhists earnestly advised me to stop in the island to learn Pâli. I saw other priests, but Sumangala seems to be the most renowned there.

There is one Colonel Olcott, an American, who professes himself to be a Buddhist. In India and in Ceylon he has formed a great many branches of the Theosophical Society of which he is the founder. I do not know his real motives, but, at all events, he has roused the Buddhists of the island from their slumber. He is working hard, and preaching almost daily in different places. But I had no chance of seeing him during my stay here, although he was willing to see me, as he expressed it in his letter from some distant place to one of his friends at Colombo.

After all, I was much pleased with this my stay in Ceylon, and I think I learned some things there which otherwise I could not learn in Japan. Some Buddhists at Colombo showed me kindness and civility, and promised to keep up communication with me hereafter.

The steamer Sindh, of the Messageries Maritimes Company, arrived in the harbor yesterday, two days earlier than it was expected. I hastily embarked on board the steamer. The ship is still in the harbor, but, as I do not find anybody who would go to shore and post this letter for me, I shall forward it from the next station, that is, from Singapore. The ship will leave here very soon.

I remain, Sir,

Yours very faithfully,

K. KASAWARA.

TOKIO, JAPAN, 25 *November*, 1882.

MY DEAR SIR, — After twenty-six days' voyage since I left Ceylon, I safely arrived at Yokohama at seven o'clock in the evening on the 17th last. As I wrote to you before, at the time when I was in Ceylon, I thought I was nearly recovered from my disease. But this was an illusion. After the Sindh arrived at Singapore the weather became very changeable, and after we left Hong-kong the wind was so strong that the steamer could not resist it, and three times was obliged to take refuge in some small Chinese harbors. All the while I felt myself weak, although by that time I had become quite a good sailor. The cough was often troublesome, which proved to be the returning symptom of my former condition. There were two or three unnaturally warm days, which made me very ill.

After two days' stay at Yokohama, where I had something to do with my luggage, I came to Tokio. In Tokio I find one old friend now remaining, who is a priest of our sect (and who had chiefly taken charge of sending money to Nanjio and me while in Europe). Even he has now no longer any connection with the affairs of Higashi Hong-wan-zi. He however kindly came to the railway station to meet me when I arrived in Tokio. Next morning (21st) I went to consult Mr. Ikeda, one of the Imperial physicians, and he carefully examined my chest and back. He was of opinion that my condition has lately been aggravated, and that I should avoid the coming winter in some warmer place. I thought I might go to Kobe, which was at once healthy and near Kioto. But he said Kioto was worse; and that he should rather recommend me, had I not returned from those regions, to go to Ceylon or Saigon, as Japan was hardly a better place than England with regard to cold weather. He said, as I was here, I might go to Atami, a place far better than Kobe, only twenty-seven Japanese or about fifty English miles from Tokio, where I might remain till next March, but without doing any work. I had been quite prepared for hearing such words of the doctor, otherwise alarming. I therefore determined to hurry to Atami. I need not say that it has been an unpleasant thing to me to return home on account of my illness, but I should have been consoled if I had found a brighter state of things at home on my arrival. I expected to see Ishikawa Shuntai in Tokio (who was my teacher and advised us to go to Europe), but to my great disappointment he too has taken part in the recent quarrels, and is now in extreme difficulties. I am writing a long letter to Mr. B. Nanjio, and shall inform him of these things at length.

My dim recollection of the mazy streets of Tokio does not enable me to find places I want to go to. In fact I know Tokio less than London. Besides, I am forbidden to go out except from eleven to four o'clock, nor does anything attract me. I have taken my lodgings in one of our paper houses. The room I use is roofed very low, where a small man like me seems like a giant. Three sides of the room are sheltered with sliding paper screens, and the other side is divided into two portions. One is made a covert, and the other a niche in which an image on paper is hung, and a porcelain pot placed, with flowers in it. As I have passed one fifth part of my life in Europe, my habits have been Europeanized. What is most inconvenient at present is, to sit down on my calves, as our rooms are not furnished with tables and chairs. I am almost unable to write and read at a Japanese desk nine inches high. It is highly injurious to lung diseases. I have not yet put on a Japanese dress. As you know, Tokio is not my home. I must have complete suits of Japanese clothes newly made, top split socks, girdle, clogs, etc. If I send to my home for those things, they will not come to me in less than thirty days.

I have seen very few people here. Some of the young students who are priests by birth, and are studying English in Tokio at the expense of the monastery at Hong-wan-zi, have sometimes come to see me. It is somewhat strange that most of them are destined to study philosophy. Every one of them speaks of Mill and Spencer, as if there were not more sensible men in the world. I cannot say anything as yet of the prospect of the study of Sanskrit here, and those young philosophers do not at present seem to have any desire for learning Sanskrit. We must endeavor to break the earth for our cultivation, but this is a land of frequent earthquakes and destructions.

I shall write to you something more very soon.

I am, Sir, your obedient pupil,

KENJIU KASAWARA.

ATAMI, JAPAN,
7 Dec., 1882.

MY DEAR SIR, — I have made inquiries about the old palm-leaves and the destiny of the copy of the Kathâvatthupakârana-atthakathâ, presented by you to the Higashi Hong-wan-zi through our Minister Iwakura.

As to the former, you have I suppose been informed of the matter before, viz., that it was privately granted by the Minister to photograph the palm-leaves (which formerly belonged to the Horiuji monastery). The reason why it was delayed is this. The old leaf is now, as you know, among the imperial treasures at Nara, which no one has acccss to but by imperial order. It was intended, as I am told, to bring them to Tokio, and some months ago an officer was actually despatched for Nara. The officer, however, resigned his office before he left

Tokio, and his resignation was granted while he was *en route*. This altered everything. He went to Kioto on some other business without staying at Nara. I do not know whether this matter is considered to be not a very pressing business, but it is certain that no officer has since been despatched for the purpose. Unless the palm-leaves are brought to Tokio, there will be no chance of their being photographed; for those treasures are sealed up at Nara, and no keeper is there who is free to open them. I do not say I understand the matter very well. But Susuki and Ota, the latter of whom you know by name, both tell me the same. Ota, being a mere young student, has no intimate access to Iwakura, but the former, I am sure, is able to beg of the Minister anything about the matter. I urged him not to neglect to make further inquiries. The matter being in such a state, delay seems inevitable. Although I shall urge my friend to seek every means to accelerate its progress, I am afraid you cannot delay your publication so long.

I have written letters to some of my old friends, but none of them, even by this time, has written any answer. I do not know what they think of me, but my illness and my withdrawing to Atami have put me into oblivion.

I came to Atami on the 4th last. It is only about fifty English miles from Tokio, and famous for its hot springs. The place has come to particular notice since foreigners began to praise its healthiness as well as its waters. This is one of our few places which know the faces of ministers and foreign ambassadors. It has the advantage of its position, forming a little bay, surrounded by considerably high hills, embracing the warmth of the sun in the southeast. But the road to this place was very bad till some four or five months ago, and only since that time small vehicles drawn by men can pass carrying invalids. The hills around are not so easy to climb as at Malvern, the footpaths being stony and neck-breaking. This naturally stops us from going astray, and we are confined in this small village, where there is nothing to see and nothing to amuse us. But I like this nook of the earth very well as my present asylum.

I am not able to work much, and am forbidden to do so, but as I have no one to speak to in my room, I naturally have recourse to my books. By the way, my store of books, which I call my honeycomb, arrived safely from England in Tokio, but now the books no longer follow me so easily wherever I go.

I presume you and all your family are quite well. Please remember me to Mrs. Max Müller and the rest. My parents are well, and very glad of my safe arrival, and, though they and I both regret that I cannot go to see them at present, yet they are quite satisfied with my being here. They well know that their place is too cold for me, and they cannot attempt to come to me. To them this part of Japan may still seem, as it seemed to me when I was a boy, as strange a land as Turkey or Egypt may seem to you, and the difficulty of travelling even now is actually greater. They are extremely thankful to you for your great kindness to me during my stay in Oxford.

I hope that the Japanese gentlemen in Oxford are in good health, and continue their important studies.

I am, Sir, your obedient pupil,

K. Kasawara.

OTANIKIOKO, TOKIO,
14 *June*, 1883.

MY DEAR SIR, — Since I wrote my last letter to you two months have passed, but I am sorry to say I have nothing to tell you that is new and bright.

I have passed these six weeks, and especially these few last days, in very bad health. A bad cough is the principal symptom, but now my bodily strength too is failing. Tokio is not my home. I have remained here in suspense, neither having been able to set out for home, nor having been able to find a comfortable abode here. No one looks after me: to a sick man very few remain as friends. Now the best way for me is to surrender myself entirely to medical treatment. Dr. Baeby, a German in the service of the Government Hospital at Tokio, is now very famous. I am using the medicine prescribed by him for me. I have resolved to go into the hospital from to-morrow. This will be to my satisfaction, as I shall have better accommodation and good medical treatment.

I received the "Athenæum," in which a review of your Cambridge Lectures is found. I thank you very much, and read the review with pleasure. This reminded me of our pleasant Cambridge tour last year, and my last efforts in copying. How different are things around me this year!

Your kindness did not stop there. You also made an application that the physicians attached to the English Legation here should attend me. But I had been under the treatment of Dr. Baeby, so that I have gone on with him. I hope you will pardon this careless writing, as I am weak, and require to sit quiet.

I am, Sir, your humble pupil,
KENJIU KASAWARA.

JULIUS MOHL.

(1800–1876.)

WHEN, in the beginning of the year 1876, the French papers announced the death of Julius Mohl, a member of the French Institute, and professor of Persian at the Collège de France, it was felt by Oriental scholars in France, England, Germany, and Italy, that not only had they lost a man on whose kind sympathy, prudent advice, and ready help they could always rely, but that some centre of life, some warm-beating heart was gone, from which Oriental studies, in the widest sense of the word, had been constantly receiving fresh impulses and drawing active support.

The French, better than any other nation, know how to do honor to their illustrious dead, and when the duty of writing Mohl's *nécrologe*, or bidding a last farewell to their *confrère*, was intrusted to such men as Laboulaye, Maury, Renan, Regnier, Bréal, and others, we may well believe that all that could be said of Mohl's life and literary work was said at the time, and well said.

The mere story of his life is soon told. It was what the world would call the uneventful life of a true scholar. Nor is there anything new that we could add to that simple story, as it was told at the time of his death by his friends and biographers. His more special merits, too, as editor and translator of the great epic poem of Persia, the "Shah Nameh" of Firdusi, have lately been so fully dwelt on by Persian scholars both in France and England, that little could be added to place his literary achievements in a new and brighter light. Since his death, his widow has rendered one great service to her husband's memory by publishing his translation of the "Shah Nameh," or the "Livre des Rois," in a more accessible form.[1] But there still remains another duty to be performed to Mohl's memory, and that is a reprint of his annual reports on Oriental scholarship, delivered before the Asiatic Society of Paris, and now scattered about in the volumes of the "Journal Asiatique."[2] It is in these reports that we seem to read Mohl's real life; and whoever wishes to study the history of Oriental learning in Europe, from 1840 to 1867, "the heroic age of Eastern studies," as M. Renan justly calls it, could not consult better archives than those contained in the "Rapports Annuels faits à la Société Asiatique, par M. J. Mohl."

Before entering more fully on the importance of those reports, it may be useful to give, as shortly as possible, the main outlines of Mohl's life, drawn partly from the biographical notices published at the time of his death, partly from private papers kindly communicated to me by his widow and other members of his family.

1 *Le Livre des Rois,* par Abou'lkasim Firdousi, traduit et commenté par Jules Mohl, publié par Madame Mohl. Paris: Imprimerie Nationale, 1878. 7 vols. 8vo.

2 These annual reports have since been collected and published by his widow, Madame Mohl, under the title of *Vingt Sept Ans d'Histoire des Etudes Orientales, Rapports faits à la Société Asiatique de Paris de 1840 à 1867 par Jules Mohl.* Ouvrage publié par sa veuve: 2 vols. Paris, 1879–1880.

Julius Mohl was born at Stuttgart the 23d October, 1800. His father was a high official in the civil service of the kingdom of Wurtemberg, and his three brothers all rose to eminence in their respective branches of study—Robert, the eldest, as a jurist and liberal politician; Moritz, as a national economist; Hugo, as a botanist. The education of these four boys was carried on, as is generally the case in German families, as much at home as at school, for the German system of sending boys to a gymnasium, which is a Government day-school, throws a great deal of responsibility and actual work on the father and mother at home. As is generally the case with distinguished men, we hear that in the case of Mohl, too, his mother was a lady of a highly-cultivated mind, combining a great charm of manner with force and originality of character, and devoting herself quite as much to the training of her children as to the humbler cares of her household. Julius showed early signs of love of knowledge, though we may hope that his rising every day at four o'clock in the morning to read books, when a mere child, may be a slight exaggeration, such as often creep into the *Evangelia infantiæ* of men who have risen to great distinction in after-life. Be that as it may, Julius Mohl finished his school career at eighteen, and went to Tübingen to study theology. He was a contemporary there of Christian Baur, who afterwards became the founder of the new critical school of theology, commonly called the Tübingen school; and he seems also to have made at that time the acquaintance of David Strauss. Becoming dissatisfied with the narrow and purely theological treatment of Christianity, Hebrew proved to him, what it has proved to many scholars, a rail to slide from ecclesiastical to Oriental studies. Though in 1822 he was actually appointed to a small living, Julius Mohl felt more and more attracted by Eastern studies, and resolved in 1823 to go to Paris, where alone at that time there existed in the Collège de France a school of Oriental learning. He attended at first the lectures of De Sacy on Arabic and Persian, and of Abel Rémusat on Chinese. He did not at once, as is so much the fashion now, devote himself to one special language, but tried to become an Oriental scholar in the true sense of the word. He wished to become acquainted, as he expressed it himself at the time, "with the ideas that have ruled mankind," particularly in the earliest ages of Eastern history. He seems soon to have endeared himself to several of the leading Oriental scholars at Paris, and the society in which they moved, the charm of their manner and conversation, the largeness of their views, seem to have produced a deep impression on the mind of the young scholar, just escaped from the narrow chambers of the Tübingen seminary and the traditional teaching of its learned professors. After all, there is no society more delightful than good French society; nor should it be forgotten that much of its ease, its lightness and brightness, is due, not only to perfect manners, but to deeper causes, a general kindliness of heart, and a much smaller admixture of selfishness and self-righteousness than is found elsewhere. Alexander von Humboldt was at that time in Paris, and the friendly relations which commenced thus early between him and Mohl remained unaltered through life. Cuvier's house also was open to young Mohl. In 1826 the Wurtemberg Government, wishing to secure the services of the promising young Orientalist, gave him a professorship of Oriental languages at Tübingen, allowing him at the same time to continue his studies at Paris. In 1830 and 1831 Mohl went to England, and here gained the friendship of several Oriental scholars, some of them servants of the old East India Company. He then seems to have conceived the plan of passing some years in India; and when he failed in this, he returned to Paris, which had already become his second home.

At Paris he continued for some time his Chinese studies, and produced as their fruit his edition of a Latin translation of two of the canonical books, the "Shi-king" and "Y-king" (1830, 1837, and 1839). These translations had been made by two Jesuits, Lacharme and Régis, in the first half of the last century, but had never been published.

At the same time, Persian became more and more his *spécialité*. So early as 1826 the French Government entrusted the young German student with an edition and translation of the "Shah Nameh," the famous epic poem of Firdusi. The poem was to form part of the "Collection Orientale," a publication undertaken by Government, and carried out in so magnificent and needlessly extravagant a style that it altogether failed in the object for which it was intended, viz., to bring to light the treasures of Eastern literature. To Mohl this undertaking became the work of his life; nay, it was not quite finished at the time of his death. In preparation for his great work he published in 1829, with Olshausen, "Fragments Relatifs à la Religion de Zoroastre." The printing of the first volume of the Persian epic began in the year 1833, and in the same year he resigned his professorship at Tübingen, where he had never lectured, and determined to settle at Paris. The first volume of the "Shah Nameh" appeared in 1838, the second in 1842, the third in 1846, the fourth in 1855, the fifth in 1866, the sixth in 1868. The last and concluding volume was left unfinished at his death, some portions of it having been destroyed at the time of the French Commune. His former pupil, and worthy successor at the Collège de France, M. Barbier de Meynard, undertook to finish the work of his friend and master; and we have it now before us in two forms—in the *édition de luxe*, which the French Government uses for presents to people the least likely to make any use of it, and the reprint of the French translation only, in seven small octavo volumes, published at the expense of his widow, and likely to find its way into every library which pretends to contain the masterworks of poetry in the principal languages of the world.

It would require an article by itself to show the importance of the "Shah Nameh" as one of the six or seven great national epics of the world, still more to explain the light which Firdusi's poetry throws on the intricate problem of the transition of mythology into heroic poetry and actual history. Nowhere can that transition be watched to greater advantage. No Persian on reading the exploits of Feridun would ever doubt that he was reading the history of one of the ancient kings of his country, nor would it be easier to convince him that the great Feridun was originally a purely mythological conception, than to convince an ancient Greek or a Greek scholar of to-day that Helena was a mere goddess, long before she became the wife of Menelaos, or that the siege of

Troy was the reflection of a much more ancient siege. In Persia, fortunately, we can transcend the limits of epic poetry, and trace the names of some of the principal heroes of the "Shah Nameh," in the corruptions which the names of the old deities of the Zend-avesta underwent in Pehlevi and Parsi. Feridun, as Eugène Burnouf was the first to prove, occurs in Pehlevi as Fredun, and that Fredun is a corruption of the Zend Thraêtaona, corresponding to a Sanskrit form, Traitana, a patronymic of the Vedic god Trita. The tyrant, Zohak, of the epic poem is likewise, as Burnouf was again the first to point out, the same as the Ashi dahaka of the Zend-avesta, whom even Firdusi still knows as Ash dahak, while the true explanation of his nature and real origin can only be found in the Ahi, the serpent of Vedic mythology. We can see in Persia, step by step, the growth of mythology, of legend, and at last of history, while in other countries we generally have the second or third stages only, and must frequently depend on the etymology of the names of half-historical, half-legendary heroes, or appeal to the character of their exploits, in order to show that an Odysseus, no less than a William Tell, was evolved from "the inner consciousness," and was never seen, whether in Ithaca or Switzerland, in flesh and blood. Some of these questions, particularly the character of the materials collected and used by Firdusi when composing his epic, are fully treated in the prefaces to the different volumes of Mohl's edition of the "Shah Nameh," and they deserve to be carefully considered by every student of comparative mythology.

By accepting the task of editing and translating the "Shah," for the French Government, Mohl must have seen that he would have to spend the best years of his life in France.

It has sometimes been a matter of surprise why Mohl should have declined to return to the university of Tübingen, which was so anxious to receive him back, and should have preferred to live and work at Paris. He himself, when asked in later life, found it difficult to give an answer. But first of all it should be remembered that in 1830 men were still far more cosmopolitan than after 1848, and that Paris was then the most cosmopolitan city in the world.

We may quote on this point the opinion of M. Renan in his "Rapport sur les travaux du Conseil de la Société Asiatique," in 1876 :—

"Le meilleur fruit," he says, "du grand et libéral esprit qui régna en Europe depuis la fin des orages de la Révolution et de l'Empire jusqu'à la funeste année qui a déchaîné de nouveau le typhon de la haine et du mal, fut la facilité avec laquelle l'homme voué à une œuvre sociale consentait à transporter ses aptitudes et le libre exercice de son activité dans un pays différent du sien. Il résultait de là des échanges excellentes de dons opposés, des mélanges féconds pour le progrès de la civilisation. Et comme une pensée vraiment haute présidait à ces changements de patrie, le pays le plus hospitalier était celui qui en bénéficiait le plus."

Secondly, friendships, and more than friendships, seem to have had much to do with his unwillingness to leave Paris. Such men as De Sacy, Rémusat, Fauriel, Fresnel, Saint-Martin, Ampère, Eugène Burnouf, were not easy to find at Tübingen. Nor was there, in the then prevailing state of Government, any place in Germany where a young professor would have found such a sphere of usefulness and independence as Mohl had at Paris. He was able to live there on easy and pleasant terms, not only with the greatest scholars of the day, but also with such men as Guizot, Villemain, Cousin, Thiers, and others, all of them at a later time his colleagues as members of the Institute, and at the same time Ministers of State, ready to listen to his counsels, and willing to carry out any plans that he or his friends might submit to them for the furtherance of Oriental studies. Nor must it be forgotten that his being a foreigner was at that time a recommendation rather than an impediment in his career at Paris. Mohl was not only welcome to do the work or take a place for which no Frenchman happened to care, but the highest and most honorable appointments were given to him in no grudging spirit. In 1844 he was elected a member of the French Institute ; in 1847 he received the chair of Persian at the Collège de France; and in 1852 he was appointed Inspector of the Oriental Department at the Imperial Press. While these appointments gave him an independent and honored position among his French colleagues, he was able to devote a considerable portion of his leisure to the *Société Asiatique*, of which he was first the assistant secretary, then the secretary, and finally the president. That society was in fact his pet child through good and evil days, and it was through that society that Mohl rendered the most valuable and most permanent services to Oriental scholarship.

The best record of these services is to be found in the Annual Reports delivered by him regularly every year from 1840 to 1867. It is but seldom that he tells us what share he himself has had in encouraging, guiding, and supporting the work of other scholars. Still we can recognize his hand in several of the most brilliant discoveries of those days. He generally begins his annual address by giving an account of the work done by the members of the Asiatic Society during the year. He dwells on the losses sustained by the death of some of its prominent associates, and some of his biographical notices are perfect gems. We need only mention his *nécrologes* of James Prinsep, Gesenius, Csoma Körösi, Schlegel, Burnouf, Lee, Fresnel, Hammer Purgstall, Wilson, and Woepke. After enumerating the principal papers published during the year in the Journal of the Asiatic Society, and dwelling on the larger literary undertakings, which the society had either recommended for Government support or supported out of its own resources, Mohl passes in review all Oriental publications, whether in French, English, German, Italian, or some even of the Eastern languages, which seemed to him to constitute a real addition to the stock of Oriental learning in Europe. Scholars whose works are recorded in those pages may well look upon such record as the Greek cities looked upon the honor of being mentioned in Homer's catalogue. There is perhaps more praise than blame in Mohl's judgments, yet to those who have ears to hear, it is easy to perceive where he looks upon any publication as a real and permanent conquest of new territory, or as mere skirmishing and reconnoitring in search of literary glory. It would be impossible, of course, to give anything like an adequate account of the work performed by Mohl in his annual censorship in every branch of Oriental learning. But we think it due to his memory to show, at least in one case, how he suggested and silently directed discoveries, the credit of which he was himself the first to ascribe and to leave undiminished to others.

One of the most brilliant and truly light-bringing discoveries of our age has no doubt been the unearthing of the palaces of Babylon and Nineveh, and still more, the deciphering of the wedge-shaped inscriptions with which the walls of those ancient palaces were covered.

If one asked any educated Englishman, supposing he cared at all about Oriental antiquities, who it was that discovered the bulls at Nineveh, he would answer, Sir Austen Layard. And if he were asked who first deciphered the cuneiform inscriptions, he would say, Sir Henry Rawlinson. Yet both these statements are utterly and entirely wrong, and we have the less hesitation in saying so, because Sir Austen Layard's merits in bringing the Nineveh bulls and many other antiquities to light, and Sir Henry Rawlinson's merits in copying and translating some of the most important cuneiform inscriptions, are so great that they are the very last persons who would wish to see themselves bedecked with feathers not their own. Long before Sir Austen Layard ever thought of Nineveh, and before Sir Henry Rawlinson published any of the cuneiform inscriptions of Behistun, we find M. Mohl pointing out to his French friends the importance of the discoveries that might be made on the historic soil of Mesopotamia. He was then already carrying on an active correspondence with Schultz, the unfortunate traveller, who had been sent to Armenia to copy the arrow-headed inscriptions which were known to exist in the old castle of Van. In the very first of his reports, of the year 1840, Mohl had to announce the death of Schultz, who was murdered while engaged in copying these inscriptions. It was Mohl who rescued his papers from oblivion, and who urged the French Government to publish the most important materials collected by his unfortunate friend. He tells us at the same time, in the same report of 1840, what had been hitherto achieved in the deciphering of the cuneiform alphabet. After Grotefend had proved that these bundles of wedges with which the walls of the ancient palaces of Persepolis were covered, were really meant for inscriptions, consisted, in fact, of consonants and vowels, and exhibited clearly at the beginning of certain inscriptions the names and titles of Darius and Xerxes, kings of kings, kings of Persia, little progress had been made till the year 1836, in which Burnouf and Lassen published, almost contemporaneously, their Memoirs on the Cuneiform Inscriptions, then accessible from the copies made by Niebuhr during his Persian travels, and by Schultz. The results at which they arrived were almost identical; but the first idea which proved so effective in unlocking the remaining secrets of those ancient documents, i. e. the looking in them, not only for the proper names of kings such as Cyrus, Darius, and Xerxes, but also for geographical names, more particularly the names of the provinces of the Empire of Darius, seems to have come from Burnouf. By the labors of these two pioneers, the whole alphabet of the Persian cuneiform inscriptions had been recovered: there remained only a few doubtful letters, some of which were cleared up soon after by Beer at Leipzig, and by Jacquet at Paris. One letter only, the *m*, remained to be determined by Rawlinson, while the discovery of inherent vowels was due, at a still later date, to Hincks and Oppert.

What was at that time most sorely wanted was a new supply of trustworthy copies. The inscriptions of Hamadan were furnished in Schultz's papers. Rich completed those of Persepolis. The great desideratum was an accurate copy of the trilingual inscriptions of Behistun. Schultz, who was to have copied it, had been murdered. It was known, however, that Colonel Rawlinson was in possession of a copy of at least three out of its four columns, and Mohl, so early as 1840, expressed a hope that this copy would be published immediately, to satisfy the impatience of all Oriental scholars.

Though this hope was not then realized, we find Mohl indefatigable in urging on his friends in Paris and elsewhere the necessity of collecting new materials. In his report of the year 1843, he calls attention to the first publication of Oriental cylinders by A. Cullimore, and to a similar collection then preparing under the auspices of M. Lajard, a French scholar, best known by his vast researches on the worship of Mithra, and not to be confounded with Austen Henry Layard, who will appear later on the stage. In the same year Mohl announces a more important fact. M. Botta, then French Consul at Mosul, had carried on excavations at Nineveh, encouraged to do so by M. Mohl. M. Maury, as President of the Académie des Inscriptions et Belles-lettres, tells us: "C'est surtout d'après ses indications que Botta retrouvait les restes des palais des rois de Ninive." Botta's first attempts were rewarded by the wonderful discovery of Assyrian bas-reliefs and inscriptions. Mohl, on communicating M. Botta's letters to the Asiatic Society of Paris, says, "These are the only specimens of Assyrian sculpture which have hitherto come to light, and the excavations of M. Botta will add an entirely new chapter to the history of ancient art." The French Government, justly proud of the discoveries of its consul, lost no time in securing the treasures he had found. Mohl did all he could to persuade the French authorities to give Botta the aid he required in order to continue his explorations, and he impressed on the members of the Asiatic Society the duty of publishing as many of the newly-discovered inscriptions as their means would allow. He felt, in fact, very sanguine at that time, that after the progress which Burnouf and Lassen had made in deciphering the first class of these inscriptions, namely, the Persian — the two other classes, the so-called Median and Babylonian, would soon have to surrender their secrets likewise. They were all written with the same wedge-shaped letters, and though it was easy to see that the number of independent signs, or groups of wedges, was far larger in the Median than in the Persian, and again far larger in the Babylonian than in the Median inscriptions, yet as there existed trilingual documents, and as it was known in particular that the great inscription of Behistun was repeated three times, on three different tablets, in three different alphabets, and in three different languages, it seemed but natural that after the Persian edict had been deciphered, the Median and Babylonian could offer no very formidable resistance. In this expectation M. Mohl and his friends, as we shall see, were sadly disappointed. Still, every year brought some new light, and in every one of his annual addresses M. Mohl reports progress with unflagging enthusiasm.

In 1844 he says: —

"It was reserved for a member of your society, M. Botta, to lift a corner of that veil with which time had covered the history of Mesopotamia. Last year he wrote to you that he had found at Khorsabad, at about five leagues' distance from Nineveh, the ruins of a building covered with sculptures and inscriptions. The excavations which he has carried on since have only added to the importance of his discoveries. Everything at present seems to show, that these ruins are truly Assyrian; but much more abundant materials will soon be forthcoming. The French Government has sent M. Flandin to make drawings on the spot. M. Botta himself has bought the whole village beneath which the ruins are found, and the Louvre will soon possess a splendid museum of Assyrian antiquities."

But while thus telling the world of the wonders revealed from year to year in the Assyrian Herculaneum and Pompeii, Mohl never ceased to point out the duty incumbent on Oriental scholarship in Europe of deciphering the three cuneiform alphabets, and reading the three ancient languages in which the old kings of Babylon, Nineveh, Media, and Persia had recorded their achievements for the benefit of future generations. He dwells again and again on the labors of Mr. Rawlinson, the fortunate Consul-General at Bagdad, who was in possession of the great trilingual Behistun inscription, and therefore was supposed to hold in his hand the key that would unlock, not only the remaining secrets of the Persian, but likewise the as yet only guessed at contents of the Median and

Babylonian tablets. Yet that inscription was still withheld, and such was the impatience of the learned public in Europe for new materials and new light, that the small kingdom of Denmark sent Westergaard to Persia, to copy cuneiform inscriptions, and to study the ancient language of the Zend-avesta, which, as Burnouf had shown, supplied in reality the most advanced trench from which the language of the Persian mountain records of Cyrus, Darius, and Xerxes could be attacked. A large number of the Assyrian inscriptions copied by Flandin and Coste were published in 1843, at the expense of the French Government. Many hands were at work, if not to decipher these inscriptions, at least to draw up lists of all the letters, which, in the Assyrian and Babylonian alphabet, amounted to several hundreds instead of the thirty-three consonants and vowels of the Persian; to find out, in various transcripts of the same inscription, what letters could be replaced by other letters, which signs were ideographic, which syllabic, which phonetic; in fact to carry out some kind of preliminary sifting, and to establish a certain order in what seemed at first a mere chaos of arrows and wedges. A real assault, it was felt, would be premature until the Behistun inscription became *publici juris*. It was known then that Colonel Rawlinson had copied as much as four hundred and fifty lines of Persian text, containing probably ten times as many words as all the other Persian inscriptions put together. Coste and Flandin had been on the spot, and had prepared careful drawings of the sculptures of Behistun, representing Darius with his captive kings before him, protected by Auramazda, the god of the Avesta, called Ahuramazda in Zend, and Ormazd in modern Persian. But the most important part of the monument, the inscriptions, they had left uncopied.

The next year, 1845, brings us news of the unearthing of the first complete palace. M. Botta had then two hundred workmen at his disposal, consisting chiefly of those unfortunate Nestorians who had escaped being massacred by the Kurds. Two thousand *mètres* of wall covered with inscriptions and bas-reliefs were laid open, one hundred and thirty bas-reliefs were copied by M. Flandin, two hundred inscriptions were carefully transcribed by M. Botta. The most striking specimens of the Assyrian sculptures had been shipped off on the Tigris, and had actually arrived at Bagdad, ready to be taken to Paris. There were only the two gigantic bulls, and two statues of men throttling lions in their arms still waiting to be packed with care. M. Botta was expected back at Paris, and his whole museum was to follow as soon as the shallow Tigris would allow it.

The best account of what had been achieved in recovering the antiquities of Mesopotamia up to the year 1845 may be found in "Lettres de M. Botta sur ses découvertes á Khorsabad prés de Ninive, publiées par M. Mohl, Paris, 1845." We have only to add that Westergaard was then publishing his first essay on the Median inscriptions, and that Colonel Rawlinson's papers containing the Persian text of the Behistun inscriptions complete, about one-third of the Median and one-tenth of the Babylonian tablets, were in the hands of Mr. Norris, the indefatigable secretary of the Royal Asiatic Society in London.

In 1846 Mr. Layard appears on the stage. Attracted by the fame of Botta's discoveries, he set to work digging at Nineveh with that pluck, that energy, and at the same time that discriminating judgment which he has since shown on other occasions. There was enough, and more than enough, to disinter for both France and England; yet there can be no doubt that England, leaving its representatives far greater freedom of action than France, obtained in the end far greater results, owing chiefly to the energy and undaunted perseverance of such men as Rawlinson, Layard, and Loftus. Cargoes of antiquities soon arrived in London. One was unfortunately wrecked on its way from Bombay. In France the Government seemed satisfied with the collection sent home by Botta, and spent large sums on publishing the description of his discoveries in so extravagant a style that again its very object was defeated. This is a point on which Mohl speaks out in almost every one of his reports. Doing full justice to the French Chambers, and their liberal grants for sending out learned expeditions and publishing their results, he shows that the sumptuous way in which these works are got up, and the enormous price at which they are sold, keep them altogether from those in whose hands alone they would be most useful. He shows how much more sensible and practical the English system is of leaving the publication of such works to private enterprise, and he tells the Government that while Mr. Layard's works on Nineveh are read in thousands of copies, yielding at the same time a good profit both to author and publisher, M. Botta's "Monuments de Ninive," published at an enormous expense by Government (Paris, 1848), was so dear that the two men who would have made the best use of it, Mr. Rawlinson and Mr. Layard, were unable to buy it. Here was indeed a *reductio ad absurdum*, but like other *reductios* of the same kind, it seems only to have confirmed the Government in its perverse course.

In 1848 M. Mohl is able to announce that Rawlinson's paper on the Behistun inscription has been published at last in the Journal of the Royal Asiatic Society for 1847. Though at that time there were no more discoveries to be made in deciphering the alphabet of the Persian cuneiform inscriptions, yet the publication and translation of so large a document marked a new epoch in the study of Persian antiquities. How well the alphabet was known at that time was best shown by the fact that Mr. Norris, then secretary of the Asiatic Society in London, was able to point out mistakes in the copies of the Behistun inscription sent home by Colonel Rawlinson, with the same certainty as a Latin scholar would correct clerical blunders in a Latin inscription. Mohl, though fully recognizing the principle that priority of publication constitutes priority of discovery, does the fullest justice to Rawlinson's industry and perseverance, and to the real genius with which he had performed his own peculiar task.

After Rawlinson's Memoir was published, the Persian cuneiform inscriptions were disposed of; their ancient texts could thenceforth be read with nearly the same certainty as an ancient Greek or Latin inscription. The question now was, what could be done for the Median and Assyrian inscriptions? Westergaard had proved that the language of the second class of the so-called Median inscriptions was Scythian or Turanian. With regard to the third class, the inscriptions found at Babylon and Nineveh, all scholars who were then at work on them, such as Grotefend, Löwenstern, Longperier, De Saulcy, Hincks, were agreed that they were written in a Semitic dialect. The inscriptions of Van only gave rise to doubts, and Hincks, in a paper "On the Inscriptions at Van," suspected that they were composed in an Aryan language.

The difficulties, however, of reading either the Median or the Assyrian inscriptions, even after the Behistun texts had been published, were far greater than had been expected. First of all, the Median and Babylonian transcripts at Behistun were imperfect. Secondly, they were written in an alphabet that was not only, like the Egyptian, at the same time ideographic, syllabic, and phonetic, but, what was much worse, employed the same sign to express different powers, and different signs to express one and the same power. We enter in fact into the long controversy of the Polyphony and Homophony of the Babylonian alphabet, a problem which made several scholars give up the whole matter as hopeless, which roused a general skepticism among Oriental scholars, and still more among the public at large, and which even now, after twenty years of continued research, continues a constant stumblingblock to Assyrian and Babylonian scholarship.

Mohl was fully aware of all these difficulties, but he goes on year after year announcing new triumphs, and exhorting to new victories. In 1849, the French Government withdrew its patronage from the field of excavation. M. Botta was removed from Mosul to Jerusalem, and the rich mine which he had opened was left to be worked by Mr. Layard. At home the chief advance made in deciphering was in the Median line. Colonel Rawlinson had succeeded in copying nearly the whole of the Median text at Behistun, and promised to send his copies home; M. De Saulcy gave the results of his own independent studies, on the Median inscriptions, so far as they were then known, in several papers contributed to the "Journal Asiatique."

In 1851, we receive the first account of Mr. Layard's splendid discoveries at Koyunjik, and somewhat later at Babylon. This Koyunjik proved the richest field of Assyrian discovery. There are within the precincts at Nineveh two artificial hillocks, the one called the Koyunjik, the other the Nabbi Yunus. It was the former which yielded its treasures to European excavators, while the latter, being supposed to contain the bones of the prophet Jonah, and protected by a mosque, was considered too sacred to be surrendered to them. The Pasha of Mosul, however, though forbidding the infidels to disturb the peace of the prophet Jonah, had no scruples in digging himself, and his labors were soon rewarded by two bulls, nineteen feet high, which were not exactly what he was looking for. ("Rapport," 1856, p. 49.) At the same time Mr. Loftus was sent to the Lower Euphrates to explore the ruins of Warka and Senkereh, while another expedition to Susah was in contemplation at the expense of the English Government.

At home the linguistic excavations were carried on quietly by Botta, De Saulcy, Rawlinson, Norris, and especially by the Rev. E. Hincks, who at that time was the most advanced pioneer, and the first to lay the solid foundation for a grammatical study of the Assyrian language. His labors, scattered about in different journals, are now in danger of being almost forgotten; and it would be but a just tribute to his memory if the Irish Academy or some of his surviving friends and admirers were to publish a collected edition of his numerous though not voluminous contributions to the study of the cuneiform inscriptions.

In 1853, Mohl reports with great satisfaction that M. Place, the successor of M. Botta as French consul at Mosul, has been directed to continue excavations. His labors at Khorsabad were soon rewarded by most valuable results. "He found new halls, subterranean vaults, long passages in enamelled bricks, Assyrian statues, the cellar of the castle containing vessels still filled with dried-up liquors, bas-reliefs, inscriptions, articles in ivory and metal, and, quite recently, a depôt of iron and steel instruments, and a gate of the town or the palace in splendid preservation, covered in by a vault supported on both sides by bulls, and built in enamelled and ornamental bricks." In spite of these splendid discoveries, which, as M. Mohl said, would at last bring the Assyrian Museum at the Louvre up to the level of the British Museum, the French Government, it was feared, would again stop M. Place, as they had stopped M. Botta, in the midst of his campaign. M. Mohl did all he could to plead the cause of Assyrian discovery before the Société Asiatique, before the Institute, before the Ministers, and it was again chiefly due to his never-ceasing intercessions that his friend M. Fresnel, who had been for years devoting himself to the collection of Himyaritic inscriptions in the south of Arabia, was sent out with MM. Oppert and Thomas, at the head of a well-equipped scientific expedition, destined to explore the ruins in the basin of the Lower Euphrates. When the disturbed state of the country frustrated the original intention of Fresnel's expedition, he and his companions concentrated their work on Babylon. At about the same time Mr. Loftus was hard at work at Susah, and had discovered there a palace like those of Persepolis, and inscriptions in the Persian cuneiform characters of the time of Artaxerxes. Mr. Layard had published an account of his wonderful discoveries at Koyunjik, and had explored a large portion of Lower Mesopotamia, the ruins of Arban, Van, Babylon, Niffar, and Kalah Sherghat. At home, Rawlinson's Memoir on the Babylonian text of the Behistun inscription had been published in the fourteenth volume of the Journal of the Royal Asiatic Society (1851), and in the first number of the fifteenth volume of the same Journal (1853). Mr. Norris, in publishing for the first time the Median transcript of the same document, had confirmed Westergaad's opinion that its language was Turanian, without determining, however, whether it was more closely allied to the Turkish or to the Finnish branch of that extensive family, or rather class, of speech.

In the next year, 1854, while Mr. Loftus was continuing his work at Warka and Senkereh in Lower Mesopotamia, while Mr. Rassan was hard at work for England at Koyunjik, M. Mohl has to announce that the French Government has really stopped the excavations undertaken with so much success at Khorsabad by M. Place. The next year brings sadder tidings still. That precious cargo, containing the harvest of the combined labors of M. Place at Khorsabad and M. Fresnel at Babylon, was completely wrecked at Basra on its voyage home. Fresnel, who for years had held his own against the Government, who had declined to be recalled, and was meditating at Bagdad the establishment of an archæological school, on the model of the French school at Athens, died in 1855, and with his death the excavations in the East at the expense of the French Government came to an end. While Loftus was still collecting fresh materials among the ruins of Mugheir, Abu Shahrein, Tel Sifr, Senkereh, Warka and Niffar; while Rawlinson was looking for new treasures at Babylon, nothing remained to the French expedition, now entrusted to M. Jules Oppert, but to save what could be saved, and to return home. With Fresnel's death M. Mohl's interest in the antiquities of Mesopotamia seems to flag. In spite of his constant efforts, the enterprises which he had encouraged and directed had not led to the results which he anticipated. Even the deciphering of the Babylonian and Assyrian inscriptions had somewhat disappointed him. In speaking almost for the last time of the subject, in drawing attention to the "Rapport adressé à S. E. le Ministre de l'instruction publique, par M. Jules Oppert: Paris, 1856 (tiré des Archives des missions)," he expresses a hope that the difficulties created by the polyphonous and homophonous character of the Assyro-Babylonian alphabet may be overcome; but with regard to the theory then started for the first time by M. Oppert, that the cuneiform alphabet was originally invented by people speaking a Scythian language, and afterwards adapted as well as might be by the Babylonians to their own Semitic speech, he says: —

"Il faut réserver son jugement, attendre le développement des preuves, et, si elles sont concluantes, réformer nos idées préconçues. Il est impossible qu'une découverte immense, comme celle de Ninive, et cette restauration subite de langues et presque de littératures perdues depuis des milliers d'années, ne révèlent des faits qui s'accordent mal avec des opinions formées sur l'ancienne histoire de l'Asie d'après des données imparfaites. Il est probable, au reste, que l'histoire ancienne, telle que l'on a construite d'après la Bible et les auteurs grecs, sera plutôt enrichie que changée par les résultats des études assyriennes ; car nous voyons que tout ce que nous avons appris sur l'Egypte, l'Inde, et la Perse, n'a fait que grandir l'autorité d'Hérodote. C'est un cadre qui se remplit, mais qui ne change pas dans ses parties essentielles. On n'est qu'au commencement de ces études, et la route est longue et ardue ; mais les progrès sont très-réels et deviendront plus rapides à mesure que les matériaux seront plus accessibles."

We can give this one instance only, to show how conscientiously Mohl performed his work as the recognized contemporaneous historian of Oriental learning, and how much may be learnt from his pages that is apt to be forgotten in the hurry of our life. No doubt Persia was always nearest to his heart, and hence his warm interest in these cuneiform researches, which, resting chiefly on the decipherment of the edicts of the ancient kings of Persia, such as Cyrus, Darius, and Xerxes, threw a new light on the history of the Persian language, both before and after their time. Hence, also, his sincere admiration for Burnouf's labors for the recovery of the sacred writings of Zoroaster, and the full appreciation of Burnouf's philological method as the only one that could lead to trustworthy results in the interpretation of the Avesta as well as of the Veda. But though these personal predilections had their influence, we shall find in reading his annual reports that he treated every other subject, too, with almost the same accuracy and thoroughness of appreciation. Every really important publication, whether in Arabic, Hebrew, Syriac, Armenian, Sanskrit, or Chinese, is carefully chronicled — nay, we meet again and again with paragraphs which form short but complete treatises on the history and the true value of whole branches of Oriental literature.

Whoever wishes to know how we came possessed of the Himyaritic inscriptions, and what their bearing is on the history of the Semitic languages, should read Mohl's account of Fresnel's and Arnaud's wanderings on the coast of Yemen, chiefly suggested and encouraged by Mohl himself. (See Rapports for 1840, 1844, 1845, 1846, 1856.)

The practicability of substituting the Roman letters for the numerous alphabets of Oriental languages is discussed by Mohl in 1841, and again in 1865. In answer to those who twitted the English Government with the slow progress they had been able to make in persuading the natives to write Hindustani with Roman letters, while the Mohammedans had succeeded in a very short time in making the Persians adopt the Arabic alphabet, he drily remarked that the Mohammedans punished all who continued to write Persian with the old Pehlevi, and not with Arabic letters, with death (p. 25). Though Mohl does not give his authority for this statement, we have no doubt he could have given chapter and verse for it.

The discovery of the Syriac and Coptic MSS. by Tattam in 1842, and subsequently by Pacho, the first specimens of these new treasures such as the three undoubtedly genuine letters of Ignatius published by

Cureton, and lastly the excellent catalogue of the whole collection by Wright, — all this is described in a masterly way in the Report for the years 1846, 1847, 1848, 1864.

Students of Arabic will find an accurate account of all important publications, particularly some instructive chapters on the life of Mohammed, doing full justice to Sprenger's treatment of the prophet on one side, and to Sir W. Muir's very different treatment on the other. The gradual formation and sifting too of the traditions concerning Mohammed and the growth of his new religion will interest many readers, as containing significant and useful hints on similar phases in the history of other religions. Full justice is rendered to Lane's Arabic Lexicon, but not without an expression of regret that it should have been restricted to the so-called classical language only.

The reports on Chinese literature are very complete, Chinese having been for a long time one of Mohl's favorite occupations. When Stanislas Julien published his translation of the travels of Buddhist pilgrims from China to India, he nowhere found a more appreciative, yet discriminating critic than in Mohl.

In all the subjects hitherto mentioned Mohl was perfectly at home. The languages were familiar, the literatures a subject of constant interest to him. But even in other branches of Eastern learning, in Sanskrit, for instance, and Indian literature in general, few could have more surely distinguished the important from the unimportant, few could have better pointed out the duty which Sanskrit scholarship owed to the learned world at large, than Mohl. Beginning with his first report, in 1840, he calls the attention of Sanskrit scholars to the Veda. *Hic Rhodos, hic salta!* he seems to say whenever his survey brings him to the frontiers of India. He welcomes with real joy every attempt at filling the gap in our knowledge of Sanskrit literature, which scholars such as Sir W. Jones, Colebrooke, Mill, and Wilson had indicated rather than filled. He shows how Indian literature must for ever remain a baseless fabric unless its truly historical foundation, the Veda, can be recovered. As early as 1840 he tells us that the old East India Company had ordered the text of the four Vedas to be published by the learned Brâhmans of the College at Calcutta after the best MSS. of Benares. "C'est une grande et magnifique entreprise," he says, "qui fera honneur au gouvernement anglais, et qui livrera aux études des savants de tous les pays un monument littéraire dont il est difficile d'évaluer l'importance pour l'histoire de la civilisation." It is well known, however, that neither learned Brâhmans nor trustworthy MSS. were forthcoming in India. Brâhmans who were able were unwilling, those who were willing were unable, to produce an edition of the text and the commentaries of the Veda; and European scholarship had at last to undertake the work, and give to the Brâhmans the first complete edition of their own sacred books.

Mohl tells us at the same time that during several years the French Government had then been buying MSS. of the Veda and its commentaries in India, and that several boxes of them had already arrived at Paris. This was chiefly due to Burnouf, who, besides Rosen, was at that time probably the only Sanskrit scholar who had gone beyond Colebrooke, and penetrated furthest into the outworks of Vedic scholarship, and to the enlightened patronage of M. Guizot. Even so late as 1869 M. Guizot, in announcing to the writer of this article his election as a foreign member of the French Institute, remarked: "Je ne suis pas un juge compétent de vos travaux sur les Védas, mais je me félicite d'avoir un peu contribué à vous fournir les matériaux, et je vous remercie d'en avoir gardé le souvenir."

Hardly a year passes in which Mohl does not give us some new information on the gradual advances made by Sanskrit scholars in their attempts to master the difficulties of the Veda; and in his simple and clear treatment of the importance of the native traditional literature on one side, and the freedom of European scholarship on the other, we see again the maturity of his mind and the impartiality of his judgment, in strong contrast with the wranglings of one-sided pleaders.

But deeply impressed as Mohl was with the importance of Vedic studies, other branches of Indian literature were not passed over by him in silence. Troyer's edition of the Râ*g*atarangini, the history of the Kings of Kashmir, Prinsep's discovery of the Pâli alphabet, Gorresi's magnificent edition of the Râmâya*n*a, Foucaux's translation of the Tibetan version of the Life of Buddha, Lassen's Indian Antiquities, Boehtlingk and Roth's as well as Goldstücker's Sanskrit Dictionaries, Woepke's original researches on Indian numerals and mathematics, Nève's and Weber's works, all receive their recognition; all are represented to us as marking definite stages in the slow but safe advance of the small and valiant army of Oriental scholars.

It is not easy to form an idea of the work entailed on a really conscientious scholar who undertakes to write such annual reports. Those only who have tried to do it know how much time is required in collecting the mere materials, how much care in determining what amount of recognition, of praise or blame, is due to each work. Though each of these annual reports fills only from fifty to a hundred pages, a considerable portion of Mohl's leisure must have been consumed in their preparation.

Other societies have published similar reports, but seldom with such regularity as the Société Asiatique during Mohl's secretaryship — never with that due proportion which Mohl knew how to preserve in the general plan of his annual review. If such reports become too complete, they degenerate into mere catalogues; if they are too minute and searching, they grow into treatises on a few leading publications. There have been annual *rapports* published by those who succeeded Mohl as secretaries of the Asiatic Society of Paris. These *rapports* are written, no doubt, in more classical French, and are full of most valuable materials. But they have gradually become less and less comprehensive, and are now restricted to a survey of the work done during each year by the Oriental scholars of France only.

Still greater, perhaps, was the difficulty of maintaining throughout that judicial position which Mohl took in his reports from beginning to end. Of himself we hear little—almost nothing. It is only by accident that we find out how much was due to him personally in several of the greatest undertakings patronized by the French Government. In some cases he seems to carry that modesty too far. The

French, we know, are very sensitive on this point. They dislike the pronoun "I." Yet there is danger of good taste sinking into mannerism even here. When speaking of his edition of the "Shah Nameh," it would have sounded more simple and natural, even in French, if Mohl had said, "A new volume of my edition of the 'Shah Nameh' has been finished," instead of telling his friends, as he always does, that "a member of their Society has finished a new volume of the 'Shah Nameh.'" However, as a German writing in French, Mohl no doubt felt himself bound to observe French etiquette even more carefully than a Frenchman, and if he erred, he erred, at all events, on the safe side.

What is, however, even more creditable to him is the reserve with which he speaks of his personal friends. Mohl could not have been the scholar he was, without having both strong sympathies and strong antipathies with regard to other scholars or would-be scholars, whether in France or elsewhere. But it would require a very delicate ear to discover any trace of these personal feelings in his official reports. When delivering these annual addresses he speaks with a full consciousness of his responsibility. He seems to feel that the honor of the Société Asiatique is in his keeping. He never abuses the trust committed to him, he never allows himself an unfair advantage. When reading again through his reports from the year 1840 to the year 1867, we meet with few lines which he would now wish to see unwritten, though time has laid its disenchanting hand on many hopes and many schemes in the field of Oriental scholarship. No doubt Mohl disappointed many, either by his silence or by his measured praise.

He made himself, we believe, more enemies than friends by his faithful stewardship; but he retained through life, in spite of many disappointments, an unshaken trust in truth.

It is delightful to see the unanimous testimony borne to Mohl's uprightness by his colleagues at the French Institute. His position at Paris was by no means an easy one. True, he had old and faithful friends, but he had also — and how could it be otherwise? — enviers and enemies. He was loved by some, liked by many, respected by all, even by those who neither liked nor loved him. Men, so high-minded as Maury, Renan, Regnier, and others might truly say that they had almost forgotten that Mohl was not a Frenchman. In his last farewell Alfred Maury exclaimed: "Adieu, Jules Mohl; nous te saluons à ta dernière demeure, non seulement comme un confrère, mais comme un compatriote. La science, au reste, n'a pas de nationalité; ou, pour mieux dire, elle est de toutes les nationalités; elle travaille à les rapprocher à les unir, et cette conciliation nous aimions à la rencontrer en toi."

But it would hardly be fair to expect the same elevation of thought and feeling from smaller minds, least of all from those whose pretensions Mohl had occasionally to check, or whose interests he had sometimes to cross. Mohl, though he seems to have been a welcome guest at several courts, had never learnt to be a courtier. Life to him was not worth having, if it required any economizing with truth. All his friends agree that there was a certain *brusqueness* in him, which he could never overcome to the end of his life, and which they kindly ascribed to his German blood. M. Barbier de Meynard says of him: —

"L'amour du vrai, l'horreur du charlatanisme et de l'intrigue donnaient à son abord ce je ne sais quoi de réservé et de brusque qui ne permettait pas d'apprécier du premier coup d'œil tout ce qu'il y avait en lui de bonte naturelle et de chaleureuse sympathie."

That brusqueness, however, was not merely a national peculiarity; it had a deeper source, it arose from his sense of the sacredness of science. The *profanum vulgus* never forgave him for that.

M. Laboulaye says of him with perfect truth: —

"Mohl avait au plus haut degré le sentiment de la responsabilité qui pesait sur nous; pour lui, la science était une religion, et il voulait écarter du temple tous les profanes."

M. Renan speaks in the strongest language of the influence which Mohl exercised in all elections, whether at the Institute, the Collège de France, or elsewhere, simply because it was known that to him science was sacred, and no personal feelings would ever sway his vote: —

"Le grand titre de M. Mohl à la reconnaissance des savants est cependant, avant tout, l'influence qu'il a exercée. Il sut présider à nos études avec une solidité de jugement et un esprit philosophique qui seuls peuvent donner de la valeur à des travaux épars et sans lien apparent. Ce lien, il le créait par sa judicieuse et savante critique; son autorité aidait les amis de la vérité à distinguer le mérite sérieux des succés faciles qu'on trouve souvent auprès du public en flattant ses goûts superficiels. Par là M. Mohl a occupé dans nos études une place de premier ordre; le vide qu'il a laissé ne sera pas de sitôt rempli. Ami du vrai et du solide en toutes choses, il ne faisait aucun part à la vanité, à l'envie de briller. Sa direction a été aussi efficace qu'éclairée. M. Mohl était pour nous tous une des raisons que nous avions de vivre et de bien faire."

How true it is to say of such men as Mohl, "They make us live and do well." They keep us from making concessions, from taking what is called an easier view of life, from making to ourselves friends by the mammon of unrighteous praise. That his friends at Paris should have allowed him to maintain that independent position through life, that they should have yielded to his silent influence, that they should not have resented his occasional reproofs, reflects the highest credit on the French character. No doubt, it was but human nature that Frenchmen who found themselves opposed by Mohl should sometimes, when all other arguments had failed, be heard to murmur grumblingly, "*Ah! cet Allemand.*" Frenchmen would not be Frenchmen, Englishmen would not be Englishmen, Germans would not be Germans, if they did not think that on some point or other they were better judges than anybody else. There were the *dii minorum gentium* in Paris too, who shrugged their shoulders when Mohl's Rapport was out, and thought it very hard that the censorship of Oriental studies in France should have fallen into the hands of *cet Allemand.* But when we read these annual Reports now, after the lapse of many years, and compare them with the reports of presidential addresses of other academies or learned societies, we shall be better able to understand the influence which their high judicial and moral tone exercised at the time. Nowhere do we see any traces of *communiqués*, but thinly veiled by the honored name of a president or secretary. Nowhere is there a sign of his yielding to that great temptation of saying a kind word of our friends, or passing a slur on our or their opponents. It was because every one felt that the Secretary of the Société Asiatique was a man of honor, most sensitive and jealous for the good name of his Society, and still more for the honor of science, that his addresses were listened to and his judgments accepted by the whole world. It was because in other cases that charge has been committed to men of less sensitive minds and less clean hands, to men who look upon scientific studies as a mere amusement or a road to social distinction, that the honor of this or that learned society has been tarnished and sacrificed to the petty ambitions and the impotent jealousies of a small *clique.* When we read through the long list of Mohl's "Rapports" without meeting with one single line that could be traced to personal favor or personal spite, one word of blame or praise that would make the members of the Société Asiatique regret having entrusted their honor to their German assistant-secretary, secretary, and president, we shall be better able to understand what M. Renan meant when saying of Mohl, "Il était une des raisons que nous avions de vivre et de bien faire."

But we should carry away a very false impression of Mohl if we thought of him only as the stern censor. Among his more intimate friends Mohl was full of kindliness and humor, though later in life there was a cloud of melancholy that threw a shadow over the twinkle of his bright and piercing eyes. Mohl spoke three languages, — German, French, and English, — and it might be said of him what was said of Ennius, that he had three hearts, or rather that he had a large heart, large enough to appreciate and love all that was good and noble in the German, the French, and the English character; strong enough to despise and shun all that was bad and mean, whether German, French, or English. He was German by nature, French by taste, English by love, and he had true friends in every one of these countries. He had learnt more particularly from his own personal experience how the French and German characters might supplement each other in their strong and weak points; and during the whole of his life he looked forward to a future when these two nations should better understand and appreciate each other; should forget their vulgar military rivalry, and work together for the highest achievements in literature and art. There was a time when that dream seemed more than half-realized, and there can be no doubt that the silent but never-ceasing influence of such men as Mohl did much towards the realization of such a dream. During Louis Philippe's reign the spirit of German science might be felt in the best works of French scholarship, literature, and art. There was a "Revue Germanique" published in Paris, intended to show to the more fastidious French public that there was solid gold to be found in the crude ore of German science, while in Germany the name of Humboldt alone is sufficient to show how German science had begun to be quickened by French *esprit*. These happy days came to an end almost from the beginning of the Napoleonic *régime*. If there was a place where Louis Napoleon was hated with an unwavering hatred, it was the *Institut de France*. One might have written over its portals, "No Bonapartist need apply." When Leverrier was forced upon the Institut, Biot, the veteran astronomer, was heard to say in a bluff voice, "*Qui est cet homme là?*" and when told that it was Leverrier, he muttered to his friends, "*J'ai connu Laplace; je ne connais pas Leverrier.*" When about the same time Napoleon insisted on having the name of the *Institut de France* changed into *Institut Impérial de France*, Villemain was chosen to draw up an historical memoir, showing how under the most glorious kings of France, during the Republic, and during the reign of the *great* Napoleon, the Institut had always been called simply *Institut de France;* and if a change was now required, the Minister was requested to send his architect to erase the golden letters placed on the façade of the *Palais de l'Institut* by the architect of Richelieu.

Nor was there among the *Membres de l'Institut* one who saw and dreaded the fatal influence of the Napoleonic rule more than the one German member of that illustrious assembly, Mohl. No political successes, no outward splendor, no offers of patronage to literature and science, could dazzle his eyes. His conviction remained unshaken from first to last, that the system of government introduced by Louis Napoleon and his court must ruin France, and through the ruin of France ruin the peaceful development of the whole of Europe. He lived to see his prophecies come true. The last years of his life were passed in deepest sorrow at the utter destruction of the fairest dream of his youth, the union and friendship of France and Germany, as the champions of the intellectual freedom of the future. His friends in Paris, though their ranks had been thinned by death, remained loyal to him, and to the honor of French men of science it should always be remembered that even in those darkest days, when all that was German was detested in France, Mohl was able to occupy his chair at the Institute without one single member of the Academy forgetting the respect they owed to him, to themselves, and to the noble traditions of the place in which they were assembled. It was he who wished to retire and to withdraw himself from society; and though he patiently and silently continued his useful work, no one who knew his happy countenance before the days of 1848 would have known him again after the days of 1871. His house, however, continued what it had been for many years, a kind of free port, open to all who came to Paris to see what was most worth seeing there. During the days of the Empire it happened sometimes that Royal visitors, staying at the Tuileries, came to the Rue du Bac to make the acquaintance of men whom neither the Empress could attempt nor the Emperor command. When the storms of the *Commune* had subsided, the old free port was open again, and many of his English friends will long preserve the recollection of pleasant hours spent with him during the last years of his life, though chiefly talking over old days and mourning over old friends. What the charm of his society was, all his friends know. No one has a better right to bear his testimony than he with whose words we shall close this tribute of respect and gratitude: "Sa maison, grâce au tact et à la profonde connaissance de la société française que possède Mme. Mohl, continuait les meilleures traditions d'un monde plein d'esprit et de charme, qui n'est plus qu'un souvenir. Tous les étrangers de distinction s'y rencontraient; toutes les opinions s'y donnaient la main."

CHARLES KINGSLEY.[1]

(1820–1875.)

"Of the dead nothing but what is good" is an old and beautiful saying, of more profound truth than is commonly supposed. Though at first sight it may seem to convey no more than that it is unchivalrous to speak evil of those who can no longer defend themselves, it discloses a far deeper meaning if we look at it more intently. Let us remember that of most people we know, as of the moon, one side only, the side which they present to us as we pass them by in the throng of life. We may try to complete and correct our own impressions by the favorable or unfavorable impressions which the same people have left on others. But most of these, too, judge by outward appearance only, and how little is that compared with what lies hidden in the soul of man, which never rises to the surface, nay which in our society, as it now is, never can rise to the surface. And what is stranger still, most people are inclined to believe evil rather than good report. Even if we hear nothing but good of a man, we often hesitate in our judgment, as if we could not believe that any one could be so good, so much better than we ourselves. We wish to be cautious, we wish to wait and see, for after all we do not even trust ourselves, but only hope that we may be as good as we seem to be. Thus life passes

[1] Charles Kingsley, his *Letters and Memories of Life*. Edited by his Wife.

away: and during the whole of it we probably give our perfect trust, our full love, to five or six people only. Of these we never believe anything evil, whatever the evil world may say of them. And happy the man who out of the small number of those whom he called his own, has never lost one! Happy the man who never had cause to rue the bestowal of his unbounded confidence!

Very often such disappointments and losses are our own fault. We can all understand our own faults, and explain them and thereby more or less excuse them; but with regard to the faults of others we seldom practice the same advocacy. If we see the smallest spot on the surface, we quickly conclude that the whole fruit must be rotten to the core; and yet how often are these spots but traces of the heat of the day on the bloom of the peach, while the flesh is sound, the sap fresh, and the flavor of the whole fruit pure and delicious!

Such thoughts often pass through the mind when we are standing by the grave of a friend, or when we read the biography of a man whom we have known well, or whom we have often met on our way through life. We can then hardly believe that our eyes have been so blind, and it is only when it is too late that we learn that there may be on earth angels without wings. When we examine a life-like portrait or read a beautiful biography, the good points often seem too prominent, the weak ones too much veiled; but by the side of a closing grave we suddenly learn the art how to discover what is good, and how to understand what is bad, in man. At the grave the old human love breaks through at last. The scales fall from our eyes, and we need not ask what scales they are that so often prevent us seeing what is good and beautiful in man. Certain it is that, as our life is at present, we really do not know men truly till they have joined the company of saints.

Such thoughts were rising again in my mind when reading the Biography of my old, lately departed friend, Charles Kingsley. In England this work seems to have produced this spring the same wide and deep impression which was made some years ago by the Life of Prince Albert and the Life of Bunsen. In a few months five large editions were sold. Our newspapers and journals are full of it, and though during the season and during the session the Eastern Question threw every other question into the back-ground, the Life of Charles Kingsley has held its own, and has become what is called in England "the book of the season."

What hard judgments had been uttered of these three men, Prince Albert, Bunsen, and Charles Kingsley, during their life-time! There was a certain similarity between them all, and they were well acquainted with each other. It would really be a useful undertaking to make a selection from all the attacks which appeared against these three men in the newspapers and journals, and preserve them for posterity as an appendix to their biographies. It might be of use to coming generations. I do not mean to say that all these attacks proceeded from malice, hatred, and ill-will. On the contrary, some of them, I know, come from men who were as good as those whom they attacked. But this very fact, that good men may misunderstand, hate, and persecute good men, would be the best lesson to posterity. No one would venture to say that these three men, whom I have here mentioned together, were entirely free from weaknesses and faults. But what is strange is that, during their life-time, we heard constantly of their weaknesses and faults, while all that is good and beautiful and noble in them was taken as a matter of course. Only when death has lifted the veil from our eyes, do we begin to see clearly, and recognize, when it is too late, the pure, and beautiful, and noble image of man, aye, the long-despised master-work of a divine art.

Among Kingsley's works, Hypatia is probably the one most widely known and appreciated, not only in England, but in Germany, France, and Italy also. Though a mere novel, it represents the struggle of the old Greek world with the new powers of Christendom with truly dramatic art. What Bunsen thought of Hypatia may be seen from what he wrote in a preface to the German translation of it: "I do not hesitate to recognize these two works, Hypatia and the Saint's Tragedy, as the two most important and most perfect creations of his genius. It is in them that I find the justification of a hope which I here venture to express, namely, that Kingsley should continue Shakespeare's historical plays. For many years I have freely confessed that Kingsley seems to me the genius called upon in our century to place by the side of the greatest modern dramatic Epos, beginning with King John and ending with Henry VIII, a second series of national plays, beginning with Edward VI and ending with the landing of William of Orange. It is the only phase in European history which combines all vital elements of dramatic poetry, and which we might watch on the stage without overpowering pain. The tragedy of Saint Elizabeth shows that Kingsley not only knows how to write a novel, but that he has mastered the more severe rules of the drama also, while his Hypatia proves that he can discover in the history of the past all that is truly human and eternal, and place it full of life before our eyes. All his works testify to his ability to catch the fresh tone of the life of the people, and to make broad humor a powerful ingredient for dramatic effect. And why should he not do it? There is a time when the poet, the true prophet of our time, must forget the unpoetical events of the day, which seem important only because they are so near, and say to himself, Let the dead bury their dead! Kingsley it seems to me has arrived at that point, and he ought to decide."

In England Kingsley has been loved and revered for many years as a writer and a poet. But he has been much more than that. He formed part and parcel of the people; nay, one might say he formed part of the English conscience. He was one of the men of whom one thought at once, whenever a social, or a religious, or a great political question stirred the people. If there are in England the "Upper Ten Thousand," who are the leaders of what is called society, there are also the "Upper Hundred," the leaders of public opinion, whose judgment on the great questions of the day is really asked for and cared for by the people at large. A man belongs to these *Centumviri*, not because he is a minister, a member of parliament, a bishop, a professor, or a *millionaire*, but because he is believed to be true, honest, clear-sighted, free from prejudice, unselfish, and independent of party. They are the true salt of the English people. Kingsley was one of these Hundred; nay, English papers went so far as to call him one of the

Twelve who during the last generation have most powerfully impressed and guided the thoughts and feelings of the English nation. This does not mean that his judgment was always trusted or his advice always followed. On the contrary, he was often called a dreamer; yet people wished to know what he would feel, think, and say about matters which lay within the sphere of his interests, because they knew that he would always say what he felt and thought. His correspondence now shows how many telegraphic wires, not only from England, but from the English Colonies and from America, ended in the quiet rectory at Eversley, and how many electric pulsations radiated from the large heart which beat in the breast of a simple and thoroughly honest country clergyman. People abroad have no idea of the minute organization of public feeling in England. If newspapers represent the muscles of the social body, the personal relations between men of mark and the thousands who look up to them, form the nervous system from which alone the muscles receive life and vigor.

This close intellectual organization is favored in England by many circumstances. The number of Public Schools is limited. Of Universities there are, or there were till lately, two only. Most men of note are acquainted with each other from school or from university, and whoever has gained the trust and love of his friends at Eton or Oxford, retains it mostly through life. Besides, though everything in England is on a grand scale, there is also something which in Germany would be called *Klein-städtisch*. Almost everybody knows everybody, and the great families, and clans, and counties hold so closely together that whenever two Englishmen meet abroad they soon find out that they are either distantly related or have at least some friends in common. Add to this the innumerable societies, clubs, charitable institutions, political associations, and last, not least, the central hearth in London, Parliament, where everybody appears from time to time, if only to have a warm shaking of hands with old friends and acquaintances, and you will understand that England hangs more closely together and knows itself better than any other country in Europe. As a natural result of all this, there is a very sharp control. A man who has once attracted public attention is not easily lost sight of. Each man feels this, and this produces a sense of responsibility, or, what the French call, solidarity, which forms the safest foundation of a political organization. True, Kingsley was only a writer and country clergyman, but from his earliest appearance we see that he is conscious of belonging to a great people. He knew he could not hide himself, but that his convictions must out, however offensive they might sound to that class of society in which he moved, nay, however opposed they might seem to be to the interests of the clergy to which he himself was proud to belong.

Kingsley came of a good, old family, and moved in the best society. But when in the year 1849 the socialistic agitation of the working men frightened not only the thoughtless, but even the thoughtful statesmen of England, he wrote his novel, "Alton Locke, Tailor," and declared himself openly a Chartist, in the truest sense of the word. He was then known everywhere under the name of Parson Lot, much criticised, abused, and even threatened, but never troubled for one moment in his conviction that Chartism had its justification, and that it was the duty of every true statesman and patriot to recognize the good elements in socialism, and with their help to keep down its dangerous elements. Much as he was blamed for the part he took, all, even those whom Kingsley attacked most fiercely, felt that his action was entirely unselfish, and that by his advocacy of the extreme views of the working classes he forfeited all chance of Church preferment. He sacrificed not only his time, but his money also (of which he had very little at the time), in order to help in improving the condition of the laboring classes, not only by word, but by deed also. What would people have said in Germany, if he had thundered into their ears that whosoever does not devote at least one tenth part of his time and one tenth part of his annual income to public and charitable purposes, belongs to the most dangerous class and fosters the growth of social democracy!

Thus he marched on, straight as an arrow. Though devoted heart and soul to the English Church, he stepped forward as the defender of Frederick Maurice, when the Bishops deprived him of his professorship at King's College, because he denied the doctrine of Eternal Punishment.

When, during long-continued rain, the Bishops ordered a general prayer for sunshine, he declined to read it from the pulpit, first, because even his limited knowledge of the laws of nature told him that much rain was necessary; secondly, because with his limited knowledge of the laws of nature he would not criticise the decrees of the Highest Wisdom.

At the end of a sermon which he had been asked to preach in London, the clergyman to whom the church belonged rose and warned the congregation against the heresies to which they had had to listen. This was something quite unheard of, and the excitement became threatening. Kingsley bowed in silence, pacified the people who had gathered round the church, published his sermon, and succeeded in making the Bishop of the diocese acknowledge that there was nothing in his sermon in any way opposed to the true spirit of old and genuine Christianity.

At the time when nearly the whole of what is called Good Society declared in favor of the Southern States of America, Kingsley remained true to the North, not because he did not admire the heroism of the rebels, but because he clung to one simple principle, that slavery is wrong, and that the victory of the South would have been the victory of slavery.

In the year 1866, when but few Englishmen saw the true meaning of the war of Prussia against Austria, Kingsley wrote to me ("Letters," vol. ii., p. 238): —

"My dear Max, — What great things have happened for Germany, and what great men your Prussians have shown themselves. Much as I was wroth with them about Schleswig-Holstein, I can only see in this last campaign a great necessary move for the physical safety of every North German household, and the honor of every North German woman. To allow the possibility of a second 1807–1812 to remain, when it could be averted by any amount of fighting, were sin and shame; and had I been a Prussian, I would have gone down to Sedowa as a sacred duty to wife and child and fatherland."

Again, when towards the close of the Franco-German War the sympathies of nearly all the most eminent men in England, and particularly of the Liberal party, went over from Germany to France, he remained faithful to the end. Knowing how my best friends had then turned against me, he wrote to me ("Letters," ii., p. 323): —

"EVERSLEY, *August* 8, 1870.

"Accept my loving congratulations to you and your people. The day which dear Bunsen used to pray, with tears in his eyes, might not come till the German people were ready, has come, and the German people are ready. Verily, God is just; and rules too, whatever the press may think to the contrary. My only fear is, lest the Germans should think of Paris, which cannot concern them, and turn their eyes away from that which does concern them, — the re-taking Elsass (which is their own), and leaving the Frenchman no foot of the Rhine-bank. To make the Rhine a word not to be mentioned by the French henceforth, ought to be the one object of wise Germans, and that alone. In any case, I am yours, full of delight and hope for Germany."

Later on there follows another letter, in which he pours out his whole heart on the Franco-German war: —

"*August* 31.

"And now a few words on this awful war. I confess to you that, were I a German, I should feel it my duty to my country to send my last son, my last shilling, and, after all, my own self to the war, to get that done which must be done, done so that it will never need doing again. I trust that I should be able to put vengeance out of my heart — to forget all that Germany has suffered for two hundred years past, from that vain, greedy, restless nation; all even which she suffered, women as well as men, in the late French war: though the Germans do not forget it, and some of them, for their mothers' or aunts' sakes, ought not. But the average German has a right to say, 'Property, life, freedom, has been insecure in Germany for two hundred years, because she has been divided. The French kings have always tried to keep her divided that they might make her the puppet of their ambition. Since the French Revolution, the French people (all of them who think and act, viz., the army and the educated classes) have been doing the same. They shall do so no longer. We will make it impossible for her to interfere in the internal affairs of Germany. We will make it an offence on her part — after Alfred de Musset's brutal song — to mention the very name of the Rhine.' As for the present war, it was inevitable, soon or late. The French longed for it. They wanted to revenge 1813–15, ignoring the fact that Germany was then avenging — and very gently — 1807. Bunsen used to say to me — I have seen the tears in his eyes as he said it — that the war must come; that he only prayed God that it might not come till Germany was prepared and had recovered from the catastrophe of the great French war. It has come, and Germany is prepared; and would that the old man were alive to see the 'battle of Armageddon,' as he called it, fought, not as he feared on German, but on French soil. It must have come. The Germans would have been wrong to begin it; but when the French began, they would have been 'niddering' forever not to have accepted it. If a man persists for years in brandishing his fist in your face, telling you that he will thrash you some day, and that you dare not fight him, a wise man will, like Germany, hold his tongue till he is actually struck; but he will, like Germany, take care to be ready for what *will* come. As for Prussia's being prepared for war, being a sort of sin on her part — a proof that she intended to attack France — such an argument only proves the gross ignorance of history, especially of German history, which I remark in average Englishmen. Gross ignorance, too, or willing oblivion of all that the French have been threatening for years past, about 'rectifying their frontier.' The Germans had fair warning from the French that the blow would be struck some day. And now that it is struck, to turn the other cheek in meekness may be very 'Christian' towards a man's self, but most unchristian, base, and selfish towards his women, his children, and his descendants yet unborn. There can be no doubt that the French programme of this war was, to disunite Germany once more, and so make her weak and at the mercy of France. And a German who was aware of that — as all sensible Germans must have been aware — had to think, not of the text which forbids us to avenge private injuries, but of that which says, 'They that take the sword shall perish by the sword;' not of the bodily agony and desolation of the war, but of Him who said, 'Fear not them that can kill the body,' and after that have nothing left to do; but fear him — the demon of selfishness, laziness, anarchy, which ends in slavery, which can kill both body and soul in the hell of moral and political degradation. As for this being a 'dynastic war,' as certain foolish working men are saying — who have got still in their heads the worn-out theory that only kings ever go to war — it is untrue. It is not dynastic on the part of Germany. It is the rising of a people from the highest to the lowest, who mean to be a people, in a deeper sense than any republican democrat, French or English, ever understood that word. It is not dynastic on the part of France. The French Emperor undertook it to save his own dynasty; but he would never have done so, if he had not been of opinion (and who knows the French as well as he?) that it would not be a dynastic war, but a popular one. Else, how could it save his throne? What could it do but hasten his fall, by contravening the feelings of his people? But it did not contravene them. Look back at the papers and you will find that Paris and the army (which between them, alas! constitute now the French people) received the news of war with a delirium of insolent joy.

"The Emperor was mistaken . . . in spite of all his cunning. He fancied that after deceiving the French people — after governing them by men who were chosen because they could and dared deceive — that these minions of his, chosen for their untruthfulness, would be true, forsooth, to him alone; that they would exhibit, unknown, in a secret government, virtues of honesty, economy, fidelity, patriotism, which they were forbidden to exercise in public, where their only function was, to nail up the hand of the weather-glass, in order to insure fine weather, as they are doing to this day in every telegram. So he is justly punished, as all criminals are, by his own crimes; and God's judgments are, as always, righteous and true."

On September 5, 1870, he wrote again: —

"EVERSLEY, *September* 5.

"Since Waterloo, there has been no such event in Europe. I await with awe and pity the Parisian news of the next few days. As for the Emperor, whilst others were bowing down to him, I never shrank from expressing my utter contempt of him. His policy is now judged, and he with it, by fact, which is the 'voice of God revealed in things,' as Bacon says; and I at least, instead of joining the crowd of curs who worry where they lately fawned, shall never more say a harsh word against him. Let the condemned die in peace if possible; and he will not, I hear, live many months."

In this manner Kingsley spoke, wrote, and acted throughout the whole of his life, always the sworn enemy of all hypocrisy, meanness, and selfishness; always the open friend of all who meant well, who professed openly whatever they had discovered to be true, and who lived for others rather than for themselves. He was by nature the defender of all who were unjustly persecuted, or borne down by the Juggernaut of public opinion. That such a man should have enemies, and bitter enemies, was but natural, but in all the battles which he had to fight he proved himself, not only a brave, but likewise a generous antagonist. The rules of chivalrous courtesy were sacred to him, and to a German reader his courtesy and modesty may sometimes seem carried too far. But this modesty was part of Kingsley's nature, and in some sense the respect which he showed to others arose from self-respect; and the modesty with which he spoke of his own achievements, prove only his truthfulness towards himself. He was in this respect a true nobleman, one of nature's true gentlemen. We remember one case only where he seems to have forgotten himself. He had been shamefully attacked and maligned. Then, instead of saying quietly that his opponent had stated the opposite of what was the fact, he allowed himself to imitate an old Father of the Church, and to fell his enemy to the ground, with the words, *Impudentissime mentiris.*

His most famous controversy was that with John Henry Newman, the High Church theologian, who ended by becoming a Roman Catholic. The controversy was the old controversy, whether it is allowable within the Christian Church to suppress truth from respect for authority. To Kingsley that ecclesiastical policy was not only unchristian, but simply inhuman, and, with all due respect for the historical importance of the papal church-government, he often spoke with the strongest indignation against what he called the un-English character of the Roman priesthood. This called the learned and clever theologian, John Henry Newman, into the arena, as the defender of his new co-religionists, and led to a literary duel which will retain an historical character, if only by having called forth Newman's "Apologia pro vita mea." Strange to say, public opinion was in favor of Newman. He was the cleverer, sharper, more sarcastic fencer, and while Kingsley came down with heavy blows, his opponent inflicted many painful wounds.

In spite of his secession Newman enjoys great popularity in England. He is loved and esteemed, because after all he is looked upon as a martyr to his convictions. The Roman Catholics themselves fear him, or at least do not quite trust him, and he who has done more for the Roman Church than any other English convert, has never been admitted to an influential position in the Church.[1] Personal sympathies and a certain delight in his swordsmanship secured the sympathy of most newspapers and journals in favor of Newman; and Kingsley himself, in his frank, honest way, confessed openly that "he had crossed swords with a man too strong for him." And yet, whoever is able to separate the outward shell from the real kernel of the question, will easily see that Kingsley defended a strong position badly, while Newman defended a weak position cleverly. Kingsley fought with his heart, Newman with his tongue. The one cared for truth, the other for victory.

During this long controversy in the years 1864 and 1865, Kingsley's friends observed the first symptoms of decreasing force and health, and it required his iron will during the last ten years of his life to produce so much and to sustain throughout the glow of his thoughts and the splendor of his language. But he was weary. Nay, through the whole of his life, full of work as it was, we can hear a deep note of sadness and of longing for peace and rest in the grave. Even in his first work, the "Saint's Tragedy," he sang his touching song:—

"O that we two lay sleeping
In our nest in the churchyard sod,
With our limbs at rest on the quiet earth's breast,
And our souls at home with God!"

His lot on earth could hardly have been happier. But in the midst of all his happiness as husband, father, friend, teacher, preacher, and poet, his eyes seem always lifted beyond the earth towards the

[1] Written before he was made a Cardinal.

Eternal. He has died young; and of his life, if we mean by that a chain of great events, there is little to relate. He was a country clergyman, a Professor of History at Cambridge, then Canon of Chester and Westminster, and died on the 23d of January, 1875, in the fifty-fifth year of his life. The interest of the two volumes in which his wife and his friends have collected his letters and the memoirs of his life centres entirely in the man himself, in the magnificent human soul that speaks to us on every page. Whoever wants to know England and its real strength, should read these volumes.

But the book has also a charm of its own, and whoever can watch a beautiful sun, setting in the west after a glorious course, and illuminating by its refracted rays the whole sky with its clouds, and the whole earth with its mountains and valleys, will delight in watching the glorious course and the beautiful setting of a human soul which in life has warmed, nourished, strengthened and gladdened many a heart, and which was never more grand and glorious than in its death.

In conclusion, I add a few extracts from a preface which I was asked to write soon after Kingsley's death for a new edition of his "Roman and Teuton:"—

"Never shall I forget the moment when for the last time I gazed upon the manly features of Charles Kingsley, features which Death had rendered calm, grand, sublime. The constant struggle that in life seemed to allow no rest to his expression, the spirit, like a caged lion, shaking the bars of his prison, the mind striving for utterance, the soul wearying for loving response,— all that was over. There remained only the satisfied expression of triumph and peace, as of a soldier who had fought a good fight, and who, while sinking into the stillness of the slumber of death, listens to the distant sounds of music and to the shouts of victory. One saw the ideal man, as Nature had meant him to be, and one felt that there is no greater sculptor than Death.

"As one looked on that marble statue which only some weeks ago had so warmly pressed one's hand, his whole life flashed through one's thoughts. One remembered the young curate and the Saint's Tragedy; the chartist parson and Alton Locke; the happy poet and the Sands of Dee; the brilliant novel-writer and Hypatia and Westward-Ho; the Rector of Eversley and his Village Sermons; the beloved professor at Cambridge, the busy canon at Chester, the powerful preacher in Westminster Abbey. One thought of him by the Berkshire chalk-streams and on the Devonshire coast, watching the beauty and wisdom of Nature, reading her solemn lessons, chuckling too over her inimitable fun. One saw him in town-alleys, preaching the Gospel of godliness and cleanliness, while smoking his pipe with soldiers and navvies. One heard him in drawing-rooms, listened to with patient silence, till one of his vigorous or quaint speeches bounded forth, never to be forgotten. How children delighted in him! How young, wild men believed in him, and obeyed him too! How women were captivated by his chivalry, older men by his genuine humility and sympathy!

"All that was now passing away — was gone. But as one looked on him for the last time on earth, one felt that greater than the curate, the poet, the professor, the canon, had been the man himself, with his warm heart, his honest purposes, his trust in his friends, his readiness to spend himself, his chivalry and humility, worthy of a better age.

"Of all this the world knew little; — yet few men excited wider and stronger sympathies.

"Who can forget that funeral on the 28th January, 1875, and the large sad throng that gathered round his grave? There was the representative of the Prince of Wales, and close by the gipsies of the Eversley common, who used to call him their Patrico-rai, their Priest-King. There was the old Squire of his village, and the laborers, young and old, to whom he had been a friend and a father. There were Governors of distant Colonies, officers, and sailors, the Bishop of his diocese, and the Dean of his abbey; there were the leading Nonconformists of the neighborhood, and his own devoted curates, Peers and Members of the House of Commons, authors and publishers; and outside the churchyard, the horses and the hounds and the huntsman in pink, for though as good a clergyman as any, Charles Kingsley had been a good sportsman too, and had taken in his life many a fence as bravely as he took the last fence of all, without fear or trembling. All that he had loved, and all that had loved him were there, and few eyes were dry when he was laid in his own yellow gravel bed, the old trees which he had planted and cared for waving their branches to him for the last time, and the grey sunny sky looking down with calm pity on the deserted rectory, and on the short joys and the shorter sufferings of mortal men.

"All went home feeling that life was poorer, and every one knew that he had lost a friend who had been, in some peculiar sense, his own. Charles Kingsley will be missed in England, in the English colonies, in America, where he spent his last happy year; aye, wherever Saxon speech and Saxon thought is understood. He will be mourned for, yearned for, in every place in which he passed some days of his busy life. As to myself, I feel as if another cable had snapped that tied me to this hospitable shore.

"When an author or a poet dies, the better part of him, it is often said, is left in his works. So it is in many cases. But with Kingsley his life and his works were one. All he wrote was meant for the day when he wrote it. That was enough for him. He hardly gave himself time to think of fame and the future. Compared with a good work done, with a good word spoken, with a silent grasp of the hand from a young man he had saved from mischief, or with a "Thank you, Sir," from a poor woman to whom he had been a comfort, he would have despised what people call glory, like incense curling away in smoke. He was, in one sense of the word, a careless writer. He did his best at the time and for the time. He did it with a concentrated energy of will which broke through all difficulties. Though the perfection and classical finish which can be obtained by a sustained effort only, and by a patience which shrinks from no drudgery, may be wanting in many of his works, he has but few equals, if any, in the light and fire of his language, in the boldness of his imagination, and in the warmth of his heart.

"He cared little for fame; but fame has come to him. His bust will stand in Westminster Abbey, in the Chapel of St. John the Baptist, by the side of his friend Frederick Maurice; and in the Temple of Fame which will be consecrated to the period of Victoria and Albert, there will be a niche for Charles Kingsley, the author of Alton Locke and Hypatia."

INDEX.